Agile Software Construction

John Hunt

Agile Software Construction

 Springer

John Hunt, BSc, PhD, MBCS, CEng, MEng
Experis Ltd.
Chippenham
Wiltshire
UK

British Library Cataloguing in Publication Data
A catalogue record for this book is available from the British Library

Library of Congress Control Number: 2005930512

ISBN-10: 1-85233-944-6   Printed on acid-free paper
ISBN-13: 978-1-85233-944-9

Printed in the United States of America   (TB/MV)

9 8 7 6 5 4 3 2 1

Springer Science+Business Media
springeronline.com

Contents

1

Introduction

1.1 Why This Book?

Lets start of with a basic question "Why should you read this book?" The answer, as I hope you will see, is because it brings together a range of the most popular *Agile Methods* and presents them back to back allowing you, the reader, to gain an insight into what it means to be agile, what agile methods are (and are not), what Agile Modelling is and what XP (Extreme Programming) is. However, it goes further than this and considers how some of the approaches can be used together, how you can plan larger agile project (using a feature-driven approach) and how you can introduce agile methods into your organisation. All of this is done in a practical, no-nonsense manner that cuts through the hype and tells it to you straight!

That is, you should read this book because it tells you how to actually plan, organise and approach software systems in an Agile Manner. It does not try to sell you an evangelical, purist or (pardon the pun) extreme view. Instead it introduces the core concepts and methods in a concise and easy digested form. It also evaluates how successful the core techniques, such as Extreme Programming (often referred to as XP) and Agile Modelling can be, as well as what problems may be encountered. It then shows how some of these problems have been overcome on real-world projects by combining XP, Agile Modelling and Feature-Driven Development.

Without a book like this you can be left wondering what to do with Extreme Programming on a large software project. You might find yourself asking "must I always pair program if I wish to be agile?" or "should I do any design at all if I want to be agile?" or "how can I plan a project to be delivered to a client who uses a PRINCE 2 project management method when I am developing using an agile approach?" With this book you will know!

1.2 A Bit of History

I first encountered Extreme Programming early in 2000 when I was running a software development project, to create a data import and export utility for a large logistics company. The tool to be created need to be interactive, supporting data preview facilities, XML, Excel and database formats and to have excellent error reporting tools. Two of the developers on the project started talking about working on some of the more difficult problems "Extreme" style. It was somewhat to my surprise that this seemed to mean that they worked on the problem together, with the two of them working on a single machine. Intrigued, I let them continue – partly to see what happened and partly to understand what they were up to. The result was that they dealt with the problem quickly and effectively. They continued to work in this way for the remainder of the project. The delivered system not only worked, but also was well constructed and very maintainable (as many subsequent changes were required as the clients software requirements kept changing).

As my interest in this "Extreme" style grew, I found that many of the aims and objectives of the agile movement fitted well with my own. I also found that I could immediately identify with many of the issues being addressed and began to incorporate them more and more into the projects I was involved in running. This did not mean that we immediately adopted a 100% pure Extreme Programming approach. Rather we gradually became more and more agile on a project-by-project, and client-by-client, basis. One of the more obvious aspects of this to me was that people became more comfortable with working together and in asking for help, input or feedback.

Are the projects I work on agile? Yes, I believe they are. Do they use Agile Modelling techniques – yes, I believe they do. Do we always use an Extreme Programming approach – actually no, it depends on the project and the developers involved, but then to me that is the point. We use each technique where and when we feel it is appropriate – we are pragmatists rather than evangelical purists!

1.3 What Is Agile Software Development?

Agile software development is an attempt to put the software being developed first and to acknowledge that the user requirements change. It is *agile* because it can respond quickly to the users' changing needs. Agile software development, in general, advocates frequent and regular, software releases. This allows new versions of the software to be released to users quickly and frequently. In turn, users can respond frequently and quickly to these releases with feedback, changing requirements and general comments (such as "that's not what we meant!"). As the releases are frequent, the time taken for the users to see the results of their comments is short and they are then able to respond to the new version quickly. This is particularly useful in a volatile environment, such as the environment of the web during the late 1990s and early 21st century.

In turn, agile software development puts the software first, because almost any activity undertaken must be to the benefit of the software that will be delivered. For example, if I create a model of some problem domain, then that model is not the actual delivered software, although it may help me to understand the problem better, in order that I can write the executable software. However, if the only use I make of the model is to help me understand the problem, then I shouldn't worry about updating it after the implementation varies from the design – at least not until I need the model again. That way, the effort is focussed on developing the software, rather than spending time on other supporting (but ultimately less productive) activities.

1.4 Why Be Agile?

You may be wondering at this point "Why would I even want to be agile?," "What difference can agile software development make?" or "What has Extreme Programming and Agile Modelling got to do with me?" The answer to these questions is in this book, but the essence of the whole of the agile movement is the production of working software systems, on time and within budget.

So why should you consider adopting agile development methods – the answer is simple – because they can help you produce software within budget and agreed timescales, that actually does what the users want! And we all want that right!

Of course, you might well argue that you have "seen it all before," and that this is what software engineering has been promising for decades. And you would be right, but things change. Today we live in a fast-moving, uncertain world, in which users' requirements seem to be as changeable as the weather (here in the UK) and software needs to have been delivered yesterday!

Traditional, single iteration, waterfall development approaches often can't cope. Other approaches have been proposed and new technologies created. Yet, still software is late, or over budget, or both. Even when delivered it often has numerous requirements removed or contains undesirable features/bugs.

Being agile doesn't guarantee the removal of all bugs, nor does it guarantee an easy ride, but it does help produce useful software within a project framework that can adapt to changing requirements.

In the current climate, everyone needs to be Agile!

1.5 What This Book Is About?

This book is about exploiting as many features of the agile movement as possible to enhance our software development processes. It is about selling you the concept of agile software development. It is about how to make your projects agile. It is about what tools you should use to become agile.

This book is about not rejecting anything out of hand just because it seems radical, but also of not just accepting all of a concept just because the literature says you should. It is about being realistic about what you can achieve in your organisation/team/situation.

It is not a detailed in-depth presentation of any of the agile methods (there are already very good books available that focus on each approach in depth – so why write another one?), it is not a diatribe for, or against, any particular method, nor is it a prescription for all of software development's ills.

This book is thus a *guide to the agile software development* methods currently available!

1.6 Implementation Languages

For the most part, this book is agnostic when it comes to a particular programming language, as we are dealing with issues relating to programming and software development rather than the actual software development itself. However, there are times when the book does refer to a particular programming language or to a particular technology or tool used with one programming language or another. In these situations, the book tends to use the programming language Java for its examples. This is intentional – it is the environment that I am most familiar with and within which all my training; mentoring and development work takes place. This does not mean that if you are a hardened C++ developer, or a newly trained C# developer, this book is not of interest to you – merely that the few code examples will be less relevant. However, even here the issue may be blurred as some of the UML diagrams happen to be generated from java code, but would essentially be the same if they were generated from C#, for example.

1.7 The Structure of the Book

The remainder of the book has the following structure.

Chapter 2 : Agile Methods and the Agile Manifesto
This chapter covers the basics of the ideas and the philosophy behind the agile movement. It explains what it is to be agile and presents a summary of the agile manifesto. The manifesto, produced by the *Agile Software Development Alliance*, expresses all the common philosophies that underlie the agile movement. As such it is the heart of what it is to be agile! The chapter then describes the different methods that are loosely grouped under the Agile banner including Agile Modelling, Extreme Programming (XP), The Dynamic Systems Development Method (or DSDM), SCRUM and Feature-Driven Development (FDD).

Chapter 3: Agile Modelling
Modelling has a great number of misconceptions associated with it. This chapter first attempts to dispel these myths. It then introduces Agile Modelling. Agile Modelling can be seen as the design-side equivalent of the coding-oriented Extreme Programming. It tries to bring agile principles to the act of application modelling.

Chapter 4: How to Become an Agile Modeller
In this chapter, we will look at how agile modelling can be implemented, what it means to be an agile modeller and how agile modelling practices can be put into practice.

Chapter 5: Extreme Programming (XP)
Extreme Programming or XP is part of the agile movement that focuses on the writing of the software that will implement the system required by the end users. This chapter introduces XP by presenting the four key values of XP. It then describes the 12 practices that essentially form XP. Note that XP is comprised of a set of practices and is thus a very lightweight process and is actually more of a set of guidelines than a methodology!

Chapter 6: XP in Practice

Chapter 5 describes in more detail the practices that make up XP; however, these practices on their own provide very little in the way of guidance on how to run an actual XP project. This chapter therefore describes how to implement XP on a software project. It takes the XP practices and gives guidance on how to actually make them work.

Chapter 7: Agile Modelling and XP

This chapter considers how to use Agile Modelling within an XP project. It also considers how agile modelling and XP relate to one another.

Chapter 8: Agile Modelling and XP Reviewed

This chapter reviews agile modelling and XP in light of various experiences including the authors' own experiences. It also considers applying agile modelling and XP to larger scale projects. It concludes by considering the best situations within which to apply these techniques.

Chapter 9: Feature-Driven Development

This chapter discusses an agile development process based on Features. A *Feature* is a schedulable piece of functionality, something that delivers value to the user. It considers the role of FDD in planning agile development projects.

Chapter 10: An FDD Example Project

The aim of this chapter is to present an example of a project that employs agile principles but that has been planned using an FDD approach.

Chapter 11: Agile Methods with RUP and PRINCE 2

This chapter considers how Agile Modelling and the Rational Unified Process can fit together. It concludes by briefly discussing how agile methods and PRINCE 2 can work in tandem.

Chapter 12: Introducing Agile Methods into Your Organisation

In this chapter, we consider strategies for introducing Agile Development methods into an organisation.

Chapter 13: Tools to Help with Agile Development

Life can be made a great deal easier if you choose the appropriate toolset to use. In this chapter, we discuss some of the tools that can really help to simplify life on an agile development project. In particular, we discuss the make-like tool ANT, the use of version management software such as CVS (Continuous Versioning System), unit testing software such as JUnit and IDEs such as Eclipse.

Chapter 14: Obstacles to Agile Software Development

This chapter discusses what obstacles may be encountered within an organisation, what problems may occur and the difficulties relating to agile development methods. It also considers some strategies for mediating these issues.

1.8 Where to Get More Information?

There are now many books available on various subjects within the agile movement (there are even books, technologies and organisations that are trying to jump on the agile bandwagon and make themselves appear agile). So which books might you consider? In this section, I list the six or seven books that provide the best coverage of the core aspects of Extreme Programming, Agile Model and Feature-Driven Development (the main subjects covered in this book).

The definitive book on Extreme Programming is

- *Extreme Programming Explained: Embrace Change.* K. Beck, Addison-Wesley, 1999.

Although there are many other books on Extreme Programming, two standout from a practical perspective, these are:

- *Extreme Programming Applied: Playing to Win* (The XP Series), Ken Auer, Roy Miller, Addison Wesley - New York, 2002.
- *Extreme Programming Installed*, Ron Jeffries, Ann Anderson, and Chet Hendrikson, Addison-Wesley, ISBN: 0201708426, 2000.

A very good book that helps to introduce pair programming into an organisation is:

- *Pair Programming Illuminated*, Laurie Williams and Robert Kessler, Addison-Wesley Professional, 0-201-74576-3, 2003.

The definitive Agile Modelling book is by Scott Ambler:

- *Agile Modeling: Effective Practices for Extreme Programming and the Unified Process*, Scott W. Ambler, Wiley and Son, Inc., 0 471 20282 7, 2002.

Books relating to Feature-Driven Development include the following books. These books focus on the use of the Together toolset, but include valuable information on helping to plan agile projects by basing project planning around desired features.

- *Better Software Faster*, A. Carmichael, D. Haywood, Prentice-Hall NJ, 0-13-008752-1, 2002.
- *Java Modeling in Color*, P. Coad, E. Lefebvre and J. De Luca, Prentice-Hall, Englewood Cliffs, NJ, 1999.

1.9 Where to Go Online?

There is also a wealth of information available online. There are websites out there that deal with the agile movement in general, with Extreme Programming, with Agile Modelling, etc. Some of these are listed below.

Agile Movement in General
 www.agilealliance.org Agile Software Development Alliance
Agile Modelling
 www.agilemodeling.com Agile Modelling mailing list
Extreme Programming
 http://extremeprogramming.org/
 http://www.xpuniverse.com
 http://www.pairprogramming.com/

2

Agile Methods and the Agile Manifesto

2.1 Introduction

In this chapter, you will be introduced to the concept, motivations, goals and principles behind the Agile Movement. You will also learn what the common features of all agile methods are. Following this, a brief review of a number of the core agile methods currently available will be presented, before a brief summary concludes the chapter.

2.2 What Is Agile?

Okay so what does "Agile" mean? And what are the methods that can be defined as Agile in this context? This question has become somewhat muddied of late as more and more people have jumped onto the Agile bandwagon. I have even seen adverts on public television by Microsoft advocating that they are an "Agile Organisation." It is therefore worthwhile setting out our stall before continuing.

The Oxford Paper Back dictionary defines Agile as:

Agile *adj.* nimble, quick-moving

And possibly surprisingly for a computing term this actually reflects the primary goal of the various methods that have been grouped under the term agile. That is, they aim to be nimble and quick moving in response to changes in requirements, to the people that comprise the development teams and to issues that arise during the software development process.

These methods are not trying to be "nimble" just for the sake of it; instead they have focussed on the fact that the primary purpose of software development is to produce a working piece of software! This might sound like a major case of telling your grand-mother how to suck eggs but just think about it for a moment. How many times have you or a colleague stopped developing the actual software that is to be delivered, to produce (for example) a set of view charts in PowerPoint to give a presentation to the senior management explaining the progress you have made, what you have achieved and what you will achieve during the next period. Don't get me wrong, I am not saying that such reporting is completely unnecessary; however, it might not need some fancy PowerPoint slides in order to have achieved the same goal. And that is the essence, do what is useful, productive and generally good for the development of the software and question anything else that you are doing.

Of course, the necessity for other deliverables will depend on the nature of the software being developed and the length of time it is likely to exist for. Take, for example, a simple web application that will be used to register members for a small club. This web application must take a member's name and address, charge them £10 for the privilege and send them a confirmatory email message. What sort of documentation will this require? You might well argue that it will need at least a requirements specification, a detailed design document, test specifications, installation manual, etc. But what if this system is only intended as a stopgap until the main all singing, all dancing web application is produced that includes member only areas, a content management system, online database, etc. At this point much of the documentation you may have developed may well be thrown away as soon as the stopgap is phased out.

Possibly, you will argue that such a situation is unlikely to occur. My answer to that is it has and indeed I was involved with the design and implementation of this system.

So agile methods are methods that try to focus on the primary goal of software development, i.e., the creation of working (defect-free) software. This is distinct from "hacking" up code as quickly as possible, hence the inclusion of "defect-free" in the previous sentence. Thus, agile also implies being both effective and sufficient for the current situation. By this I mean:

- *effective* in terms of producing working, defect-free (as far as possible) software,
- *sufficient* in terms of meeting its requirements both in the short-term and in the long-term (for example, the documentation required to support a long-lived project will be greater than for a short-lived one).

Note the use of the word "sufficient," this also implies that it should not be over sufficient. That is, engineering support into your software for things that might never be needed is in general considered unnecessary.

So what is an *Agile Methodology*? Well, it is a method that tries to be responsive to the needs of the software development process, that is based on practise and experience, and that focuses on being effective and sufficient!

Okay, so that is a little bit vague, so in the next section we will look at the Agile Manifesto that really coalesced the ideas being developed by a disparate group of people.

2.3 The Agile Manifesto

There is a growing movement that promotes the use of an agile development philosophy. This movement (see references at the end of this chapter) came together in February 2001 to form the *Agile Software Development Alliance* (often referred to as the *Agile Alliance*). They produced a manifesto that they hoped embraced the philosophies that they commonly supported, and that they believed to help produce better software. From this manifesto, they defined a set of principles for Agile Software Development. The manifesto proposed the following values (very briefly) summarised below:

1. *Individuals and interactions over processes and tools.*
   This refers to the fact that it is the people involved and how they communicate that typically has the largest bearing on the success (or failure) of a software project. Yes, software development processes, methodologies, tools, etc., can help but they are still not the overriding influence. Thus, you should encourage the best people and group interactions.
2. *Working software over comprehensive documentation.*
   There are times when (and I am sure I am not alone in this) you can feel that all you seem to be doing is producing reams and reams of documentation. Sometimes, this is aided (even determined) by the CASE tool you might be using and sometimes it is merely the process being followed. However, at the end of the day it is the software produced by a development project that will be used by a user and not the documentation. Therefore, documentation should not be a major goal in and of itself. Instead, it should be a supporting medium for the actual product – the software.
3. *Customer collaboration over contract negotiation.*
   Remember these are values – thus, time should be spent on working with customers and in getting them involved in the software development rather than on detailed contract negotiations. However, of course in the real world this can be difficult, as although your direct clients may buy into this philosophy, their legal and financial departments may not. For example, we have worked with a number of clients where the legal (and/or financial) departments have imposed a contract and associated negotiations because they want something to hit us with, if things go wrong.
4. *Responding to change over following a plan.*
   Finally, agile software development embraces change rather than saying "it's not in the requirements or the plan, so we can't do it." That is development progresses in response to user feedback, rather than as a reaction to a fixed plan. Note that does not mean that there is no plan and that planning isn't important – actually, it is very important but the project adapts itself to its environment – that is it is agile!

Based on these value statements, a set of 12 principles have been identified. The aim of these principles is twofold. First, they are intended to help people gain a better understanding of what agile software development is all about. Second, they can be used to help to determine whether you as a developer are following an agile methodology or not. Note that these principles do not specify a method, etc., but rather define a set of guiding statements that any approach that wishes to be grouped under the banner "Agile," should conform to. Thus, agile methodologies should conform to these principles:

1. Highest priority is to satisfy the customer.
2. Welcome change.
3. Deliver working software frequently.

4. Business people and developers must work together daily.
5. Build projects around motivated individuals.
6. Face-to-face communication is best.
7. Working software is the primary measure of progress.
8. Promote sustainable development.
9. Continuous attention to technical excellence and good design enhances agility.
10. Simplicity – the art of maximising the amount of work not done – is essential.
11. The best architectures, requirements and design emerge form self-organising teams.
12. Introspection – teams should regularly review itself and its processes to try and improve.

Some of the above may seem obvious and others may appear more contentious. In general, they appear quite vague ("Welcome Change"). However, they have been defined to help guide agile methodologies rather than to actually be a methodology. For example, an agile methodology should promote the frequent delivery of working systems rather than a single big bang delivery. One way this can be interpreted is that an iterative and incremental approach is better than the more traditional waterfall approach to software production.

Of course, this last statement is a little simplistic and it would be more accurate to state that the "Agile" movement has a desire to meet the needs of the sort of rapidly changing and uncertain business world that we find ourselves working within today. From this, agile methodologists have tried to devise methods that move from

- heavyweight to lightweight processes,
- document-oriented to code-oriented objectives,
- predictive to adaptive methods,
- process-oriented to people-oriented activities.

2.4 What Are Agile Methods?

The common theme about agile methodologies is that they are all focussed on trying to produce a working solution and be able to respond to changing user/client requirements. Of course traditional development methods are also trying to develop working solutions, but it is in the focus on changing requirements that the core difference lies. For example, consider the following diagram.

This diagram tries to illustrate the difference in emphasis of agile methods compared to more traditional methods. That is, in an agile method it is the time available and the resources available that are generally considered to be fixed, while the functionality is considered more flexible. Thus, the aim is usually to set a fixed delivery date at which point something will be delivered and to prioritise the functionality that must be implemented so that what can be implemented will be implemented, but to acknowledge that not everything may be delivered. In contrast, many software development projects have overrun because management has considered the functionality to be fixed, but the time available and the number of resources that can be applied are variable. There are of course situations where all the functionality must be provided, but in many (most?) cases, functionality varies between the *must* have, the *nice* to have, the *may possibly* be useful and the *never* used at all! Thus, prioritising such functionalities can result in a leaner, more effective solution being delivered on time and within budget.

For example, a fundamental assumption of DSDM (outlined below) is that nothing is built perfectly first time, but that a usable and useful 80% of the proposed system can be produced in 20% of the time it would take to produce the total system. The implication being that the remaining 20% may never be required, or at worst will be required in later deliveries.

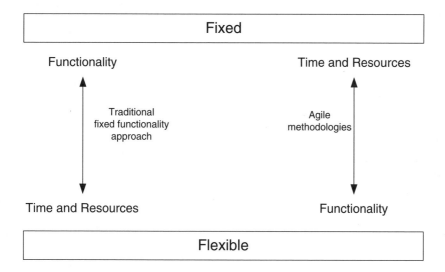

It is interesting to relate a recent project that I was involved in that was started originally in 2002. The original specification led to an initial green field prototype being built. This prototype convinced users and management that a system similar to this was needed but that it would change in significant ways. A detailed requirements document was drawn up and the functionality prioritised. An initial time period for the first delivery was determined and the development started. This resulted in a system being delivered on time and at the budget originally stated. Following this, the functionality that had not yet been implemented was re-evaluated. Interestingly, there were many changes to the priorities of various features/functions at this time. Some of the *must haves* that could not be implemented within the original time scales slide down and (eventually over the next 2 years) dropped off the list altogether.

This is not to say that the lists were wrong initially – on the contrary, given the users understanding of their own requirements at that time the functions were ordered appropriately. However, once things got going and incremental deliveries were made, and real end users started working with the tools, the requirements both changed and were understood better. In addition, actual working patterns altered as a result of the new software that lead to different end user needs.

Because an agile methodology was being followed (the management of which was based on Feature-Driven Development (FDD)) we were able to respond to these changes easily, resulting in an extremely high quality of service to the client. That is, they got what they actually needed, when they wanted it and for a mutually agreed cost. The software was even put forward as an example of good practices within the client organisation.

Okay, so that is the theoretical part, what are these so-called Agile Methods? Without trying to provide a complete list of every possible method that might try and bring itself under the umbrella of the term Agile, there are five core methods being worked on and with at the present time. These are Agile Modelling, eXtreme Programming (or XP), DSDM, SCRUM and FDD. I will not try to cover all of these in depth within this book, instead I will try to provide a flavour of each approach here and focus on three of these methods later in the book.

2.5 Agile Modelling

Agile Modelling applies the philosophy of the agile movement to the software modelling process. It tries to find an appropriate balance between too little modelling, and too much modelling, at the design stage. That is, the point at which you have

> modelled enough to explore and document your system effectively, but not so much that it becomes a burden (Ambler, 2002).

It is certainly not a methodology in its own right and rather more of an approach or philosophy towards the modelling stage of a project. As such it can be used as the modelling approach adopted within, for example, a RUP project. Indeed, it might be clearer to state that Agile Modelling provides guidelines on how to create effective models and how to be an efficient modeller. This does not necessarily mean that less modelling will be performed while adopting Agile Modelling rather that the models that are produced are those required for useful, necessary purposes. Like other Agile Methods, it is trying to promote lightweight processes, in this case within the modelling arena (as opposed to the programming arena with XP). To this end it has three main goals:

1. The definition and promotion of a set of values, principles and practices that help to produce the appropriate models.
2. Guidance on how to apply modelling to an agile software development.
3. Guidance on how to apply agile modelling to other software processes (such as RUP).

This results in the concept that an agile model is just good enough for its purpose (of course non-agile models may be "just good enough for their purpose" but often they provide far more information than will ever be useful or indeed used at a later date). This is defined in terms of a set of criteria that an agile model should meet, these are:

- *Agile models provide positive value.* That is, is there a real need for the model, will it help in the general aim of producing the final deliverable software? If not, then within the Agile Modelling philosophy it is not required.
- *Agile models fulfil their purpose (and no more).* For example, if that purpose is for John to explain to Steve and Dave how their code should integrate with his, then a drawing on a white board may be good enough to serve its purpose (so don't use a heavyweight tool such as Rational Rose to do this!).
- *Agile models are understandable* to their intended audience but not necessarily to everyone. That is, the level of detail and the content needs to be appropriate for Steve and Dave, but not necessarily to any software engineer from any other project.
- *Agile models are sufficiently accurate.* Recently, I had to explain how the Java-Mail API worked to some colleagues. I was doing so in order that they could have a general understanding of what our software was doing (but they would not be involved in the actual software development, rather they would be administering the email accounts). As it had been a while since I had last looked at the JavaMail API, I gave then an overview in which I got the general ideas across (using a mixture of UML like diagrams and flow charts). I was even unsure of the exact names of some of the classes but I still got the point across!
- *Agile models are sufficiently consistent.* If one model has more detail in than another, so what! As long as they are both understandable by their target audiences it does not matter.
- *Agile models are sufficiently detailed.* For example, when John explains to Steve and Dave about the structure they need to integrate with, many details not relevant to them can be left out – it may be sufficient merely to get the general concepts across.
- *Agile models are as simple as possible.* The less information within a model, the easier it is for the reader to absorb. Within UML, there are a wide range of notational elements that can be applied to most diagrams. However, very few UML diagrams employ as many of these as is possible and in my experience very few of them need as many as they have.

As such Agile Modelling is far more of an art than a science or indeed a prescriptive design method! In addition, it does not claim that documentation is unnecessary – indeed models are a form of design documentation and with any design model there are elements that cannot be captured easily within diagrammatic models. However, the documentation associated with the design of the system can be associated, where appropriate, with agile models and can be focussed on the models. Thus, the concept of Agile Documentation is born, such that the documentation being created meets the overall goals of agile modelling, namely, that is, as simple as possible, as minimal as possible, has a distinct purpose but is as effective as possible for the intended target audience.

The principles of Agile Modelling are supported by a set of core and supplementary practises. These practises (if adopted) help to achieve an Agile Modelling environment.

We will return to Agile Modelling in more detail in Chapters 3 and 4.

2.6 XP: eXtreme Programming

Extreme Programming, or as it is more commonly known XP, was originally designed as a way of supporting small development teams working within uncertain and changing requirements. That is, it was a response to many of the more traditional heavyweight approaches that are often overkill for small software developments. However, it was not an attempt to throw everything away and just program (which is a common misinterpretation of XP). Rather, XP was designed as an approach based on software engineering principles, but focussed on the timely delivery of software that meets users' requirements (rather than on the sometimes over bearing processes that surround the development of software). An important aspect of XP is the empowerment of the actual developers – they should be able to react immediately to changing customer requirements, even late in the development life cycle.

XP also places great emphasis on the software development team and teamwork. The team, in turn, incorporates management, technical personnel and end users all cooperating towards the common good. It takes as one of its aims that teams communicate and constantly pay attention to all the details necessary to make sure that the software being developed matches the user requirements, to help to produce quality software.

Underlying XP are four basic principles, these are:

- *Communication* – it is good to talk (particularly, between users and developers).
- *Simplicity* – keep it simple and grow the system as and when required.
- *Feedback* – let users provide feedback early and often.
- *Courage* – to go with such an approach.

These four basic principles have led to the following key ideas presented within XP:

Code in pairs. This is probably the thing that people first hear with relation to XP. The idea is that all software is developed in pairs (i.e., with two programmers at one screen). The concept is that if code reviews are good, because they force at least one other person to consider your code, then constantly working in pairs results in constant reviewing of code and feedback between the two developers.

Stay in contact with the customer. For example, place a customer representative in the team, so that you have access to them all of the time. Meet regularly with the customer to give information and receive feedback.

Create tests before coding then test heavily. Developers should write the unit tests before the code to be tested. Part of the argument is that if you can't write the test (i.e., don't know what the inputs and outputs should be), then you shouldn't be writing the code. You should then automate testing so that you can regularly re-run the tests to make sure that nothing that has been done breaks earlier results.

Short iterations. Each iteration should be relatively short allowing for rapid and frequent feedback. Thus, a minimal system may be produced and possibly even put into production quickly and the system will grow in whatever directions prove most valuable.

Keep it simple. Start projects with a simple design that can evolve later as required by future iterations. This removes unnecessary complexity from early iterations. It also removes the need to code in additional functionalities believed to be required by future iterations, but which may actually never be needed.

Don't anticipate: code for current needs. That is, don't over-engineer solutions based on what they may one day need to do, rather focus on what they need to do now and leave tomorrow's functionality to tomorrow.

Collective ownership. Everyone within the team owns the software and has responsibility for it. When something goes wrong, no one should ever consider it not to be his or her problem because Bill wrote that piece of code. In turn, XP does not support a culture of blame and recrimination – everyone is responsible for all the code. As a result of this, everyone is responsible for fixing a problem when they find it rather than ignoring it.

2.6.1 The XP Project Lifecycle

We have now briefly considered the primary goals and principles of XP, but what is XP? Is it just programming in pairs? No, XP does provide a software development lifecycle model as well as guidelines on the organisation of a software development team. The XP lifecycle is presented in Figure 2.1.

2.6.2 User Stories

User stories are similar in some respects to Use Cases from the Rational Unified Process in that they aim to capture how the user will use the system. However, they are written by the users themselves and not by the development team. Note

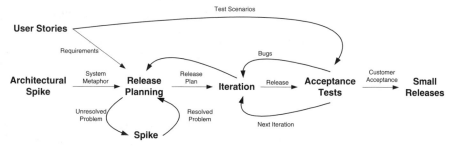

Fig. 2.1 XP lifecycle.

that the users should not be limited to describing just the user interface. Rather the user stories should describe how the user would use the system to accomplish something.

It is worth noting that User Stories are not detailed requirements. These will be obtained during the iterations, when and if the aspect of the system covered by a particular user story is to be implemented. Instead, User Stories should only be detailed enough to allow a reasonable estimate to be made of the time taken to implement them under ideal conditions for the planning meeting.

They should be short (e.g., about three sentences long) and should use the terminology of the user and not the terminology of the software development team. These user stories should feed into the release-planning meeting and to the creation of the user acceptance tests.

2.6.3 Architectural Spike

A Spike in XP terms is an attempt to reduce the risk associated with an unknown area of the system, technology or application domain. A Spike may involve some investigation, research and possibly some software to evaluate or elucidate the problem. The result of most explorations is usually not good enough to keep and so should be thrown away. Early on the overall architecture of the system to be developed is an important issue that needs to be resolved. Thus, at this stage research and analysis of the architecture to use should be carried out and fed into the release planning meeting. Other spikes are used during the project-planning phase to determine unresolved issues.

2.6.4 Release Planning

A release-planning meeting is used to create the release plan, which lays out the overall project. That is, the release plan indicates which user stories will be implemented and in which release this will happen. It also indicates how many iterations are planned and when each iteration will be delivered. This is done by negotiation between the interested parties using estimates derived from the user stories. The estimates are produced by the technical members of the team potentially with input from the users. The users prioritise the user stories possibly with input from the technical team members. From this, the timescales for the project, the delivery dates of various iterations, and the final system delivery are all negotiated. If it is found that management or users are unhappy about the proposed delivery dates, then one or more of the features of the system, the resources available or the time taken must be modified until all participants are happy. Note that individual iterations are planned just before the iteration commences, not in advance.

2.6.5 Iterations

Each iteration within the project adds to the agility of the development team. That is, at the start of each iteration changes can be made to what will be done and when it will be done. The shorter the iteration, the quicker the development team can respond to changes (indeed within XP it is recommended that iterations last only a matter of weeks). At the beginning of each iteration, an Iteration Planning meeting is held to determine exactly what will happen within that iteration (such as what programming tasks there will be and when they will be done). Such just-in-time planning is considered an easy way to stay on top of changing user requirements. If, however, it looks like the iteration will not manage to achieve all that was planned for it, then further iteration planning meetings should be called during the iteration to respond to these concerns. These meetings might need to re-estimate current and future tasks and determine what can and can't be achieved. The overriding concern here should be to concentrate your efforts on completing the most important tasks as chosen by your users rather than having several unfinished tasks chosen by the developers.

2.6.6 Acceptance Testing

The acceptance tests are created from the user stories, written at the start of the project. Each iteration implements one or more user stories; these stories will be translated into a series of acceptance tests during the iteration. To do this, the customer must specify scenarios to test whether a user story has been correctly implemented. A story is not limited to one acceptance test and may be related to many acceptance tests (depending on the complexity of the scenario). Interestingly, it is the users who assess the results of the acceptance tests and reviewing test scores to decide which failed tests are of highest priority. Acceptance tests are also used as regression tests prior to a production release. Thus, Acceptance tests should be automated so they can be run often. Indeed in each iteration, all previous Acceptance tests should be run to ensure that nothing has been broken. Indeed, contrary to some popular misconceptions, XP has Software QA at its heart and encourages the QA team to be very closely related to the development team.

2.6.7 Release

XP promotes the concept of "small releases" and "release often." The release-planning meeting should identify meaning "chucks" of system functionality that makes business sense in relation to the users and to the state of the system at various intervals. These meaningful releases should be made available to users when available. This will allow early and frequent feedback from the users rather than relying on the big bang approach and then worrying about the consequences.

2.6.8 Why Is XP Controversial?

XP has had some mixed receptions in the press and within the wider developer community. Why is this? In the following brief section, we will try to answer some of the issues that have been raised about XP.

XP is a hackers paradise or at the very least encourages hacking. Some people believe that XP is all about programming with little or no emphasis on design, documentation or indeed testing. Yet, the reality is that XP tries to focus the developer on their core activity (writing code) and not to get bogged down in less relevant tasks. However, the key here is "less relevant tasks." XP does not mean that there is no need to document, or to design or indeed to test. In fact testing is considered to be extremely important within XP and design and documentation should be carried out but when, where and as required, rather than just mindlessly created.

XP Programmers get to work in pairs! So that means that we now need double the number of programmers and that one programmer can just ride along on the coat tails of the other programmer? Yes? Well no! The idea is that two programmers working on the code together will produce more effective code, quicker and with less bugs in, because they are monitoring what each other are doing, and are both analysing the problem – i.e., two heads are better than one.

XP doesn't force team members to specialise and become analysts, architects, programmers, testers and integrators – every XP programmer participates in all of these critical activities every day. Actually this is true, but is not necessarily a bad thing, particularly in small software development teams where it can be very useful to have everyone familiar with all aspects of the development process.

XP doesn't conduct a complete up-front analysis and design of the system. Rather an XP project starts with a quick analysis of the entire system, and XP programmers continue to make analysis and design decisions throughout development. This is particularly troublesome for those entrenched in more traditional (and particularly waterfall based) development models. But then the point of XP is that it is agile, and that what might be thought to be needed upfront may change during the lifetime of the project!

XP promotes the development of the systems' infrastructure and its frameworks as you develop your application. That is, you do not develop the core of the system upfront. The intention is that you do not do needless work early on; rather you focus on delivering business value right from the start. The counter argument to this is that you may end up with an amorphous mess or need to carry out extensive refactoring as the project progresses. Of course, this may still be the case even if you attempt to create an appropriate infrastructure and set of frameworks early on as the system may evolve extensively during its lifetime.

XP does not encourage the creation and maintenance of implementation documentation. Instead within an XP project communication occurs face-to-face, or through efficient tests and carefully written code. However, code is not self-documenting and some documentation is always, and will always, be needed. However, only that which is in this category should be created.

XP is not a complete methodology. It is a lot like a jigsaw puzzle. There are many small pieces. Individually, the pieces make no sense, but when combined together a complete picture can be seen. This is a significant departure from traditional software development methods, indeed XP is not really a fully fledged development method, rather it is a development philosophy with proposed procedures, approaches and strategies.

We will return to eXtreme Programming in more detail in Chapter 5.

2.7 DSDM

DSDM or The Dynamic Systems Development Method provides a framework of controls and best practice for Rapid Application Development (RAD). It is particularly suitable for application development projects that need to develop complex business solutions within tight timeframes.

A worldwide consortium of systems developers initially designed (and indeed are still evolving) DSDM (now in Version 4.1). Their goal was to produce what at the time they referred to as a RAD methodology which has evolved into an Agile Method model that is time, quality and cost sensitive, producing deliverables quickly and accurately – rapid and right. Since its inception in 1995, more than 20,000 practitioners have been trained and thousands of developers have used DSDM successfully.

As with a number of the approaches described in this book, in DSDM, time is fixed for the life of a project, and resources are fixed as far as possible. This means that it is the requirements that will be satisfied that are allowed to change. (For the moment, we will ignore the implications of this on contracts based on requirements specifications that are often the norm in the software industry). A central tenant of DSDM is that "high-quality demands fitness for purpose as well technical robustness" rather than the need to match every requirement as described in the requirements document to the nth degree (not least because many requirements documents are at best flawed).

DSDM is based on nine overriding principles, these are:

1. Active user involvement is imperative.
2. The team must be empowered to make decisions.
3. The focus is on frequent delivery of products.
4. Fitness for business purpose is the essential criterion for acceptance of deliverables.
5. Iterative and incremental development is necessary to converge on an accurate business solution.
6. All changes during development are reversible.
7. Requirements are base lined at a high level.
8. Testing is integrated throughout the life cycle.
9. Collaboration and cooperation between all stakeholders is essential.

Some of these may seem obvious (such as the user being actively involved in the development process). However, it is not exceptional for a development team to be given a requirements document and to work solely from this and never to talk to the actual end users. Thus, a major impediment to the understanding of those requirements exists – first hand experience.

To emphasis this particular aspect of DSDM, the key users within a DSADM project are know as Ambassador Users. Ambassador Users are so called because they have an ambassadorial role between the project team and the actual end users. They promote two-way communication and compromise between the end user community and the project development team.

Of course, they are not the only users who should be involved, not least as they may only have a view of part of the whole project. Rather they help to identify other users who should become directly involved as and when necessary. If this is not practical, then they must represent the input and ideas of other users. They should not have a passive role in the project as they should be involved not only with determining the features the system must include but also in the testing, direction and overall solution produced.

However, one or more Ambassador Users still cannot provide the sort of direct and rapid feedback that getting a group of users in front of the development team or an early iteration of the tool can produce. To this end DSDM promotes the use of Facilitated Workshops. These workshops when used properly can be a useful tool for effecting cultural change in an organisation because they promote buy-in from and empowerment of participants. When used effectively, they can set the tone for the whole project. However, it is up to the project members themselves to decide whether a workshop is necessary, or whether another technique, such as interviewing or research is more applicable.

The actual DSDM lifecycle is broken down into seven different phases, these are: Pre-Project Phase, Feasibility Study, Business Case Study, the Functional Model Iteration (FMI), the Design and Build Iteration (DBI), the Implementation Phase and the Post-Project Phase. These are illustrated in Figure 2.2.

The first three phases (namely, the Pre-Project, Feasibility and Business Studies phases) are done sequentially in order. These phases set the ground rules for the rest of development process allowing users and teams to understand the world

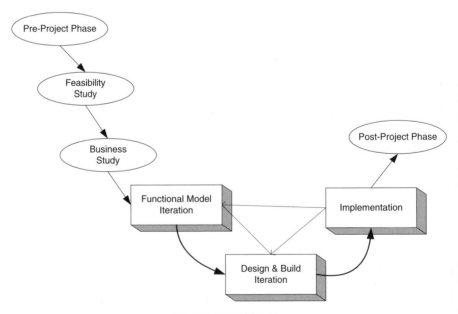

Fig. 2.2 DSDM lifecycle.

within which the application must execute as well as what will be expected of the end product.

The Feasibility Study phase is expected only to last a few weeks. The output of this phase is a "feasibility report" that assesses whether or not to use DSDM for the particular project. It should also consider issues surrounding the people and organisations involved, and define the general scope of the project and its objectives. This phase should also produce an outline plan for the development of the end product.

The Business Study phase of the project should have three outputs; these should be the Business Area Definition (BAD), the System Architecture Definition (SAD) and the Outline Prototyping plan:

- *Business Area Definition.* Identifies the high-level requirements and provides a process description of the end product.
- *System Architecture Definition.* Sketches out the architecture of end system. Note that it is likely that this will evolve over the life of the project.
- *Outline Prototyping Plan.* This states the prototyping strategy to be adopted for the development of the end product.

The core phases of the DSDM are the FMI, the DBI and the Implementation Phase.

The *FMI Phase* involves:

- Analysis of the features to be designed and implemented.
- The production of the Functional Model. This is the primary output of this phase. It may include prototype code as well as analysis models.
- Coding and prototyping. Prototypes may be used to help improve the analysis or understanding of the system. These prototypes may continue to evolve (particularly in the next phase) until the quality level achieved is high enough that they can be used in the delivered system.

The *DBI Phase* involves:

- Designing and Building the features to be implemented during this phase. This involves reviewing the designs produced so far, the functional prototypes, as well as the creation of code to implement the required functionality.
- The primary output of this state is the tested system. This system must meet all the requirements selected as essential in the particular iteration being implemented.

The *Implementation Phase* involves:

- The transfer of the completed system from the development environment to the production environment.

- The provision of other deliverables such as User training, the creation of the User Manual and the Project Review Report. If issues arise, then the project can be reiterated back to the appropriate phase.

The core three phases, the FMI, the DBI and the Implementation Phase are expected to be iterative and incremental. However, exactly how these three phases overlap and merge is left to a particular project to decide.

After the project has delivered the end product, the project team can be disbanded and the Post-Project activities initiated. This phase may cover such diverse activities as providing a help desk for users to ensure that the product operates effectively and checking that the expected business benefits have been achieved.

Within the two main product creation phases (the FMI and DBI) the primary mechanism used for handling the uncertainty considered inherent in the development process is the timebox. In any project, there is a fixed completion date, which provides an overall timebox for the work to be carried out. DSDM refines the concept of timeboxing by nesting shorter timeboxes of 2–6 weeks within the overall time frame.

Each timebox will typically pass through three phases.

- Investigation – a quick pass to see whether the team is taking the right direction.
- Refinement – to build on the comments resulting from the review at the end of investigation.
- Consolidation – the final part of the timebox to tie up any loose ends.

Each timebox has an immovable end date and a prioritised set of requirements assigned to it. Some of these are mandatory, some are of a lesser priority. The mix is essential as if all the requirements are mandatory, there will be no room for manoeuvre when things don't go perfectly to plan or when new requirements surface. The prioritisation of the requirements throughout the timebox is checked and possibly reassigned using the MoSCoW Rules.

The MoSCoW rules provide the basis on which decisions are made over the entire project, and during any timebox. As timeboxes are fixed, the deliverables from the timebox may vary according to the amount of time left. Essential work must be done – less critical work can be omitted. So, the MoSCoW rules are applied. MoSCoW stands for:

Must haves: fundamental to the projects success
"on time"
Should haves: important but the projects success does not rely on these
Could haves: can easily be left out without impacting on the project
"on budget"
Won't have this time round: can be left out this time and done at a later date.

A clear prioritisation is developed ensuring that the essential work is completed within the given timeframe.

Recent trends within the DSDM community have been to combine DSDM with XP to gain the benefits of DSDM's project management framework and business focus with XP's high efficiency and high-quality development practices, what has been called Enterprise XP or EXP (Craddock, 2002).

2.8 SCRUM

SCRUM (Schwaber and Beedle, 2001) aims to manage and control the production of software using iterative, incremental and lightweight processes (that is less intrusive processes). It does this by wrapping up existing methods (such as RUP) and agile methods (such as XP) together to provide a workable agile development methodology.

One of the interesting aspects of SCRUM is that actually it aims to help with the production of a "product" of which software is just one example. The benefits put forward by the proponents of SCRUM are:

1. The management and control of development work in an agile manner.
2. It explicitly acknowledges that requirements may be changing rapidly within its iterative and incremental approach to product development.
3. It is possible to still use existing engineering practices within SCRUM (which may help facilitate the introduction of agile methods into an organisation).
4. It is an inherently team-based approach and helps to improve communications and co-operation.
5. It scales from small projects up to very large projects.
6. It helps to identify and then remove any obstacle to the smooth development of the end product.

At its core SCRUM is a set of rules, procedures, and practices that are all inter-related and that work together to improve the development environment, reduce organisational overheads and ensure that iterative deliverables match the end users requirements. This is illustrated in Figure 2.3.

SCRUM is based on current process control theories and specifically aims to produce the best end result, given the current resources and time available. Note that it does not aim to produce the best possible piece of software given unlimited resources – rather it is based within the realities of the modern world and will help to produce the best that can be done given the situation within which it is applied. This may mean that some functionality, for example, is sacrificed (especially if that functionality is low priority functionality). Note that, as well as having an iterative cycle of only 30 days between iterative deliveries, it also employees daily reviews. These reviews should be short (of, for example, 15-min duration), and should force team members to address the basics of the process, namely they should consider:

1. What has been done by team members since the last meeting.
2. Is there anything causing a problem? Are there any obstacles to completing their tasks?
3. What will each team member do before the next meeting?

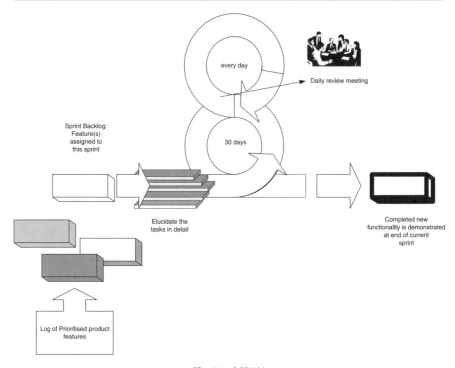

Fig. 2.3 SCRUM.

Over 50 organisations have successfully used SCRUM in thousands of projects to manage and control work, apparently with significant productivity improvements. These projects have ranged from financial products, through medial applications to internet solutions.

An interesting observation relating to SCRUM is that it can be viewed as a process that helps to wrap up existing (potentially software) engineering practices within a controlled iterative process. In doing so, it provides values, procedures and rules that can help introduce a more dynamic and responsive development process (in other words, it helps other processes to become agile!).

SCRUM can be applied from the start of a project or can be introduced during a product's lifecycle, particularly if a project is facing difficulties in completing all tasks and some form of prioritisation of tasks is required.

2.8.1 Feature-Driven Development

We have already considered four different methods which all consider themselves to be agile, why look at another? The answer lies in planning. The big advantage of using a feature-centric approach is the potential for managing an agile project, for handling the uncertainties that an agile approach introduces, for getting to grips with monitoring and reporting on the project. In many (most) situations, management will still wish to monitor the progress of a software project against some planning element and will still want to be re-assured that at the end of the day they will receive a working system. Although all of the above are primarily aimed at producing a working system, various project stakeholders still want to know what is going on.

A *feature* is a schedulable requirement associated with the activity used to realise it. These requirements may be user related requirements (i.e., be able to open a bank account), application behaviour requirements (make a backup every 10 min) or internal requirements (provide the ability to turn on debugging for system support). Each feature has a priority and a cost associated with it (for example, an estimate of the amount of person effort required to design, implement and test that feature). Thus, a feature mixes units of requirements with units of management. In addition, features should have the following attributes:

- Features should be small and "useful in the eyes of system stakeholders."
- Features can be grouped into business-related groupings (called variously feature sets or work packages).
- Features focus developers on producing elements within the system that are of tangible benefits to system stakeholders.
- Features are prioritised.
- Features are schedulable.
- Features have an associated (estimated) cost.
- Can be grouped together into short iterations (possibly as short as two weeks).

As can be seen from this list, features have many similarities with the goals and principles of the agile methods described earlier. Indeed you could use an approach such as Agile Modelling when designing each feature while applying XP principles to the implementation step of each feature.

This brings us back to the question why to consider feature-centric design. The reason for considering yet another method is that iterative lifecycles (such as those promoted by agile methods) tend to be more complex than linear one. They tend to:

- require more planning and re-planning,
- more assessment of where the project has got to go,
- more judgement of what should happen now,
- more monitoring of progress,
- be able to respond more quickly to the current situation (which potentially leads to more planning, etc.).

This involves asking some of the following questions as iterations progress:

- How are we progressing relative to the overall goal of the system?
- What are the priorities now and how have they changed?
- What issues and risks does the project now face?
- How can the issues and risks be addressed or mitigated?

Given that agile approaches are trying to keep things simple (or at least as simple as possible without undermining the overall goal of producing a working system), we need some way of managing the uncertainty inherent in an agile approach.

Feature-centric management of agile projects offers this element of control. In FDD, Coad (1999) and Palmer and Felsing (2002) present a five-step process that outlines how a feature-centric approach works, these five processes are:

Process 1: Develop an overall model of the domain and create an initial feature list.
Process 2: Build a detailed, prioritised feature list.
Process 3: Plan by feature.
Process 4: Design by feature.
Process 5: Build by feature.

We can elaborate on that by considering an iterative feature based lifecycle. This is presented in Figure 2.4.

In the diagram above, the flow illustrates the following steps:

1. First identify a prioritised feature list. This can be done by considering the systems' requirements. These can be produced in whatever manner is appropriate. For example, through use cases, a formal requirements specification or user stories. What is required is that they are elaborated sufficiently to allow prioritisation and an initial cost estimate to be associated with them.
2. This initial feature list is then used to create a plan of the iterations to be undertaken. Each iteration should have one or more features associated with it and should not be too long. Each iteration should have a timebox associated with it that specifies when it starts and when it finishes.
3. Before each iteration starts, the iteration should be planned in detail. This involves determining which features are still relevant for that iteration, any revised priorities and an ordering to the features.
4. Once a iteration starts, each iteration is addressed in turn based on their priorities. At any one time, one or more features will be worked on depending on the size of the feature and the resources available (note that no assumption is made here about how many people will be needed to implement a feature, there could be one developer per feature, two per feature or variable depending upon the step within the feature that is currently being addressed).
5. The iteration stops when the timebox finishes. At the end of the iteration, the current version of the software is tested to ensure it does what it should.
6. If this is the final iteration, then the final version of the system is delivered (if it is not the final iteration, then the current system may still be delivered to end users for early and frequent feedback). This is possible as each feature should be useful in the eyes of the various project stakeholders in their own right.

Thus, being feature-centric allows control to be regained over the agile development process as:

- features combine requirements with planning,
- timeboxes provide a structure to the plan and define how much time is available to implement the features,

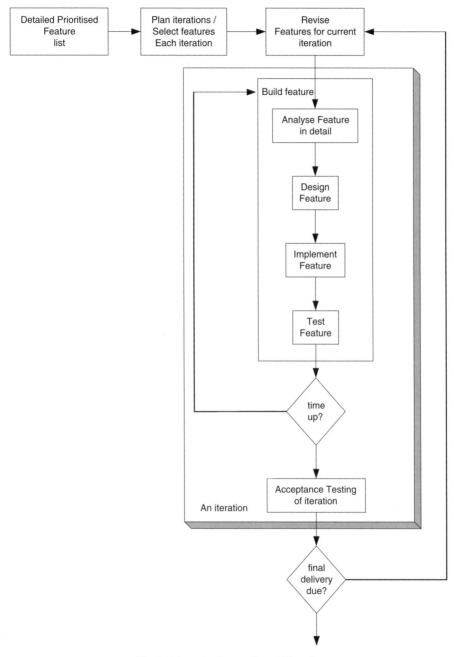

Fig. 2.4 Iterative feature based lifecycle.

- each iteration identified the features to be implemented based on the timebox and the current set of features and their priorities.

We will return to feature-centric approaches again in Chapter 9.

2.9 Summary

So what has this chapter shown us? First, that the various approaches within the agile movement have a common set of themes, namely:

- keep things simple,
- focus on producing the end product (i.e., the working software system),
- keep processes lightweight and
- remain responsive to changing requirements.

Second, that the various methods considered have different focuses and different emphasis. For example:

- Agile modelling focuses primarily on the design side of software development,
- XP not surprisingly focuses on the programming side of things,
- Feature-centric focuses on the planning side of a project.

Thirdly, that the various methods are not contradictory or even competitors. Rather that they can often supplement and support each other. For examples, a particular project may adopt a feature-centric approach, utilising agile modelling principles and practices with XP-oriented implementation steps. Indeed, this is exactly what I have done on a number of projects.

Finally, this chapter has illustrated that agile methods are not the hackers' paradise that some believe them to be. They are all grounded in sound software engineering principles and all have a significant focus on testing and quality assurance (after all the primary aim is to produce a "working" software system).

In the remainder of this book, we will return to a number of the approaches described above and will consider how an agile project can be implemented, run and supported by the software tools currently available.

3

Agile Modelling

3.1 Introduction

In this chapter, we will first consider some common misconceptions relating to models and model-based design. Once we have dispelled these misconceptions, we shall delve deeper into agile modelling. We will consider the attributes of agile models as well as what agile models look like and when they should be updated.

3.2 Modelling Misconceptions

Before discussing Agile Modelling, it is worth reconsidering some modelling myths and misconceptions that need to be clarified. These have a bearing on Agile Modelling as a modelling misconception can lead to a denial of the benefits that can be accrued from Agile Modelling.

1. *Models equal documentation.*
   Nothing could be further from the truth! A model is *part* of the documentation, but it is by no means sufficient as documentation. That is, a (UML) model, as good as it may be, cannot adequately represent all the information needed to describe how the requirements (functional and nonfunctional), behavioural and structural of a software system are to be implemented. For example, Figure 3.1 illustrates part of a Rose model developed for a real-world system built on one of the projects I have worked on. This Rose model has links to word documents (such as Overview), screen designs (such as *APS-Frame-View*), design notes (*APS-MVC-Design*), classes (*APSFrameController, APSFrameModel, APSFrameView*), Sequence diagrams (View SQM Questions) as well as class diagrams, collaboration diagrams, Visio diagrams (in pseudo UML as well as Screen layout designs indicating panels, layouts and components), Activity diagrams, etc. Thus, the models are (an important) part of the documentation of a system, but only a part.
2. *Modelling implies a heavyweight software process.*
   Again this is not true. The fact that you are using some form of modelling to describe your system does not mean that you must be using a formal software development process. It may well be that placing the modelling task within

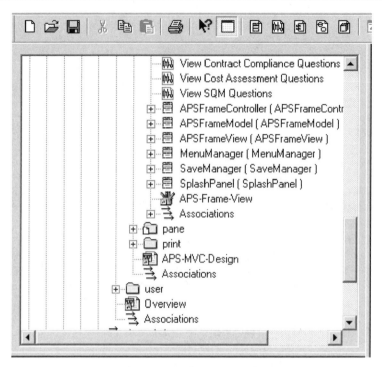

Fig. 3.1 Part of a Rose Model.

the context of a development methodology may well help, but modelling does not equate to a software process.

3. *You must "freeze" the requirements.*
   The point here is that many people believe that you must be able to freeze the requirements before you start to model. In theory this would be great. If you had all the requirements presented to you before you start modelling, then all the questions about what the system should do would be answered at the start. It would also make deciding on what should be in the model easier. However, that is theoretical, in reality requirements change (even in the smallest projects). This can be for a variety of reasons. For example:
   - Those who wrote the requirements missed out some details (that may only come to light when the development is progressing);
   - The users find their needs change during the lifetime of the project; or
   - The project is a Greenfield software system in which the requirements are difficult to ascertain upfront (or any combination of these).

   Thus, although for contractual reasons you may need to formally freeze the requirements, the reality is that these requirements will change. Thus, the design and implementation of the system may need to be "agile" enough to keep pace with these changes (either during development or in subsequent iterations).

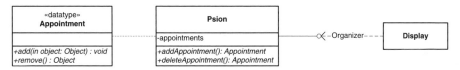

Fig. 3.2 Classes diagram produced in Visio.

4.   *Your design is carved in stone.*
     This is a leftover from the more traditional waterfall-based approaches to software development. In an ideal world, you would like to remove as many unknowns and variable elements from software development as possible. Therefore, to have the design "fixed" and never changing would be great. Again this does not work in reality. This is for a variety of reasons, including changing requirements, but also the fact that designs are an abstraction of the implementation. This means that as an implementation is progressing some elements of the design may be found to be unimplementable, inefficient or fatally flawed. Thus, during the implementation some changes may be required to the design to ensure a working system, etc. In addition, there may be some situations in which it is difficult to define more than a highly abstract model, as not enough is known at that point about how the system should work. Thus, the model will need refinement at a later date when some missing information or understanding becomes available. I know some of you may be thinking that you should not move on from the modelling phase until you have this information, but in the real world there are times when you don't have a choice.
5.   *You must use a CASE tool.*
     By this I mean that if you are going to do some modelling you must use some form of Computer Aided Software Engineering tool such as TogetherSoft's Together Control Centre or Rational's Rose. Of course, these tools may well make things easier, but they are not mandatory. Indeed in the first edition of Hunt (2003), I used the UML modelling features of the Microsoft tool Visio to generate all the models presented. As a comparison, Figure 3.2 is a diagram in Visio while Figure 3.3 is from Rose and Figure 3.4 from Together. As an extreme, I once worked for a software company, writing Smalltalk software for the financial industry, where they wanted me to use Paint to draw class diagrams. Note all of these (as well as hand-drawn diagrams) represent models.
6.   *All developers know how to model.*
     Generating appropriate, correct, well-formed, understandable models is not trivial. It takes time to get familiar with whatever tools, notation and

Fig. 3.3 Class diagram produced in Rational Rose.

Fig. 3.4 Class diagram produced in Together.

approaches are being used. Just as with programming itself, the more modelling you do, the better you get. In addition, the more you study the models generated by yourself or your colleagues, the more you will learn. Thus, just taking a developer and asking him/her to start creating a sound robust model of sufficient clarity and abstraction is generally a flawed approach.

7. *You can think of everything from the start.*
   One problem with UML style models is that they are static – that is, you cannot execute them. So, it is hard to determine whether they cover "enough" or whether you have missed out some critical areas. Therefore, believing that you can think of everything and cover all eventualities at the start of modelling is wrong for all but the simplest systems.

8. *Modelling is a waste of time.*
   I have both heard, and had to deal with, this myth. This myth represents the extreme opposite of that promoted by the waterfall boys – that is, designing models has no benefit, just get on with the coding – that's what you are delivering after all. You can of course see where these people are coming from. The model is not what gets delivered to the user and is not what will meet their eventual needs. However, let me ask you this "which would you prefer to live in, a tower block in which the architect first draws up plans, scale models and prototypes to confirm any outstanding issues or one where the builders just got on and did it?" Personally I would be happier in the one where some models were generated. And to some extent software is the same. On a personal level, I have found that working on software that can be placed within the framework of a model and in which the model provides the starting point, the basic structure and the context is extremely useful and I believe this helps to produce more robust systems. For example, on a recent project, the products of four software developers were integrated for the first time within an hour. I believe that this was achieved because we had generated appropriate designs and that at the core of these designs were the models!

9. *The world revolves around the data model.*
   That is, the data model describing, for example, the information in the database, is the centre of the universe and the object-oriented model is based on this. This is a view that is prevalent in organisations with a very strong database culture or in those that have migrated from a more data-oriented language. However, while there is certainly a mapping between the object and relational worlds it is not the case that the data model dictates the object model. The two maybe very closely aligned or they maybe quite distinct – it depends on the application, etc. It is also important to remember that the relational world of a database and the object world of, say, Java have

very different requirements when it comes to performance, maintainability and reusability and that these elements will impact on the design of their models. It is also not true that either is less important than the other. Almost every commercial system I had ever worked on had a database at its heart. Therefore, the data model used with the database is very important. However, the database was only one part of these systems and the other parts were just as important. For example, a gearbox is very important within a car; however, there are many other parts that go to make up the car and designing a car solely around its gearbox would be a mistake!

So what about the issue being discussed in this chapter – modelling in a dynamic, iterative and incremental process? Well issues 3, 4, 7 and 9 are the most important myths or misconceptions to refute. This is because these issues are in general wrong and thus we need to adopt a different approach to modelling (an agile approach).

3.3 Agile Modelling

So what is Agile Modelling? First, it is not a complete methodology in the sense that you can do Agile Modelling and that is sufficient. Rather it is an approach to the modelling aspects of a software development method. That is, it is an add-on to an approach such as the Unified Process (or indeed XP). The Unified Process is actually a framework. It has often been described as being heavyweight. This is true if you adopt the whole of the Unified Process. However, that was never the intention except for very large, very long-lived projects. Instead, you should adopt the aspects of the Unified Process that meet your requirements and integrate additional methods or techniques as appropriate. Figure 3.5 illustrates this idea.

The use of Agile Modelling is just another technique that can be used to augment the Unified Process. Thus, adding agile modelling to the Unified Process is completely in keeping with the original aims of the Unified Process. This is illustrated in Figure 3.6.

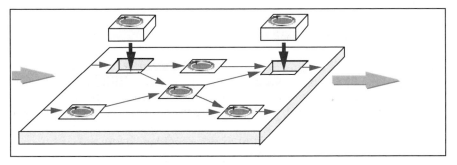

Fig. 3.5 The Unified Process as a framework.

Fig. 3.6 Augmenting the Unified Process with Agile Modelling.

Okay, so Agile Modelling is an approach to modelling and not a complete methodology. So what is that approach? If it is possible to summarise the concept of Agile Modelling into one sentence, then it is an approach that "aims to model just enough and no more!" Allied to this is the aim to use the simplest, appropriate tools for this modelling. Another way to put this is that the right tool should be used for the job. We shall come back to this issue of tools again later.

So, Agile Modelling "aims to model just enough and no more" but what does this mean? What is "just enough" and how do you know when you have done just enough! We will try and clarify some of this below but at this point let us remind ourselves of the criteria presented in Chapter 2 regarding Agile Models. Agile models should:

- *Provide positive value* in that they should have some utility, i.e. someone should need them.
- *Fulfil their purpose* (and no more) so if a model is to be used to clarify how some classes fit together, then that is all that it should clarify.
- *Be understandable* (to their intended audience but not necessarily to everyone).
- *Are sufficiently accurate* for their intended audience!
- *Are sufficiently consistent* as long as those using the models understand them.
- *Are sufficiently detailed*. For example, when explaining the structure of a group of classes, the exact set of methods, variables and constructors may not be relevant.
- *Are as simple as possible.*

We will look at each of these points in more detail below.

3.3.1 Agile Models Add Value

First, Agile Modelling assumes that modelling is a means to an end and not the final goal in itself (remember one of the principles of the Agile movement is that working software is the primary aim). Thus, you do not need to model every aspect of a software system if some of those aspects are either obvious, straightforward or may not be needed. Instead model what is actually required to understand what the software should do, how it will fit together and how it will operate? To put it another way, a model is an abstraction of the software to be produced, so by its very nature it should not be as detailed as that software, nor should it be as complete (otherwise you are writing the software just in a different language – which is generally a waste of time and effort).

3.3.2 Agile Models Fulfil Their Purpose

An associated idea is that you should model with a purpose – and not just model. This aims to help you to determine what should be modelled and at what level. For example, when creating a model you should ask yourself "why am I creating the model – how will it be used." If the answer is "I don't know," then you need to either find out or nor create the model. If the answer is "to explain to John how this part of the system is structured," then you have both the purpose and the level of detail.

3.3.3 Agile Models Are Understandable

An agile model should be understandable to its target audience. Thus, if a model is intended only for use within the modelling group themselves, then a shared awareness of basic ideas, concepts and components can be assumed and do not need to be reiterated again and again. For example, in a recent project we had numerous subsystems that employed the combination of a factory object and a singleton instance. These subsystems did little housekeeping type jobs at various points. The typical structure of these subsystems is presented in Figure 3.7.

Quiet quickly it became unnecessary to keep repeating this particular pattern of a Factory class, interface and implementation. Instead we could talk about the <X-Y-Z> *SingletonFactory*. If someone said this is using the RecoverySingletonFactory, then immediately people know that there would be a RecoveryFactory, a Recovery interface and a RecoveryImpl class. Thus, when these systems were referenced we could just draw a square box and label it appropriately. For creating white board based models this saved time and space. Of course to anyone new to the project this would have meant nothing, but within the context it was being used, the term and short hand was very meaningful.

3.3.4 Accuracy and Consistency

Another important aspect of Agile Modelling is that the models need to be only sufficiently accurate and consistent. That is, you do not need to worry about crossing every "t" and dotting every "i." Allied to this idea is that the model (or models) should be comprehensible to their intended audience (but by implication not necessarily comprehensible to everyone or at least sufficient for everyone) and sufficiently detailed for that audience. Finally, the models should be as simple as possible without losing their message. That is, unnecessary details need not be included.

For example, if I am using a street map to try to get from one location to another and I find that the map and the real world differ slightly (because of changes since the map was printed), I do not necessarily throw the map away. I

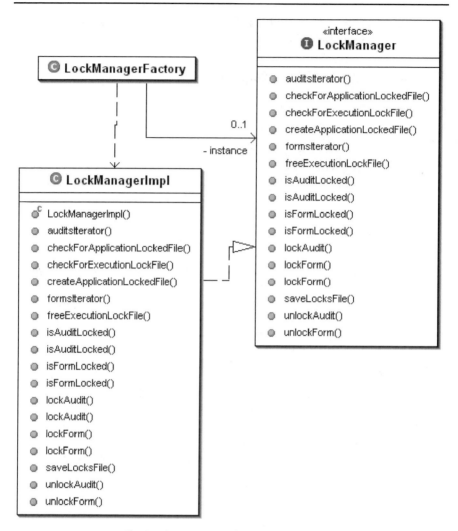

Fig. 3.7 A common implementation pattern.

may instead annotate the map at that point. Or use the map to find another route. Equally, my map probably does not show every house on my street, rather it gives an impression of a number of houses. That is enough for me to know that this is a built up area and that if I go to this street I will find houses on it. In many cases that is sufficient for my needs.

However, such a map would probably not be sufficient, accurate enough nor detailed enough for a utility company wishing to provide fibre optic cables to all the houses in my street. They would need a different type of map. Indeed such a map may well not only provide a great deal more detail of the actual houses and street, it may also show details that in my case I do not wish to know (such as what exactly is underneath the road outside my house).

3.3.5 Agile Models Are Sufficiently Detailed

It can take a great deal of time to put every element of detail into a particular diagram within a model. In many cases, the level of detail may go way beyond what is actually useful for the reader of the model. Agile modellers attempt to keep the level of detail presented (and therefore created) to the minimum actually required. For example, in Figures 3.8 and 3.9 we have the same class diagram.

In Figure 3.8, we show a great deal more detail than in Figure 3.9. However, which diagram do you think is better at showing the structure of the *EventManager* framework? Personally, Figure 3.9 shows me all the details I need to know to get the basics of the framework. And certainly early on in the design process, this may be as much as anyone needs to know other than the methods and properties that define the public interface of this framework. That is, the "contract interface" between the *EventManager* and the rest of the application. At a later date, if we need to, we can fill in the details of the classes (possibly by reverse engineering the code).

3.3.6 Agile Models Are as Simple as Possible

Agile modellers do not try to use every aspect of the notation available to them, rather they try and use appropriate notations and only try and define a minimum

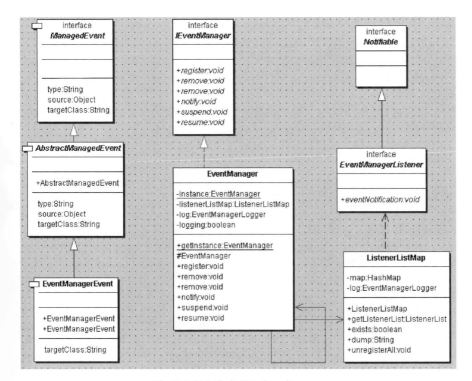

Fig. 3.8 Detailed UML class diagram.

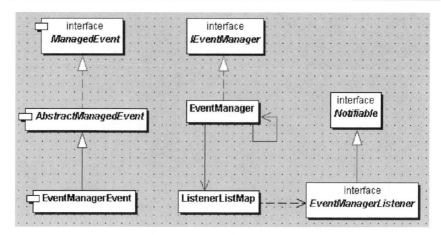

Fig. 3.9 UML class diagram with much of the detail hidden.

amount of detail within the model. In addition, if something does not impart anything useful in terms of information, then it should not be included in the model.

3.4 What Sort of Models?

Another key idea in Agile Modelling is that content is more important than presentation. For example, the hand-drawn diagram in Figure 3.10 may not be the prettiest UML diagram you have ever seen, the lines are not straight, the classes not complete, etc.; however, it is the message it conveys that is important. If this diagram is sufficient and effective in conveying that message, then that is enough!

One more point to note about Agile Modelling is that whatever a diagram or diagrams best suit the information you need to present, discussion or understanding should be done. This does not mean that you must produce many different diagrams. Merely that if what you need to describe is best presented as a class diagram, then use it. However, if it is better to use a Sequence diagram use that. In addition, if something is proving difficult to understand or work through in one type of diagram then move to another – it may be that this will help. Also do not feel afraid of mixing diagrams, placing some data modelling on a class diagram, which may well help describe your problem, etc. The key here is to use whatever tools and techniques are available to you to win the modelling battle. In general, it is likely that you will need to use multiple modelling techniques to understand a problem. Personally, I rarely find that a class diagram is suitable in isolation. In general, I will create a class diagram in parallel with at least one other behaviour-describing diagram (be it a sequence diagram, collaboration diagram, activity diagram or start chart or simple flow chart, etc.) and often more than one additional diagram.

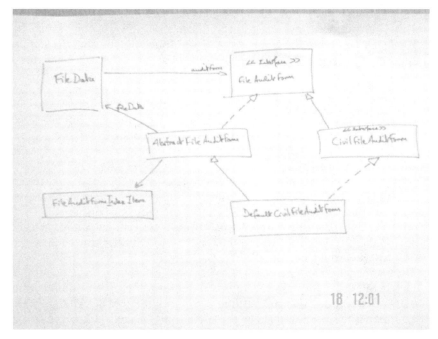

Fig. 3.10 A hand-drawn UML diagram.

3.5 Tool Misconceptions

At this point, it is worthwhile considering some misconceptions and myths relating to the use of tools, modelling and UML.

1. *UML requires CASE tools.*
   This is certainly not true – I can draw a UML diagram freehand on paper, use a simple drawing package such as Paint or indeed with a tool such as Together. It may well be true that to strictly adhere to the UML notation it is easier to use something that knows about UML (and Visio might be such a tool). It may also be true that if you want to generate code from the UML diagrams, using a CASE tool such as Rose or Together makes life easier. But it is not a pre-requisite.
2. *Modelling requires the use of CASE tools.*
   An extension of the last point is that if you are going to create models as part of your design you need a CASE tool that can manage, manipulate, cross reference, etc., your models. While these features may well be useful, they are not necessary. I can (and indeed have) used simpler tools such as Visio to perform all the modelling necessary for the design of a system. Obviously, the larger the system and the larger the amount of modelling performed, the better a CASE tool may be.

3. *Agile modellers don't use CASE tools.*
   This is a common misconception by those starting with Agile Modelling. This is partly due to the emphasis of Agile Modelling on using the simplest appropriate tool and if that tool is a white board or a piece of paper, use it. The key word here is *appropriate*. If I need to work something through with one of my colleagues, we might well use a white board or a piece of paper and not worry too much about the accuracy of the UML notation being used. If however, I am trying to describe a complex structure that will need to be referenced by a variety of developers, possibly in multiple locations, then a CASE tool might well be the most appropriate.

4. *UML is all you need!*
   Some take the view that UML is all you need in terms of notation – if you can't do it in UML (*aka* the design tool you are using), then it is either not relevant to an object-oriented system or not important enough to document. This is not true. There are many aspects of a software project that you may wish to document, but do not fit within the remit of a UML diagram, for example, GUI storyboarding, data modelling, etc.

5. *The CASE tool is master.*
   This is more a perception than a misconception. It is a perception because users often feel that they are battling with the CASE tool and that they have to work in the way prescribed by the CASE tool. Certainly, I know that some of the colleagues I have worked with over the years have an almost irrational hatred against one well known CASE tool because of the way it forces them to work. Some of this can be overcome with training and some by choosing a suitable tool. The important thing is that the CASE tool should *not* be the master but the servant. It should help you with your work and not hinder it. Thus, finding an appropriate tool (or tools) is important. For example, in one case Together proved to be particularly well suited to the organisations way of working and to the developers experience and background.

3.6 Updating Agile Models

Finally, we come to the question of when you should update the models you have created. The general gist of when this should be is "*when it hurts not to,*" that is when you actually need to.

What does this mean? Take, for example, the case on a recent project I was involved with. On that project, we created models of what we would implement, these helped us to understand what was required and the structure that would be used. However, for various memory and performance reasons, it was found that the implementations had to change to try and reuse as many Java Swing components as possible and to cache any data not actually being displayed. This necessitated quite a few changes to the behavioural aspects of the system and some changes to the structure of the system.

However, at that point we did not go back and rework the models as they had served their purpose – they had helped us to understand the requirements and how the system should be structured (in addition, they still gave a flavour of the system). If those models were never needed again, reworking them would have been a waste.

Some 6 months later, this aspect of the system was to be updated. It was at this point that a software engineer updated the models by reverse engineering the classes. He also worked through the code to update the behavioural aspects of the model. This had two effects: first, the models were updated in a timely fashion, and second, the software engineer involved gained a detailed understanding of this part of the system before he commenced further design.

In addition, some models may never be required again and can be thrown away. For example, the hand-drawn models used to allow myself and a colleague to understand how two areas of the system will interact do not necessarily need to be saved for posterity. The existing models may be more than suffice. Therefore, the hand-drawn model (created to help our understanding) can be thrown away. This means that it does not need to be maintained, fully documented, recorded, reviewed, etc. This can be taken further for more formal models, created using tools such as Rose. However, I tend towards caution and tend to feel that if the model was established enough to have been created in a CASE tool, then it should at least be stored in a version control tool (such as CVS or SCCS) so that it can be retrieved if necessary at a later date (otherwise the effort used to create the model may be lost altogether!).

3.7 Summary

In this chapter, you have seen that the act of modelling does not require expensive, complex modelling tools, but rather that modelling may involve anything from a scrape of paper up to and including powerful tools such as Rational Rose, Together Control Centre or a UML tool embedded in Eclipse. It depends on the motivation behind the model and the purpose to which the model will be applied.

You have also seen that Agile Modelling is truly a set of guidelines or principles that try to help the model to remain responsive to change and thus agile. As such Agile Modelling is clearly more art than science and inevitably you will get better at it the longer your try to be an agile modeller.

What you may have noticed with Agile Modelling is that we have not discussed the Agile modelling lifecycle or the steps you must go through or indeed the milestones that must be achieved. This is because Agile Modelling (as was previously stated) is not a stand along design process, rather it is more of an approach to modelling that can be applied to other methodologies (as an example see Chapter 7).

In the next chapter, we will consider steps you can take to help you become an agile modeller.

4

How to Become an Agile Modeller

4.1 Introduction

This chapter seeks to consider how you can make yourself an Agile Modeller or how a team of designers can promote Agile Modelling. We will do this by expanding upon the Agile Modelling practises discussed back in Chapters 2 and 3. We will then consider in more detail the supplementary Agile Modelling practises which, while not a necessary part of Agile Modelling, are useful in helping you achieve an Agile Modelling approach. We will follow this by discussing how you can maximise the modelling process (and by doing so become more responsive and adaptive and hence more agile). We will conclude by discussing how an Agile Modelling session might be run.

4.2 Agile Modelling Practices

The Agile Modelling approach defines a set of practises that help to make successful Agile Modellers. These practises are grouped into four categories of *core* practises and three *supplementary* categories. The idea is that in order to consider what you are doing to be "Agile Modelling," you must have adopted all of the core practises, where as the supplementary practises are optional.

4.2.1 The Core Practices

The core categories are:

1. Iterative and incremental practises
   - *Apply the right artefact(s).* That is, use the right type of diagrams for what you want to express (which also implies familiarity with your modelling technique).
   - *Create several models in parallel.* No single diagram type can capture all aspects of a system (or part of a system), so use different diagrams.
   - *Iterate to another artefact.* Keep moving between diagrams, particularly if you get stuck with some concept or problem. The shift may help to clarify the issue.

- *Model in small increments.* You should only attempt to model enough for what you need now and leave the rest until later.

2. Effective teamwork practises
   - *Model with others.* Do not sit all alone modelling away without any interaction, rather model in pairs; model in teams; bring in other people to help understand the problem. The resulting models are likely to be better.
   - *Active stakeholder participation.* Get users and other project stakeholders involved. This promotes rapid feedback as well as help to bring others on board.
   - *Collective ownership of the model.* Try to avoid people taking personal ownership of parts of the system model. This should ensure that no one ever says something like "Your model is wrong," as it is everyone's model. This should help to encourage a culture within which a problem in the model should be fixed and that this fix should involve those with the appropriate knowledge (including users).
   - *Display models publicly.* This ensures that people get familiar with the models and that the information within the models is shared. In some cases, a "Modelling Wall" may be set up for this specific purpose.

3. Practises promoting simplicity
   - *Create simple content.* You should aim at making your models no more complex than they need to be. Do not add complexity just for the sake of it.
   - *Depict models simply.* You should use only what you need in the notation you are using. You should also lay out your models so that they are easy to comprehend.
   - *Use the simplest tools.* Don't try to use a modelling tool such as Rational Rose when a whiteboard, note pad, etc. will do.

4. Validation oriented practises
   - *Consider testability.* That is, you should take into account how the system you are designing will be tested during the modelling phase (and not just during coding). Part of the agile mentality is to test often and test thoroughly. Thus, your designs should support this idea.
   - *Prove it with code.* At the end of the day, a model is an abstraction of what some software will do. It therefore needs to be proven in code. Within an agile approach, on iteration may be quite short and the modelling step and the implementation step close together. Thus, the model can be proved (or otherwise) by coding it up.

4.2.2 The Supplementary Practices

The three additional supplementary categories of practises are productivity, documentation and motivation.

1. Productivity
   - *Apply modelling standards.* That is, a common set of modelling conventions should be agreed upon and adopted by all modellers. This is the modelling

equivalent of having coding standards and adhering to them. It just makes life easier for all concerned. But note that this does not just mean "adopt UML," that is like saying "by adopting Java you have sorted out your coding standards." These standards should indicate the good and bad features of the notation and how they should be used. Of course, the standard should not obstruct the overall aim of being agile. Remember that understandability is more important that mindlessly following standards.

- *Apply patterns gently.* Design patterns are an extremely useful tool in designing the modern complex software system (see later in this chapter for more details on design patterns). However, applying a design pattern can (initially at least) result in more complex software than required. Thus, Agile Modellers do not try and jump in at the deep end and design in complex patterns. Indeed, as design patterns are effectively abstract design elements that must be instantiated in the current context, there is usually more than one way of "implementing" the pattern within the emerging design. As one of the goals of Agile Modelling is to keep things simple, ease into the design pattern by modelling as simple a version of the design pattern as is required to just provide what is needed. This initial model can be added to at a later date if required.

- *Reuse existing resources.* This is the Agile Modelling equivalent of "don't reinvent the wheel". An Agile Modeller will try to reuse whatever is available that does the job. Remember in many cases, designs are more reusable than code.

2. Documentation

- *Discard temporary models.* In many cases, when a model is created, it is only useful for a short period of time. This may be because the model is a work in progress prototype, or because it is only intended to clarify some concept among a group of designers, or a set of potential alternatives for an architecture, etc. If a model has fulfilled its purpose (remember Agile Models should fulfil a purpose), then the model is no longer useful and may be thrown away. If it is thrown away, then it does not have to be maintained, does not clutter up the model library and will not need further documentation provided for it.

- *Formalize contract models.* Contract models are those models that describe the interface between your project and any external resources. Examples of external resources might be an external database, a DTD defining XML files sent between your project and other systems, an external API (application programming interface), etc. These interfaces are fixed constraints on what you can do at these points and need to be formally defined and maintained. However, you should aim at minimising the number of these in order to travel light and keep things simple.

- *Update only when it hurts.* When should you update a model? This issue has already been discussed in the previous chapter. It is sufficient to state here that if a model is never used again, then there is no benefit in maintaining it; thus, the ideal time to update a model is just before you will use it, because this is the point at which it would hurt to have an out-of-date model. The implication of this is that model maintenance is done on a Just In Time (JIT) basis, meaning that many models may never be updated or may be revised years after they went out of date. This minimises the effort needed to maintain potentially obsolete models.

3.   Motivation

This deals with the basic question "when should you model". Agile Modelling puts forward two motivations for carrying out any modelling; these are model to communicate and model to understand.

- *Model to understand.* This is the commonest role of modelling, that is, modelling to understand the domain within which your system must be implemented and modelling to understand how the system must be structured to meet its requirements.
- *Model to communicate.* The second reason to model is to communicate your ideas with one or more people. For example, creating a model to discuss how two subsystems will interact or how a particular instance of a generic concept must be crafted.

4.2.3 Interactions Between Practices

Although Agile Modelling defines a set of practises that will promote its main aims, it is not necessarily very clear how they relate. (Figure 4.1) shows at the category level, how the four core categories support each other.

This diagram shows that "simplicity" makes testing easier and helps drive small increments. The application of the "simplicity" principle may also result in an increment that re-factors the design to improve simplicity. In turn, each increment should be validated and this validation (or at least the results of the validation) may influence the next (or later) iterations. "Teamwork" also has a bearing on iterations as it allows multiple stakeholders to be involved in each increment. In turn, smaller increments give more opportunity for those stakeholders to be involved. "Simplicity" also helps as it lowers the barriers to entry into the modelling world for various stakeholders.

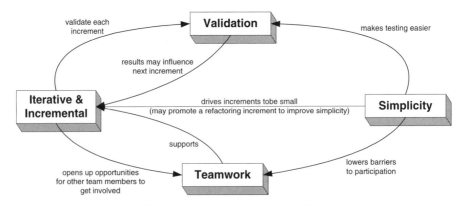

Fig. 4.1 Interactions between practises.

4.3 Adopt the Core Agile Modelling Practices

Having outlined the four core practise categories above, how do you go about achieving them or at least promoting them. In this section, we will consider this question.

4.3.1 Iterative and Incremental Modelling

First, let us consider how you can promote incremental change. That is, model in small increments (where small is relative to the size of the system). These small increments should then be validated (for example by implementing them) before moving onto the next piece of modelling work.

Incremental modelling promotes rapid feedback in the form of peer review comment, proof by implementation or from discussion groups. Part of this emphasis on small increments and rapid feedback is that if you find you need to throw away the modelling you have just done (perhaps because it has been shown to be un-implementable), then you are not throwing away a great deal.

This means that you are always modelling relevant and pertinent aspects of the system (i.e., they are about to be implemented) and are not modelling potential features that may never be implemented. It also means that any corrections to the model identified during implementation can be feed directly back to the model if appropriate.

Taking the concepts of modelling with a purpose and incremental modelling, we can now draw a flow diagram illustrating the overall Agile Modelling process. This is presented in Figure 4.2.

Figure 4.2 illustrates the basic Agile Modelling process. First, identify the issue (or features) to be analysed. This may involve client discussions, group analysis

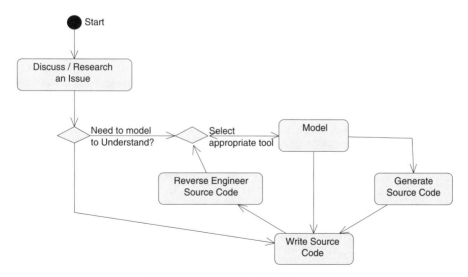

Fig. 4.2 Agile Modelling flow diagram.

or some form of research. Once this is done, the first thing you need to ask is "do I need to carry out any modelling to understand this in more detail?" If not then you can immediately start to write the code. For example, if what you are doing is writing a single class that loads images from a file and writes images back to files then you probably don't need to model it.

4.3.2 Working as a Team

This is easy to say but harder to achieve, because many developers tend to unconsciously take ownership of "their" part of the system. This means that one may try to blame, for a problem(s), other people's parts of the system and may only consider how they can improve or revise their own parts. They may also resist change to their "baby".

Agile Modelling promotes the concept that it is the team that takes ownership (and thus responsibility) for the whole system. This helps to avoid a culture of blame and also promotes humility – it is rare for one single person to know all aspects of a system and the environment that it is developed within!

There are a number of steps that can be taken to promote effective teamwork within Agile Modelling, these include:

1. Modelling with others
2. Active stakeholder participation
3. Collective ownership
4. Public model display

We shall consider each of them below.

1. *Modelling with others*
    One big problem with modelling is that it is an abstraction of what you are going to be implementing. Thus, at some level, some details are left out (otherwise you are not modelling but developing the code). Because of this, it is very hard to verify a model by inspecting it – it doesn't have all the details. Thus, you can't run a model and say "oh no! I have missed out this issue, feature, function, etc."). By modelling in pairs or in teams, there is far less chance of these features being overlooked. In addition, as the modelling process progresses, more than one person will be considering how the model fits with other areas of the model, how it will operate, what problems may occur, etc. Certainly, we have found that modelling sessions involving two or more people have produced very effective models. This does not mean that the whole modelling process needs to be done in teams. Our experience has been that a suitable room with whiteboards, etc., is ideal for the modelling session, and then one or more people are tasked with formalising what has been discussed. This more formal model (if required) can then be reviewed at a later stage, entered into an appropriate tool, etc., as required.
    An obvious problem for organisations adopting an Agile Modelling approach (which is shared with Extreme Programming) is that, organisations that traditionally had a divide and conquer approach to design may perceive that

they are "wasting effort" by using more than one person on a design task. Our experience is that this is not justified as the resulting models tend to require less revisions and are more robust than those produced by individuals in isolation.

2. *Active stakeholder participation*

   What does this mean – essentially that all those who are involved in the project, or have an influence on the project, should buy into the project. This may seem obvious, but it includes stakeholders such as senior management, end users, system owners, development and production support teams, etc. For example (and particularly if this is the first Agile Modelling effort being undertaken within the organisation), senior management must publicly and privately support what is being done, how it is being done, etc. End users (or system owners) must be prepared to and able to share their knowledge with the team as and when required. For example, having an end user who knows what is required available all the time is essential. This does not necessarily mean that they are physically available within the office (although this is a very good option) but that you can contact them (possibly by email or phone) at any time to confirm requirements, check out workflows, validate your assumptions, etc.. Certainly, I have brought them into modelling sessions before now to help work through what options should be available and how various workflows will actually operate. Other less obvious stakeholders include representatives of systems that you might integrate with (be they legacy or otherwise). I have been involved in projects where the biggest problem during design was not communication with the end users but with other developers in other groups due to the pressures and timetables they were under.

3. *Collective ownership*

   This comes back to the idea that no one person owns any part of the evolving model. There should be no one who thinks, "Your model is wrong" because all models are everyone's. Thus, if a model is wrong, then everyone has the responsibility to fix it. Although in theory, anyone can fix the model, in practise, for larger projects, there needs to be some control over this. One way of handling this is a list of models that need to be revised. These can then be reviewed by a team, and revisions and alterations introduced.

4. *Display models publicly*

   That is, let everyone see the models. This can be done on a "modelling wall" where all models are displayed. Although for large projects, this may not be possible and thus making all models available for scrutiny within a central resource or having regular "model fests" where models are put up and described using a projector can be done. Why do this? There are a number of reasons; first, everyone gets to see the models as they are evolving and take on board what is being done. They can learn from each other (that's a nice way of doing this) as well as consider how what they are doing fits in. Indeed, this can help to overcome issues related to integration between features at a later date. Second, it also helps to breakdown the cultural barriers associated with showing colleagues your work. If everyone does it from the most senior designer downwards, it becomes natural. Another benefit is that if anyone looks at the public models, then they can see how things progress (which may be important in convincing senior management that Agile Modelling is actually producing something).

4.3.3 Promoting Simplicity

Agile Modelling (along with other agile approaches) promotes simplicity in what you are doing. That is, you should try to adopt the simplest model that does what is required and no more (or less). The simpler a model is, the easier it is for others to understand it and to potentially find problems within it.

There are in effect two aspects to simplicity, the first relates to the way in which you model and the second to the content of your models. We shall consider both below.

Way in which You Model

Avoid making your modelling diagrams more complex than they need to be. For example, Figures 4.3 and 4.4 show the same class structures. However, in Figure 4.3, a lot more detail has been added. Does this actually add to the comprehension of the diagram or just make it larger. The version in Figure 4.4 has reduced the information presented partly by limiting the UML notation used on the associations

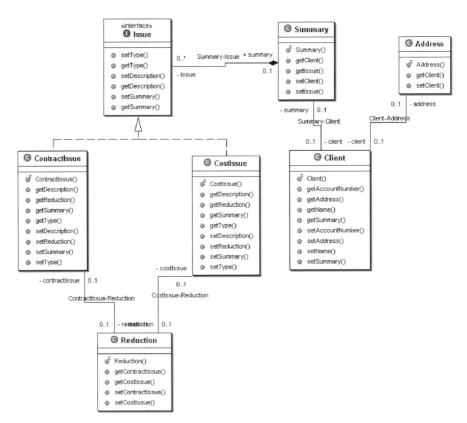

Fig. 4.3 A detailed class diagram.

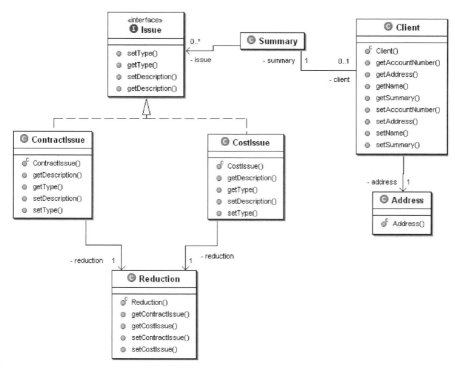

Fig. 4.4 A simpler class diagram.

between the classes. It has also hidden some of the class details shown in Figure 4.3. Depending on the purpose of the model, this may well make things easier to understand and simpler to comprehend.

Keep your modelling diagrams as clear and simple as possible. Even if you attempt to keep your diagrams clear of clutter, there are still lots of ways in which you can make it easier for the reader of the diagram. For example, you can explain about crossing lines, curved lines, diagonal lines, mixing top down layouts with horizontal or diagonal layouts (for inheritance etc.). Attention to apparently such minute will help to make your diagrams simpler for the reader.

Use the simplest modelling device available. This goes back to the points made in the last chapter about not necessarily needing a CASE tool. Rather, you should use the tool most appropriate to the situation. If I want to create a one off model to explain to my colleagues how the LockManager works, then drawing it on a large whiteboard in the meeting area might well be the best thing to do. Similarly, if I am creating a model that is expected to be refered by a lot of people on a regular basis, then creating it within a CASE tool might also be appropriate. Thus don't use a CASE tool where a whiteboard (or back of envelope) will do or vice versa.

For example, if you need to carry out some modelling to help in understanding your task (or how it integrates with other elements of the system, etc.), then you need to select the most appropriate modelling tool and do some modelling. Notice that this is a two-way process. I might start off by modelling on a paper or a whiteboard. I might use this as a medium for discussion and peer review. Once I am happy with the model (and decide that the model is worthy of preservation – see later), I can select a different modelling tool (such as a CASE tool) to represent the final version of the model. Once I have completed my modelling task, I can write the code for the model. This might be done completely by hand or may involve some automated code generation. For example, one of the very nice features of TogetherSofts' Together system is that it generates classes as you create the models. Thus, when you have to "implement" the model, the basic structure is already there. Once this is completed, you can reverse engineer the final result back into your modelling system (this happens automatically in Together) so that the model remains up-to-date. Various plugins for Eclipse give you the same functionality.

Travel light – create just enough models and documentation to get by. Another issue is how much modelling and associated documentation are required. This is of course a "how long is a piece of string" question. However, from personal experience, I have found that in many cases, detailed models that I have lovingly created have never been referenced or had to undergo major revisions long before they were actually used again. What does this tell me? First, it is hard to predict what will be actually needed in the future and second, don't try to create models just for the sake of it. Rather, create models where and when they are needed. If the model you create is on a whiteboard and it is wiped off after it has been used, then that's fine; if you create a model in a CASE tool because it will be referenced by many others, then that is why you took the effort to use a CASE tool. There will of course be many situations which lie between these two extremes, but in these cases, use the "update only when it hurts" principle so that if you have created a model and it isn't being used you do not revise it (at least not until you need to). The same is true for the documentation you are likely to create to go along with your models (see Agile documentation later in this chapter).

Content of Your Models

Avoid over-architecting your system to support potential future requirements. One of the key principles of the agile movement is to only do what is required now in order to "get the system out" and not to try to engineer features which may or may not be needed in the future. While this may seem an obvious statement and akin to telling your grandmother to suck eggs, it can be a hard one to resist. In many organisations that have adopted an object-oriented approach, the first thing to be done is to create the architecture within which the rest of the system will be created. But what does this mean? What is the rest of the system? Is it the current iteration or is it the full system that might be built within the next 2 years over many iterations. The temptation (certainly among software engineers who want to do the right thing) may be to design an architecture that will provide plugins for all possible future features; however, this may take a very long time and may result in features being engineered, which are never actually used. For the agile movement, the focus is on what is to be delivered now and thus the architecture should focus on that. But even here, things can be difficult, for example, a common object-oriented approach is to program to an interface. Thus, different implementations can then be provided for these interfaces. But what if there is only one implementation at

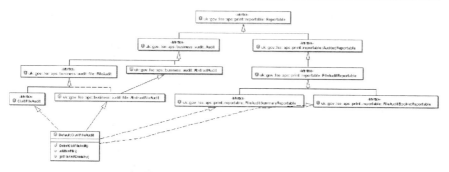

Fig. 4.5 A complex class hierarchy.

the moment – then why have an interface. With tools such as Eclipse, it is a simple task to re-factor the design at a later stage to use an interface instead of the class.

Avoid developing a complex infrastructure early on. This point is related to the above point. That is, don't try to over-engineer your solution early on for what you think will be required later – it will almost certainly have to change anyway. For example, creating a set of interfaces and a hierarchy of abstract classes that provide more and more functionality for a single concrete class may prove beneficial in the future or may not, but it is probably not required at the present time. As an example, consider the class hierarchy presented in Figure 4.5. In this figure, there is one single concrete class but there are two abstract classes and eight interfaces. This may result in a very flexible architecture for the future, but for a single concrete class, this seems excessive!

Assume simplicity. Assume that the simplest model is the best solution. This of course has to be taken within the context of the caveat that, what is referred to here is the "simplest model that does the job" is the best solution. An Agile Modeller should always strive to produce the simplest model that provides the required features, functionality, performance, etc.

4.3.4 Validating the Models

You should try to validate your models as thoroughly as you would your code unit or system test your application. In many ways, this is the Agile Modelling equivalent of the emphasis Extreme Programming places on Unit Testing. That is, you should make sure your model is correct and implementable. But how can you do this? Agile Modelling through its practises suggests that models can be validated:

1. *Within the team.* If more than one person examines a model and works through a model, then there is a greater chance that any flaws on the model will be uncovered. Use of the "modelling wall" may be an extreme version of this, but certainly opens up models to a great deal of scrutiny.

2. *With the target audience.* Although end users and those with the knowledge of the systems requirements may not be UML modellers, they can still have the

behaviour of any created model explained to them and walkthroughs of how the models would operate can certainly be carried out (personally, I am not a believer in presenting a user with a load of used case models or indeed a set of sequence diagrams and lettering them get on with it). If done with care, this can help in identifying potential future problem areas at a very early stage.

3. *Implement the model – The ultimate test.* As was said earlier, a model is an abstraction of the code that will be written. Therefore, to really test, the design code can be written to move the design from abstraction to the concrete implementation. This does not necessarily mean that you should implement the whole model to prove that the model works, rather I take it to mean that prototype code can be used to prove contentious parts of a model or areas of risk within the model. For example, to clarify if an assumption about a legacy interface, a Java feature or an operating system function is correct. It also means that within an iterative approach, such as that described in Chapter 2, you may be able to model a bit and then implement that modelling before moving to the next feature, and modelling that and implementing it. Thus, if the model for a particular feature is shown to be unimplementable (or to have less major flaws), then they can be resolved then and there and not some months later during some distinct implementation phase.

4. *Design for testability.* A final practise that should be adopted relating to validation is to consider testability when you design. That is, you should make sure that your design can be easily tested once implemented. This may seem obvious to you, but when I first encountered this concept, it almost stopped me in my tracks for its simplicity, benefit, utility and how obvious it was. However, I had not seen any writings about this before and realised that I had been failing to take testability into account at design time. That is not to say that the code was not tested, but this was not an issue considered during design. However, by considering how the code produced from the modelling phase could be tested, you can make it much easier for the person who codes the model to test it and thus make it easier to identify potential problems. Since encountering this concept, it is one of the things that I have most heartily adopted!

4.4 Consider the Supplementary Practices

Earlier, we discussed some of the supplementary practises that can be used when modelling in an agile manner. These practises are not essential but may make life easier for the Agile Modeller. As was discussed, these can be grouped into three categories.

4.4.1 Improving Productivity

The main aim here is to help you attain your goal quickly and efficiently. Using the approach "apply modelling standards consistently," in which you do not overuse the particular modelling notation being applied, and within which you reuse proven designs where and when appropriate helps productivity. This last point may seem contradictory to the earlier point about not using complex patterns too early. However, there is an important point here, we did not say don't use design patterns, but we did say "complex" design patterns. Design patterns can still be one of the most effective ways to reapply design knowledge between one situation and another.

4.4.2 Design Patterns

Historically, design patterns have their basis in the work of an architect who designed a language for encoding knowledge of the design and construction of buildings (Alexander et al., 1977; Alexander, 1979). The knowledge is described in terms of patterns that capture both a recurring architectural arrangement and a rule for how and when to apply this knowledge. That is, they incorporate knowledge about the design as well as the basic design relations.

This work was picked up by a number of researchers working within the object-oriented field. This then led to the exploration of how software frameworks can be documented using (software) design patterns (see for example Johnson (1992) and Birrer and Eggenschmiler (1993)). In particular, Johnson's paper describes the form that these design patterns take and the problems encountered in applying them. Since 1995 and since the publication of the "Patterns" book by Gamma et al. (1995), interest in patterns has mushroomed. Patterns are now seen as a way of capturing expert and design knowledge associated with system architecture to support design as well as software reuse. In addition, as interest in patterns has grown their use, representational expressiveness has grown.

Motivation Behind Patterns

There are a number of motivations behind design patterns. These include:

1. *Designing reusable software is difficult.* Finding appropriate objects and abstractions is not trivial. Having identified such objects, building flexible, modular, reliable code for general reuse is not easy, particularly when dealing with more than one class. In general, such reusable "frameworks" emerge over time rather than being designed from scratch.
2. Software components support the reuse of code but not the reuse of knowledge.
3. Frameworks support the reuse of design and code but not the knowledge of how to use that framework. That is, design trade-offs and expert knowledge are lost.
4. Experienced programmers do not start from first principles every time; thus, successful reusable conceptual designs must exist.
5. Communication of such "architectural" knowledge can be difficult as it is in the designers head and is poorly expressed as a program instance.
6. A particular program instance fails to convey constraints, trade-offs and other non-functional forces applied to the "architecture."
7. Since frameworks are reusable designs, not just code, they are more abstract than most software, which makes documenting them more difficult.

Documentation for a framework has three purposes, and patterns can help to fulfil each of them. Documentation must provide:
- the purpose of the framework,
- how to use the framework,
- the detailed design of the framework.

8. The problem with cookbooks is that they describe a single way in which the framework will be used. A good framework will be used in ways that its designers never conceived. Thus, a cookbook is insufficient on its own to describe every use of the framework. Of course, a developer's first use of a framework usually fits the stereotypes in the cookbook. However, once they go beyond the examples in the cookbook, they need to understand the details of the framework. However, cookbooks tend not to describe the framework itself. However, in order to understand a framework, you need to have knowledge of both its design and its use.

9. In order to achieve high-level reuse (i.e., above the level of reusing the class set), it is necessary to design with reuse in mind. This requires knowledge of the reusable components available.

The design patterns movement wished to address some (or all) of the above in order to facilitate successful architectural reuse. The intention was thus to address many of the problems which reduce the reusability of software components and frameworks.

Strengths and Limitations of Design Patterns

Design patterns have a number of strengths including:

- Providing a common vocabulary.
- Explicitly capturing expert knowledge and trade-offs.
- Helping to improve developer communication.
- Promoting the ease of maintenance.
- Providing a structure for change.

However, they have certain limitations. These include:

- Not leading to direct code reuse.
- Being deceptively simple.
- Easy to get pattern overload (i.e., finding the right pattern).
- They are validated by experience rather than testing.
- No methodological support.

In general, patterns provide opportunities for describing both the design and the use of the framework as well as including examples, all within a coherent whole. In some ways, patterns act like a hyper-graph with links between parts of patterns. To illustrate the ideas behind frameworks and patterns, the next section will present the framework HotDraw and a tutorial HotDraw pattern example explaining how to construct a simple drawing tool.

However, there are potentially many design patterns available to a designer. A number of these patterns may superficially appear to suite their requirements, even if the design patterns are available online (via some hyper text style browser; Budinsky et al., 1996), it is necessary for the designer to search through them manually, attempting to identify the design which best matches their requirements.

In addition, once they have found the design that they feel best matches their needs, they must then consider how to apply it to their application. This is because a design pattern describes a solution to a particular design problem. This solution may include multiple trade-offs which are contradictory and which the designer must choose between, although some aspects of the system structure can be varied independently (although some attempts have been made to automate this process for example, Budinsky et al. (1996)).

When to Use Patterns

Patterns can be useful in situations where solutions to problems recur but in slightly different ways. Thus, the solution needs to be instantiated as appropriate for different problems. The solutions should not be so simple that a simple linear series of instructions will suffice. In such situations, patterns are overkill. They are particularly relevant when several steps are involved in the pattern that may not be required for all problems. Finally, patterns are really intended for solutions where the developer is more interested in the existence of the solution rather than how it was derived (as patterns still leave out too much detail).

When Not to Use Design Patterns

Avoid applying complex patterns too soon. Much has been written about design patterns within the developer communities over the last few years and I have been one of those writing. I have certainly found that patterns have been a very useful way of designing software and providing a common language for communication within design teams. So why should you be wary of using complex patterns too soon. This is for a number of reasons, for example complex patterns are likely to make your design "more complex." This will make it harder for designers to understand the model, particularly for those who are unfamiliar either with patterns or with the pattern in hand. In addition, a design pattern is effectively a chunk of reusable meta-design which must be applied within the context of your evolving design. The way in which you apply this pattern may change as your understanding of the domain, application or system develops. In general, patterns become more useful as a design matures or as the complexity of the system is gradually built up. Thus, try to engineer into complex design patterns as and when needed rather than from day one.

4.4.3 Controlling Documentation

Documentation can be the mire which slows down any Agile Modelling project. Why? Because potentially you may feel that you need to provide additional design notes for each and every diagram you create within your model. Creating,

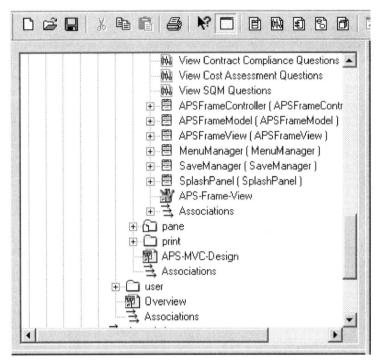

Fig. 4.6 Part of a Rose model with integrated word documents.

maintaining and updating this additional documentation is a significant investment and one which can eat into your time. For example, Fig. 4.6 illustrates part
of a Rose model developed for a real-world system built by Experis Ltd. This Rose
model has links to word documents (such as Overview), screen designs (such
as APS-Frame-View), design notes (APS-MVC-Design), classes (APSFrameController, APSFrameModel, APSFrameView), Sequence diagrams (View SQM Questions) as well as class diagrams, collaboration diagrams, Visio diagrams (in pseudo
UML as well as Screen layout designs indicating panels, layouts and components),
Activity diagrams, etc. Thus, the documentation and additional elements are (a
significant) part of the design of the system.

In fact, things are worse than implied in this diagram as some of the word
documents include screen dumps of the Rose tool illustrating the structure of the
classes and interfaces being discussed.

Maintaining these design aspects involves a significant amount of work, and
may actually accrue you little or no benefit. How then to control this volcano of
potential documentation. First, you should apply the "update only when it hurts"
principle. If you need to use a document and it is out of date, then that is the
time to update it (another way to look at it is that you update documentation in
a Just-In-Time fashion). This may seem lazy but it works very well. For example,
the person who needs this documentation is the one who notices that it is out
of date. In updating it, they gain a great deal of insight into how that area of the

system works. Once they have updated the documentation, they often understand it far better than if they had just read it.

But how do you stop this plethora of documentation being created in the first place. Two Agile Modelling principles are particularly relevant here; first, if part of your system interfaces with anything external, then this interface needs to be documented. Second, you should apply the same logic to the documentation as you apply to the models. That is, keep only models that have a reason to be kept and discard temporary models that are not needed. The same goes for documentation. If I am writing something down to explain some details to "Bob," then I should not necessarily make that part of the permanent fabric of the model. However, if I am documenting some core aspect of the system that will be accessed by numerous other areas of the system, then there may well be a need for longer-term documentation.

4.4.4 Motivations for Modelling

Finally, in this section, it is worth considering why you model at all? This may seem obvious, but I have seen situations where the motivation for modelling seemed to be to create beautiful coloured diagrams to hang on a wall and be admired. This may seem harsh, but in at least one case, once the modelling phase was completed the models seemed to be ignored. Worse during implementation the next phase of the system was being designed. The designers were using the models they had so carefully crafted a year before as the basis of the new system, but the programmers had ignored the models and were doing their own thing. There were numerous reasons for this situation and most had little to do with the models created, but at least some were down to the modellers creating very large, very detailed models that the developers found incomprehensible. The modellers had lost sight of one of the fundamental goals of modelling "To Communicate". For them, the end result was the model in all its glory. They probably considered that their primary aim was "To Understand" the application domain (which was within the credit assessment domain). And thus, they focussed on understanding the minute of their application and its domain. They failed to consider communication of their ideas to the developers. The simple act of keeping in mind that a model should communicate to others how a software system should operate can be a very useful frame of reference that can result in far more useful models being created.

4.5 Maximise Your Modelling Potential

4.5.1 Know Your Tools

As a software engineer you have available to you at any one time an array of tools to help do your job. Depending on your role or the activity you are engaged in, one or more of these tools may be appropriate for the task at hand. Knowing which tools are appropriate and when is an important factor (and this may not just be your choice) in your agility and the speed within which you can develop your models. One company I worked for over 10 years ago suggested that I use Paint as my core-modelling tool for creating OMT style diagrams. At that time, I was horrified but could not make them see why this was a problem (partly as they were only just starting to embrace object-oriented techniques and were not clear what this really meant). However, it goes further than that; it means actually knowing how to use your tools properly. Within computing, we are all subject to the "throw away the manual and try it out" syndrome. However, with today's sophisticated CASE tools, you really do need to know how to use the tools properly in order to get the most out of them.

4.5.2 Refactoring

One of the key concepts behind Agile Modelling is that you design for today and if you find tomorrow that a new feature requires you to modify your design you do so. These modifications are generally known as model refactoring when applied to your existing model. However, this is where CASE tools can be extremely useful, as many of these tools will make the task of refactoring significantly easier. For example, in tools such as Together and Eclipse, if you wish to move a Java package from one place to another, renaming all classes so that they are now in the new packages and modifying all references to those classes (in Java files and non-Java files), then this can be done with a simple drag and drop. Similarly, if you find that it would now be advantageous to have a Java interface based on an existing class and to reference this interface instead of the original class, and then this can be done from a menu option! This greatly reduces the laborious tasks traditionally associated with refactoring. This means that refactoring becomes less of an onerous task and thus one that is far easier to embrace. Thus, when doing design work, modellers are far more willing to think, "I can come back here and refactor this if I need to."

4.5.3 Test-First Design

Test-first design means that if you can design the test then you can design the model. If you can't design the tests then you shouldn't design the model. The implication is that if you don't know how the model would be tested (when coded), then you don't know enough about it to design it. There is an awful lot of truth in that statement as knowing how the model will be tested implies that you understand not only how it should operate, but also how it should not operate. Thus, you should design the test first then design the artefact to be tested.

4.5.4 Model in Increments

Incremental modelling is akin to incremental software development, in that it gives you a chance to create a piece of the model and then to test it, possibly by review, presentation or implementation, before doing some more modelling. This helps to identify problems within models early on. This is in contrast to more traditional approaches to design, in which the design phase is done up from one big step with the resulting design (and model) being implemented at a later date. Even some more incremental approaches still tend to advocate a large amount of up-front design, with the coding phase being the incremental aspect.

4.5.5 Think Small

Within the Agile Modelling movement, there is an emphasis on keeping things small, thus you should aim to keep your teams small as they require less management, less reporting and have better communications. You should aim to keep your models small, as they are easier to create, maintain and understand. Documentation should be kept to a minimum and should provide what is needed – just! In addition, you should keep your modelling sessions short so that they can be focussed and the results fed back quickly to the rest of the group.

In practise, this is fine and dandy for small projects but may not be so practical for larger projects. For example, it may not be possible to keep the overall team small because the project is a large one! But the points relate to having focussed modelling sessions and modelling diagrams that focus on various aspects of the system when they are needed can still be applied.

4.5.6 Agile Models Are Good Enough

An important point to focus on is that Agile Models are good enough for their purpose rather than being all encompassing or strictly accurate given the notation used. For example, if a hand drawn UML diagram varies from the strict letter of the UML law, then as long as those reading it still understand what is being said, what does it matter. In addition, if I create a diagram that does not include every aspect of the system but conveys to you what was required, then that is okay. It is important not to get bogged down in the detail (after all the model is not the end product, the software is that!) unless that detail is significant!

4.6 Agile Modelling Sessions

One of the key things proposed above is the use of modelling sessions during which those involved work on part of the system being modelled. This concept (rather than modelling in isolation) is not new but to model in an agile manner means that these sessions have a particular flavour to them. First off the modelling sessions need a reason. They exist to serve a purpose (and not as entities on their own right). Thus, it should never be the case that a modelling session is scheduled and at some later date the content of that session will be decided. Rather, in situations where a need arises then a modelling session should be scheduled. Remember, we are trying to "travel light" and thus do only what we need to do in order to achieve the final goal (working software). Thus, for every modelling session, there is a reason for its existence and a goal to be achieved.

Another feature of Agile Modelling sessions is that the right people are involved and only the right people. Thus, if a department thinks they should be involved in a modelling session and wants to send someone along, then they should be allowed to attend if they add value to the meeting. That is, an attendee at the meeting should have a reason for being there that promotes the overall goals (or to put it another way does it help the end user to have that person attend). It helps the overall goal of delivering the working software if the attendee can contribute information or knowledge to the session, it does not necessarily help the end goal if the attendee is there because a department does not want to feel left out!

So who are the right people to have at the modelling session and how many people should there be? First, the number of people attending should be kept to a minimum. Partly this is because of the increased complexity of communication as the number of people grows and partly this is because once the team gets too big then design by committee may ensue. Second, as a rough guide there should be at least one (and preferably two) experienced (agile) modeller(s), less-experienced modellers, appropriate project stakeholders as required (for example, database experts, operating system experts, end users, application requirements experts, etc.). These project stakeholders are not expected to actually perform the modelling but may be necessary for the modellers to achieve their goals. That is, they will provide information, clarify requirements and confirm assumptions as and when required. Obviously, in the real world having these people in hand may not be possible, but being able to contact them during the meeting for example, by video phone, email or telephone can be nearly as good. Larger meetings may also benefit a facilitator or meeting coordinator who chairs and controls the session ensuring that it stays focussed, decisions are made and actions are identified. It may also be necessary to have a "scribe" available to take down notes or minute what has been done.

Another key issue is how long the meetings are. The general philosophy is that they should be as short as possible, but as long as required to get the job done. My own personal experience is that they should never be more than a few hours long, even when the work will clearly take several days. Instead, the sessions should be broken up into half day or less sessions over several days as the breaks between sessions help promote rapid feedback with other members of the project and alleviate modelling session fatigue. Of course, modelling sessions do not need to last for hours and can be as short as 10 minutes or half an hour depending on the subject matter and the context. The key is that they should have a limited duration and a focus on a single topic.

The nature of the modelling sessions will also change over time. Early in the project's life cycle, the modelling sessions will tend naturally towards the "bigger picture" as the project team attempts to understand the domain and the application, the architecture to be adopted, what is in and out of scope etc. These modelling sessions tend to be of the longer variety and may spread over several days (although as suggested above, they should actually be comprised of several shorter sessions). As the project develops, the modelling sessions will start to focus on lower level details and are likely to be shorter and probably involve less people. These modelling sessions are likely to focus on one feature to be implemented, or part of a use case, etc. They may still last for several hours, or may just involve a couple of modellers for tens of minutes. These last very short sessions, tend to be focussed at a very detailed level and may be very iterative (that is, model a bit, implement a bit and model again).

Finally, all modelling sessions should terminate once you have achieved your goal!

4.7 Agile Models

One thing that needs to be made clear and has been hinted at before is that Agile Modelling does not focus on a single type of model. That is, when you are involved in an Agile Modelling session, you should not be doing class diagram modelling (to the exception of any other type of diagram or analysis). If you are doing this type of modelling, then you are not being agile; agile does not just mean being able to respond to changing requirements, but also to a philosophy or approach to modelling. Here it refers to the ability to move freely from one representational form to another as required by the evolving design and analysis.

To illustrate this, consider the modelling meeting room I recently set up. This room had three large fixed whiteboards on three of the walls, a digital projector and a movable freestanding whiteboard. In the centre of the room was a round table. This format allowed people to jump up and draw free hand on the whiteboards as and when required. Typically, each board might have a different view of the evolving model. One might represent a set of classes (in psudeo UML class diagram notation), another might provide a sequence style diagram and the third a description of the underlying database structures. The fourth might have a hand drawn representation of what the users screen might look like. Modellers would move between the different diagrams as and when required in a high iterative manner. This is actually natural for object-oriented designs (although sadly, it is not how modelling is done). This is because each type of diagram gives you a different perspective onto the evolving model but is not the whole thing. Merely focussing on a single type of model is a bit like trying to perceive a 3D world by only considering it from a 2D perspective. You would see only slices through that world and would fail to appreciate the overall picture. As an example, consider a person from a 2D world trying to understand the structure of a 3D orange. Rather than seeing a three dimensional orange sphere, they would see (from the side) a horizontal orange slice and would conclude that an orange was probably a long rectangular object.

Good modelling is therefore likely to cross boundaries involving, for example, the creation of class diagrams to understand the structure, sequence diagrams to consider system behaviour, and data models to consider the implications on a database, etc.

4.8 Agile Documentation

An important focus of the whole agile community is that the end goal of development is the working software and not the artefacts created along the way. Documentation is just one such artefact and is thus also not the end goal.

Therefore, to travel along the agile road, care must be taken with documentation. One of the key steps that has traditionally generated a lot of documentation is the design phase. Therefore, Agile Modelling needs to consider how documentation production can be made agile.

As with models, documentation should have been sufficient and should do what it needs to do but no more. It should have a target audience and thus be sufficient for that audience and should have a purpose.

Once again, we come to the question, what does this mean? What documentation should be created?

There are several issues here. First, the type of documentation required during development is often different from that which is required during an ongoing maintenance. Second, being agile means only producing the documentation you require now, and not trying to second guess what will be needed in the future. Third, what we mean by documentation and what form it takes changes as the project lifecycle changes. Initially, documentation may refer to requirements represented on cards or in user documents, later a large part of the design documentation will comprise models and various diagrams, later still comments in code (such as Javadoc) are part of the documentation of the system, and finally, various maintenance oriented documents may be created. Each has a target audience and a type of information that will be different. Finally, an important practical point is that few skilled technical authors are the modellers or developers who write the code.

Thus, the emphasis to be placed on producing documentation will change during the lifetime of the project. The production of very large detailed documents early on in the design phase may not actually help the production of the software. How many detailed design documents have been carefully written and then placed on the shelf hardly ever to be refered again?

This does *not* mean that Agile Modelling does not involve documentation and it is important to avoid the model's self-documenting attitude that can surface. Being agile certainly does not mean that! Rather, it means that you only create just enough documentation to get by and no more (but equally no less). How do you do this? As with models, you should produce documentation when you need it or when it hurts not having it and in an appropriate format for the audience. In addition, you should not be afraid to throw documentation away again. Not all documentation has to be written in a word processor, a set of hand written notes may well do just fine. Equally, an architectural design document intended to explain to everyone on the project the core framework may well need to be written in a more formal manner and held centrally within a version control system. It depends on the nature of the documentation, the intended audience and the duration of the utility of the documentation.

The content of the documentation should aim to provide just enough data and no more, i.e., it should be sufficient, just, it should have a purpose, it should have an audience for whom the document is meaningful (and thus to whom the level of detail is appropriate) and it should be sufficiently accurate. For example, I recently wrote a short document explaining a set of Java property files for an application we had developed. These property files had not been explicitly documented before as the source code's Javadoc essentially did that already for the developers. However, the application was now being handed over to a maintenance team who were not Java developers but would need to be able to configure various aspects of the application. Thus, concepts such as Java property files were meaningless to them, but a set of text files, with key value pairs were meaningful. In addition, the properties were described in terms of user functions rather than in terms of the Java classes they configured. The documentation was thus written just in time (on demand) and was focussed at the target audience. Until this time, the documentation had not been needed and would have had to have been revised several times as the property files had grown.

The documentation should also hold data when appropriate and refer it elsewhere when appropriate. This last point aims to apply to documentation, the same concept as is applied to the software – only hold data once, then it only needs to be updated once. Earlier, I had mentioned some design documentation that held screen dumps of Rose models. In this case, every time the Rose model was updated, the associated documentation needed to be updated even if the text was still valid!

Finally, don't document information when you expect the information to change (unless documentation is necessary to help make the change).

4.9 Summary

This chapter has taken you through some of the practises that help achieve an Agile Modelling approach. Some of the practises and principles may have sounded a bit like "home spun wisdom" but they do work. They may also not sound particularly special to Agile Modelling and many are not and could be usefully applied to many non-agile projects. The point is that by adopting all the practises, it helps you to become more agile and this should help you to be able to respond to the ever-changing demands on the typical software project, as well as to focus on the actual end goal, the production of working systems for end users. Later in this book, we will come back and review some of the practicalities of applying an agile approach in the real world on small and large projects and the experiences that have been gained. But for the moment stick with the concepts and get ready for Extreme Programming!

5

Extreme Programming (XP)

5.1 Introduction

In the last couple of chapters, we have looked at Agile Modelling, which applies agile philosophies to the modelling activities that take place within software development projects. In this chapter and the next, we will start to look at how these philosophies have also been applied to the act of programming. In our case, we will look at Extreme Programming (more commonly known as XP). XP is part of the agile movement that focuses on the writing of the software that will implement the required system. This may involve writing Java code, Smalltalk, C++, C#, database tables, XML files, etc.

XP has been widely misunderstood and is often associated with hacking, a lack of planning, avoiding the creation of documentation and of programmers wildly attacking code while working in pairs. One ex-colleague joined a company a few years ago that claimed to have adopted XP. One of their "rules" associated with XP was that the developers were not allowed to write any comments in their code (they used Java so they had rules that Javadoc was illegal). Their claim was that code was "self documenting" and, anyway with XP, you did not need any form of documentation.

All of these myths are wrong; XP does not say that you do not need documentation, or that you can hack or that there is no planning involved. Hopefully, as you will see from this chapter, XP places a great deal of emphasis on planning, and on the production of software that is as simple as is achievable, but that still gets the job done. This simplicity should help other developers understand the code; however, understanding the code often relies on good commenting, clarity of the actual implementation and consistency. It is not a hacker's paradise. Indeed, many of the practises that we will discuss later, greatly restrict (or indeed abolish) the ability to hack.

However, XP is very lightweight in terms of being a process (as was discussed earlier in Chapter 2). Thus, it is easy to take what you think you need from XP and create something which is neither XP nor particularly agile. Returning to the ex-colleague above, he recounted stories where the code within the system contained complex methods, with no comments and few if any tests. As the developers who had created the original system had all left, there was no shared knowledge available. This meant that when the system required changes, the dense code resulted in a lack of understanding on the part of new developers. This was partly due to the apparently complex design (it may have been simple but lacked enough guidance to elucidate its secrets), could not easily be retested after refactoring (which was most definitely required), was difficult to integrate back into the rest of the code and failed to follow current best practise Java coding standards. All of which breaks the guidance given relating to XP, and means that the company was not following XP and the project could not be said to be agile.

In the rest of this chapter, we will look at the values that underlie XP, the 12 core practises of XP and how they inter-relate and support each other. We will also consider the concept of a user story as used by XP as this is a core artefact often referred to within the 12 XP practises. In the next chapter, we will consider how XP can be implemented on a software project.

5.2 Core XP Values

The seminal book on XP by Kent Back is *Extreme Programming Explained: Embrace Change*, Published by Addison-Wesley (Beck, 1999). In this book, Kent outlines how XP came about and his motivations behind a great deal of what is in XP. Core to this are the four values that underlie the whole of XP. These values are presented as:

1.   Communication
2.   Simplicity
3.   Feedback
4.   Coverage

We shall examine each of these values below.

5.2.1 Communication

Communication within a software team – the very idea! Whilst this value is to many so obvious as to not require any explanation at all, it is not necessarily adopted within a software project. As two quite typical examples of what can happen on software projects, consider the following two (true) stories.

> *Some years ago (in 1995) I was asked to provide some Smalltalk and object oriented training to a small software company providing resource management software to the British Ministry of Defence (MoD). This project had 4 or 5 developers working on it, all in the same room. They had already started implementing their solution when they decided it would be useful to have some training on this new fangled object orientation stuff and on their preferred implementation language: Smalltalk. As such, during the training and mentoring sessions I tried to use examples from their own work to make things more relevant. One of the things that this did do was to help highlight the lack of communication that was going on in the team. On one occasion, I discovered that two people sitting opposite each other (but with their monitors facing away from each other) were essentially implementing the same core utility*

oriented functionality in parallel class hierarchies. They appeared to be blissfully unaware of the duplication they were currently involved in!

More recently, a company specialising in Java based web applications for academia here in the UK, wanted some guidance on applying some of the newer features in the Java 2 Enterprise Edition using JBOSS. However, their biggest problem seemed to be that their core development team were in a large room, with all the desks facing the walls around the perimeter and in which no-one ever spoke to anyone else and everyone jealously guarded their own parts of the system or the applications that they had developed. Their motto seemed to be "knowledge is power" and never talk to your co-workers, they will only steal what you know. Although some knew this was a problem, those who had been there the longest and were the most senior were the ones who were most wedded to the current ways of working.

Why do these situations occur? There are of course lots of reasons, but communication seems to be a very hard thing for computer scientists to get right. This may be due to the sort of people who are attracted to computing and software development in particular. It may be due to the practises often encouraged (and in some cases enforced) during their University education. For example, few projects undertaken in a University Computer Science degree actively encourage group working or communication of any sort. Indeed, many require the student to confirm that the project is all their own work and that they did not collaborate with anyone else!

Whatever the reason for poor communications, many problems or defects within software systems can be traced back to poor communications during the development of the system. This may be poor communication between programmers, between end users and the development team, between developers and manager, etc. For example, back in the late 1980s, I was involved in a project to create design analysis software for a large motor manufacturer. We had been working closely with two engineers to understand the processes that needed to be automated. Things seemed to be going well and we had a growing understanding of what the system needed to do. One day a third engineer was invited to join us (I don't remember now why but it turned out to be one of the most important things that happened). During the meeting, we were discussing the workflow of the proposed software system. Suddenly, the third engineer said "that's not how it is done!". Knowingly we said, "yes it is, this is exactly the same as if you were doing things manually." At which point, the third engineer turned to the other two and asked what was going on. At that point, the bombshell was dropped. One of them said, "We know, but we were keeping things simple for them, so that they wouldn't get confused!" In this case, the engineers had knowingly withheld information from us that would later have proved to have been potentially fatal to the project. Communication is everything!

5.2.2 Simplicity

A rule I have adopted and forced those working with me to adopt for many years now is to *keep things simple*. If a simple solution is adopted, then it is easier for all to understand. I have had to argue this case many times. I remember trying to convince a very talented and skilled developer that using a set of binary flags within an *int* to hold information about the state of the system was not a good idea. I proposed the use of a set of Boolean instance variables to do the same thing – each with a meaningful name. However, he was convinced that using a single *int* with each bit representing part of the system state was far more efficient, it used less memory and could be implemented using bit wise operations resulting in faster processing. The problem was that the other developers on the project were from data processing backgrounds and were not comfortable with bits and bit-wise operations. For them, this was definitely not the simplest design! Note that the application spent the majority of its time waiting for the results of database searches and in terms of performance this was the greatest bottleneck.

The simplicity value underlying XP says that you should aim for the simplest solution that does the job (echoes of Agile Modelling here). Why is this, the theory (and general experience is) that the simpler the implementation, the easier it is to implement, test, understand, maintain, etc. Thus, the easier it is to find and correct bugs in the software. This does not mean that the solution is necessarily simple or trivial; rather that it is the simplest solution to the problem in hand. In the above example, both solutions would work, but the use of boolean instance variables was a better fit with the simplicity criteria. That is, it is sufficient for its task, but no more or less.

Achieving simplicity is not easy. The simplest code may actually be harder to write in the first place. It is also hard to ignore tomorrow and not to engineer in features that would be great *if* you need this function in a future iteration. There are also other "pressures" that may limit the simplicity of the solution; these include the desire to produce some fun code or to "impress other programmers" with your skill. The problem is that the feature you thought would be implemented tomorrow, may never be implemented, or the day after tomorrow, it becomes something very different altogether!

As Kent Beck says in Beck (1999):

> XP is making a bet. It is betting that it is better to do a simple thing today and pay a little more tomorrow to change it if it needs it, than to do a more complicated thing today that may never be used anyway.

5.2.3 Feedback

It is good to get feedback. Projects should get feedback early, and often, from the customer, from the team, from real end users, from other project stakeholders, etc. It helps to identify problems early on, deal with unknowns and clarify issues. That is, it generally helps avoid nasty shocks later on.

Feedback can be at many different levels, for example, by running unit tests every time any new code is integrated into the system, any problem introduced by the new code can be identified immediately. At another level, giving frequent small releases to friendly end users, containing just enough new functionality to make it worth their while, means that they can provide feedback quickly and frequently about the evolving system (rather than waiting for a big bang delivery and then saying – that's not what I wanted!).

5.2.4 Courage

You will need courage to adopt XP. Why? Because you need courage to refactor code (that is change existing code so that it is better than it was before but such that it does not provide any new functionality), you need courage to throw away code, you need courage to code for now and leave tomorrow to tomorrow and you need courage to move management to adopt XP's way of working.

5.3 User Stories

User stories are developed any time by customers, but particularly during the planning game – a process which occurs at the start of an XP project. A user story is a description in the customers' own words, describing what the system needs to do. Conceptually, they are written by the customers, although in practise a developer may write down what a customer tells them. Each user story is captured separately; Beck (1999) recommends the use of index cards as they are relatively small, easy to move around, order and shuffle and cheap to throw away if required.

Each user story has a name, a short paragraph describing the purpose of the story, an estimate of how long it will take to implement (which may be "we don't know"), and a relative importance (such as "must have," "should have" and "nice to have").

In general terms, a user story describes something that the system must do in a way that is *meaningful* to the project stakeholders (and is thus not written in "techie talk"). It is not generally that detailed (index cards limit the amount of space available) and can be treated as a placeholder for more detailed requirements that will be obtained at a later date.

Note that it is customers, however, who can validate (and reject) stories and not developers.

A question which frequently arises is how does user stories relate to RUP's use cases or to Features in Feature Driven Development (FDD). For the moment, we will evade this question slightly and merely say that they are all trying to achieve the same goal, that is, to identify what the system must do in order that these "what the system must do" descriptions can be used to drive the development process.

5.4 The Twelve XP Practises

Given the four values presented above, twelve practises have been developed that try to translate these into a way of working that achieves the aims of XP. If you like, they are the twelve "best practises" that will allow you to fully adopt Extreme Programming on a development project.

Looking at these best practises, you may wonder at their apparent simplicity, but you should note a number of factors about them:

1. There is actually little new here – the practises are in general, well tried.
2. Where one practise is weak, another compensates – thus they work as a whole.

3. One of the important ideas behind the agile movement is to be lightweight.
4. XP is *not* a complete methodology (but we will come back to this point later).

As mentioned above, there are twelve core practises which effectively define XP. If you have not adopted all twelve, then you are not truly doing XP (although you may be very near to XP within some agile continuum).

The 12 practises are:

1. *The planning game.* This focuses on planning the next release.
2. *Small releases.* A software system is developed iteratively with small releases adding system features and allowing rapid feedback.
3. *Simple design.* Keep things as simple as possible but not simpler.
4. *Testing.* Unit tests and acceptance tests must be continually developed and the code must pass unit tests for development to continue.
5. *Refactoring.* This involves improving the system (e.g., to aid simplicity) without changing the functionality.
6. *Pair programming.* All code is developed by developers working in pairs (at a single machine).
7. *Collective ownership.* Everyone owns all the code so anyone has the right to change any of the code at any time in order to improve it.
8. *Continuous integration.* New code is integrated and the system rebuilt every time a task is completed (which may be many times a day).
9. *On-site customer.* Have a real customer as part of the team, so that they are always available to answer questions.
10. *Coding standards.* Have them and use them.
11. *40-hour week.* Work no more than 40 hours a week so that the developers are always fresh and ready for the challenges facing them.
12. *System metaphor.* Use the system metaphor to guide the whole development. It is a metaphor for how the system operates (it is similar to the architecture of the system but typically simpler).

We will come back to the practicalities of the practises in the next chapter; for the moment, we will explore each practise in more detail.

5.4.1 The Planning Game

5.4.1.1 What's in a Name

First let us deal with the name of this practise "The Planning Game". I have found that the very name of this practise causes problems (at least here in the UK). The questions I have encountered range from "what's a game got to do with serious software development?" to "why make us play a game, we want to plan the project?" The idea of this practise is far more serious than the name obviously implies. If you have a problem with calling this practise the planning game then call it something like the "Project Planning Workshop." For me, this name is a far more accurate description of what it does. However, XP has framed this practise in terms of a game to help elucidate what should happen when planning an XP project; we will therefore stick with the term "Project Planning Game" in this book.

Planning an XP Project

XP projects involve a great deal of planning. This may have come as a shock to some as they may have thought of XP as legalised hacking and thus considered planning to have no part in XP. But planning is core to XP, although it is a very different form of planning than that which might be found within a more traditional single delivery style of project.

Many times, in a more traditional development project, a large amount of time is spent crafting an elegant, complex and detailed plan using some tool such as Microsoft Project. The end result is printed proudly by the project manager on the largest printer available. They may even hang it on a wall for all to see. What happens next obviously varies, but here is a scenario that is actually an amalgam of various projects I have been in some way associated with in the past.

1. Developers begin to examine the plan and start making comments about how anyone could expect them to produce component X is 3 days, or question where the database migration task is.
2. As development progresses, developers tell their project leaders of their progress and estimated completion times, projects leaders tell their manager. At each stage, people unconsciously (or otherwise) err on the side of optimism in their estimates. Resulting in a better-estimated position than is the actuality.
3. The manager may or may not enter into the plan, the current state of the project, as he sees it.
4. At some point, some critical milestone is missed, at this point, the plan is re-assessed and it is realised that the plan and reality are out of alignment. The manager then tries to find a way of squaring the circle of the project. At this point, they may start forcing people to work excessive overtime or may negotiate a later delivery or modify the list of features to be implemented. All of which usually involve extensive discussions with the client.
5. The resulting plan may lead the whole project back to step 1 again and a new cycle of catastrophe planning.

In XP, project planning is a more incremental and inclusive process. It is incremental in that an overall plan of the project is created to determine (roughly) when each release will occur and what will be in that release (at the level of overall functionality). Then at the start of each iteration, what will be in that iteration or release are determined in detail and an implementation plan for that release is created at that point. As each iteration is relatively short, the act of planning happens very near to the point at which the work is done. There is therefore little chance for the plan and reality to become out of sync. It also means that if one iteration does go awry, then the reasons for this can be examined at the start of the next iteration and action taken to avoid this problem in the future.

The idea behind the planning game is that XP projects need to be planned just as much as any other software development project, but they need to be planned in an agile manner. Thus, they should be allowed to respond to changes in requirements, etc. Therefore, on an XP project, you initially start off by making a rough plan quickly. This plan is then gradually refined, as more information becomes available and as required features change, etc.

Agile Influences on Planning an XP Project

You are working on an XP project, so naturally you want to plan in an agile manner. That is, you wish to apply agile principles to planning your work. But what does this mean? There are a number of implications for how you will carry out any planning for an agile project that come from trying to be agile. These are:

- Plan for now
- Responsibility
- Dependencies
- Simplicity

We will briefly describe each of these below:

Plan for now. This is akin to only implementing what you need for today and leaving the rest for tomorrow. Thus, you should only do the planning that you need for the next release/next iteration in detail and no more. You can still do long-term planning, but not in such great detail. For example, you might decide (roughly) what will be in future releases, at the level of user stories but expect to come back and look at the detail of a particular release when that release is due. Part of this comes from the realisation that at the start of that release, when you consider the user stories to be implemented, you may find that a different set are required due to user feedback, or changing requirements, etc.

Responsibility. The typical project is planned top down. That is, the top-level management try and plan the project (hopefully with input from the actual developers). The end result is a plan for which the developers feel no responsibility and towards which they feel no trust. Agile planning involves the developers the whole way. They should feel that the plan is as much theirs as it is the managers. Thus, for example, the person expected to implement a particular feature is the one who must estimate it. Also, remember that in XP, an iteration should be very short and have a duration of weeks rather than months.

Dependencies. When planning an XP project, you should ignore the dependencies between parts. That is, you should not worry about whether task x is required before task y. Instead, you should focus on the highest business priorities first and allow other issues to come out in the wash.

Simplicity (in planning). You should keep in mind the type of planning that is being done at that point in time in order to keep things as simple as possible (but not too simple). For example, if you are planning to help determine the priorities and ordering of user stories, then much less detail is required. However, if you are planning the implementation of a set of tasks for a particular iteration, then far greater detail is required.

The Planning Game in Detail

The planning game relies on user (customer) stories to drive the iterations of the project. These user stories are used to determine which features will go into which iterations. From this, appropriate releases can be identified. Note that not all iterations may result in a release being produced; as it is only worth handing a release over to the users once there is something new and worthwhile for them to look at. It is qute possible that a single iteration will not result in any obvious new functionality to the end user and thus there may not be any benefit obtained by creating a release.

Although the primary output of the Business Game is the plan, it:

- allows customers to make business decisions,
- allows developers to make technical decisions.

And to combine the results into the iteration oriented plan.
Within this framework the customer determines:

- Scope – what is in and out of the system.
- Priority – what is more important, less important, must haves and nice to haves, etc.
- Composition of releases – what will be in each release.
- Release dates

In turn, the development team decides

- Estimates of how long various features will take.
- Consequences of for example, using a particular technology, for example, Linux versus Microsoft Windows XP, Java versus C#, J2EE (Java 2 Enterprise Edition) versus .Net.
- Team and Project Organisation (e.g. the organisation of the tasks)
- Risks associated with different features (e.g. will MySQL provide the required level of performance or should an Oracle database be used).
- Detailed scheduling – which features are to be done when and in what order. This involves balancing the technical risks (which will benefit from being addressed early on) with the business priorities that may be more important to the end user.

So how does the game proceed? We will only present a brief outline of the planning game here as we will return to it in more detail in the next chapter. Essentially, the planning game is comprised of two players (the Business and the Development). The business is made up of all those who can make a decision about what the system should do. The development is made up of all those who will be involved in implementing the system.

The game has three phases through which play proceeds. These phases are the exploration phase, the commitment phase and the steering phase. Although we will describe each phase sequentially, play does not necessarily flow sequentially from one phase to another, nor from one move to another within each phase.

Rather the whole process is cyclical, and play moves between steps as and when required. The steps performed during each phase are:

Elaboration phase

This phases help to identify what the system needs to do. It is compressed of the following steps:

Write a story – the business writes a user story describing some behaviour required of the system.

Estimate a story – development estimates how long the story will take to implement. If they cannot estimate the story or the story seems too big then they can ask for clarification or break the story up into smaller chunks.

Break a story up – the business must break a story down into small chunks if required.

Commitment Phase

This phase allows business to determine the scope of the release and when that release will occur (based on information provided by development and business). The steps within the commitment phase are:

Sort by value – business must sort the stories (written on index cards) into three plies (1) must have, (2) should have and (3) nice to have. This is effectively applying a relative priority to each story.

Sort by risk – Development now sorts the stories into three further piles (1) stories that can be estimated precisely, (2) stories that can be estimated roughly and (3) stories that can't be estimated.

Set velocity – development indicates how quickly they will be able to achieve the estimates (which have been made in an idealised type of time).

Choose scope – Business selects which user stories will be in the next release.

Steering Phase

The purpose of the steering phase is to allow the plan to be updated as things change over time. This phase is a little different from the last two in that the last two are likely to have happened at the same time. This phase happens later on within an iteration or between iterations as required. The players return to the game to consider what has been happening during the lifetime of the project (or at least the lifetime of the current iteration, etc.). The steps in the steering phase are:

Iteration – from each iteration the business picks the stories that will form that iteration.

Recovery – if it is realised that not all the stories can be implemented for a particular iteration, then Development must ask Business to help determine which stories should remain in the iteration and which might be moved to later iterations.

New Story – if Business realises that an important story has been omitted, then it can introduce that story to Development. This story can be estimated and the iteration re-planned. This will probably mean that one or more existing stories will be removed from the current iteration, etc.

Re-estimate – if it is clear that the current plan was over or under optimistic, then Development can re-estimate the remaining user stories and adjust the project velocity and consider the resulting implications.

By following through the planning game, a set of requirements for each iteration can be produced. Depending on the stage of the project, the current iteration may be planned in detail, with a future iteration only penned out in terms of anticipated user stories. This is okay as at the start of each iteration, the planning game will occur again. In fact, there are actually two types of planning games, they are:

1. The initial planning game
2. The release/iteration planning game.

The only real difference between the two versions of the planning game is in the level of detail. The initial planning game paints with a broad brush and plans the general set of iterations and roughly plans out the user stories for each iteration. It is only really interesting in ballpark estimates, etc. The release or iteration planning game, plans out in more detail a single iteration and explores the high level user stories by breaking them down into lower level stories.

5.4.2 Small Releases

The system being developed should be released often to the end users so that they can provide frequent and rapid feedback to the development team. Thus, the smallest possible releases that can add business value should be identified and scheduled. That is, as soon as a set of tasks can add value to the customer, it should be released to that customer. This not only allows customers frequent opportunities for providing feedback (such as that's not what we meant, or actually that's difficult to use), but also makes short-term planning easier. That is, each instance of the planning game needs to consider only the next few weeks and thus the level of unknowns and the amount that the team can have diverged from the plan is limited.

5.4.3 Simple Design

So here's a shock for some – XP does do design! However, it is design with a particular emphasis – the code that is produced. In pure XP, this design process also happens just as the code is to be implemented. XP itself does not mandate how the code is designed, it could be done merely by the pair programmers discussing how they would approach the coding, it could be done in an Agile Modelling manner, it could be done using flow charts, etc. This is beyond the scope of XP.

However, XP does present the following as being features of a simple (and thus from XP's point of view) effective design. A simple design is one that:

- Passes all the tests available for it.
- Has no duplicated logic.

- Ensures that any assumptions, or intentions, made by the developers are explicit to anyone reading the code (for example by using Javadoc or other comments in the code).
- Has the fewest possible classes and methods.

XP claims that by ensuring that your design has the following characteristics, you will produce the simplest possible design.

Note that as with Agile Modelling "the simplest design" does not necessarily mean that it is a particularly simple, small or trivial design. The key is that it is the simplest design that allows you to fulfil its purpose and no more (or less).

5.4.4 Testing

In XP, testing is all pervasive. Test are produced before any code is written, acceptance tests are generated as soon as requirements (in the form of user stories) are written, unit tests are produced before the code is implemented, all code must pass all tests from development to progress, etc.

This may seem a little extreme (but hey it is Extreme Programming we are talking about). But the idea is that no code should exist without an associated test. Indeed things are taken further with "Test first Coding" the XP equivalent of "Test First Design" described in Agile Modelling. That is, you should be able to write (and indeed should actually write) the tests for a module before you implement that module. The argument is that if you can't write the tests for the module, then you don't know enough about the module to implement it yet.

The arguments for test first coding are persuasive. I was once asked to provide training for a project that used several "Industrial Year Trainees". These were undergraduate students, who had taken a year out from their degrees to work in the industry (sometimes as a compulsory part of their course). Some of these students were asked to implement a large number of commands that would be used with an implementation of the command pattern. This pattern is used to represent a request to perform some operation on an object without hard coding that request. Instead, a *command* object is instantiated and configured to indicate the operation to perform and any parameters to pass. This also allows the command objects to be manipulated, stored, queued, sequenced and in some cases undone. The use of patterns was alien to the industrial year students, as was the application and as were client server systems (and the command pattern was being used between a client and the server). The end result was that the students implemented the commands and treated the ability to compile the code as sufficient testing to release the code to the central repository. As might be predicted, this caused chaos and resulted in a great many commands never working, and having to be re-written from scratch. If the students had been forced to write the tests first, then either they would have learned enough to understand what they needed to do, or the problems they were encountering might have been highlighted earlier. Pair programming might also have alleviated this situation by coupling those with more experience with the relatively inexperienced students.

Test first coding thus gives you:

- a complete set of tests for all code produced (as you created the tests first).
- simplest code that passes all tests.
- a clear view of what code should and should not do.
- a simple way of checking that refactored code has not altered functionality.
- a great deal of "documentation" explaining what a particular module should or should not do.

Returning to the actual tests themselves, there are in fact two types of tests that are being referred to when XP discusses testing, these are Unit Tests (produced by programmers) and Acceptance tests (developed by customers and end users).

The developers write the unit tests as they are developing the source code. In many XP projects, some form of automated unit test framework is used. For example, in Java projects, it is most common to use the JUnit unit test framework that is discussed later in this book.

In turn, customers should write the acceptance tests when they write the user stories. These acceptance tests are usually written from the perspective of the end user and thus may be harder to "prove." However, depending on the application, it may be possible to provide some form of acceptance test tool that will allow the acceptance test to be automated.

Whatever form the tests actually take, all code must pass all unit tests, before development is allowed to proceed. If unit tests are automated, then it is possible to use tools such that as a new build is created, it can automatically be tested before code is checked into the central source code repository. Tools that support this sort of behaviour include ANT (the Java source code build engine), CVS (the version control and source code repository) and JUnit. We shall return to such tools later in Chapter 13.

5.4.5 Refactoring

Refactoring is that art of refining a system's implementation without changing its functionality. This may seem unproductive, after all you have expended effort on modifying an existing system (which must have passed all its tests; otherwise, it should not have got to where it is) without changing what it does. However, there are two points at which refactoring should occur which help to elucidate why refactoring is important. The two points at which refactoring should occur are:

- Before implementing a new feature. The refactoring performed at this point may make it easier to add the new feature.
- After implementing a new feature. Refactoring at this point may help to make the resulting solution simpler.

Thus, you refactor to improve the design and implementation of the system as it progresses. You are therefore not refactoring for the sake of it, but because a new feature leads you to believe that it is necessary. That is, you refactor when the system indicates to you that you need to. For example, having added a new feature to the system, you may notice that it has a lot in common with another related feature. For example, if we are building a court records system we may have a Criminal Court Case object. At a later date, we may introduce a Civil Court Case object. Criminal and Civil court cases obviously have their difference but they also have a lot in common. Thus, you may notice that you have now introduced duplicate code into the application. This breaks the "Simple Design" principle and thus the system is telling you that you need to refactor.

At this point, you may decide that it would be useful to have an *AbstractCourtCase* object that is a parent of both the *CivilCourtCase* and *CriminalCourtCase* objects. This results in a new class hierarchy being created and the *CriminalCourtCase* object requiring some refactoring to incorporate the new abstract class.

Refactoring may mean that you end up spending longer implementing a feature due to refactoring, but the result should be that you aim to produce the simplest solution containing clean effective code, with fewer potential problem areas/black holes.

Refactoring certainly takes belief, trust and courage in what you are doing, but to compensate the Test practise helps prove that any refactoring has not broken anything in the system.

5.4.6 Pair Programming

For many, pair programming is what they think of when they think of XP. Essentially, two developers working together at one machine, with one keyboard and one mouse, write all software in the system. This is possible because the two developers play different roles:

- One focuses on the method, class or interface, etc. being implemented (this is the one with the keyboard and the mouse).
- The second focuses on the more strategic issues such as how well does this solution fit with the rest of the system, what are its implications, is there a simpler solution, do the tests cover all possibilities, etc.

The pairs that work together are not fixed, even for a particular task. Rather, pairs change as tasks change and as the code being worked on changes. For example, if you are working on an unfamiliar area of the code, then you might pair with another developer who is more familiar with it. This may change as you move to another area of the code. This may be within a task and thus you may pair with several other developers within a single task.

The benefits of this include:

1. Two brains are better than one.
2. Knowledge of the system is spread amongst the team.
3. Test coverage may be better as two people will bring two different perspectives with them.

4. Experience is spread amongst the team. If the team is comprised of a mixture of new graduates and developers with ten years experience within the application domain, then by pair programmer, the experienced developers quickly share their understanding of the domain, the technologies and the programming language with the new graduates.
5. All code is dynamically reviewed by at least one other person who also understands the scenario within which it was developed. This greatly helps to avoid the type of review that ends up focusing on the way the code is laid out rather than the quality of what has been produced.

5.4.7 Collective Ownership

Everyone owns all the system code! That is, all code is the shared responsibility of all the developers on the project. Everybody thus has the right, and indeed the duty, to make changes to any part of the system whenever they identify an opportunity to improve it.

This is something quite different from saying that the code is owned by the project (and thus no individual owns the code) as in this case, typically nobody has responsibility for the code or has a "duty" to improve it.

It is also very different from saying that developers must take ownership of their own code. In this case, each developer "owns" part of the system but not anything outside their own remit. This often results in a culture of blame where developers do their best to pass the blame for a problem to areas not within their ownership. In addition, this approach may mean that requests for changes have to be passed to the code owner when required. This code owner may then become a bottleneck in the production process.

In XP, all of the developers are responsible for the code all the time. Thus, if a problem is encountered, it can be resolved there and then. That is, the system can be refactored to overcome the problem. We can be confident in the result as all code must pass all unit tests before that code is integrated into the full release and before development can continue. If some test is not passed, then the cause of that failure must be identified and resolved before development continues.

Of course, not everyone will have the same in-depth knowledge of every aspect of the system, but if developers are concerned about their level of knowledge relating to a problem area, then they can pair program with someone who has the requisite expertise. Thus, alleviating the potential problems that might occur through unguarded revisions of existing code.

5.4.8 Continuous Integration

Every time a task is completed, the resulting code should be integrated into the current build. To do this, the new code must of course, pass all unit tests (including the new ones introduced with the new feature). Any problem encountered should be immediately resolved. In general, any problem will relate to changes made to support the new feature and will thus be easily identifiable. Once all tests are passed, the new code can be released to version control and a complete new build created. This may happen every few hours and at most daily. Thus, we can be guaranteed that the current build passes all current tests and that all the code in the version control system is part of the current build.

If a problem cannot be resolved, then the new code cannot be released and the programmers must return to the source code. They must then either rework the code until it passes the tests (and meets the other XP principles such as simple design) or throw away the code and start again. In this later case, the assumption is that the developers did not know enough about the feature they were implementing when they started (but they may do so now).

5.4.9 On-Site Customer

How many times have you looked at a requirements document, relating to the task you are about to work on and thought "what does this mean?" or "yes, but what should happen if they cancel at this point?" etc. These are questions that an expert customer (for example, an end user or someone doing the job at the moment) can answer.

In XP, such a customer should be part of the team so that such queries can be answered quickly and effectively allowing for rapid responses and rapid feedback.

On-site customers can also help to resolve disputes (over business issues relating to the system), help set small-scale priorities (is this feature or that feature more important) and review the evolving system.

Note that a user story does not (typically) provide enough information on its own for implementation to begin. Rather, the assumption is made that the on-site customer can flesh out the details for the user stories with the programmers as and when required.

5.4.10 Coding Standards

As people more between pairs, different areas of the system refactoring, produce test cases, etc., it makes life a lot easier if everyone uses the same coding standards. This has numerous benefits that have been talked about elsewhere, but at a simplistic level it means that:

- It avoids wasted arguments over silly things such as where brackets should go (on the same line or the next line) within a Java statement.
- It means that everyone gets familiar with the style of coding to be adopted which makes code easier to read.
- Simple guidelines such as "All constants in capitals" mean that as soon as such a convention is seen its meaning is known immediately.
- Helps to create an environment where code becomes de-personalised.
- Helps make activities such as refactoring and pair programming easier.

One XP-specific feature of any coding standards is that they should help promote simplicity. That is, the coding standards should help developers strive for simplicity as part of their daily work.

Coding standards can be written from scratch, evolve as a project developers or taken from the internet. The advantage of using a publicly available set of coding standards is that you are building on top of a well-tried set of standards (see the Style guidelines available from http://www.planetjava.co.uk/). The key is to have a set of standards and to adhere to them.

5.4.11 40-Hour Week

As a consultant, I have often been brought in to examine what is going wrong with a project or a development team. One particular common thread is that I will find that the actual developers are at fever pitch. They will be working 80 hours a week, be under a significant level of pressure and will often be made to feel that they are not pulling their weight or that they are lacking commitment to the project if they don't work all weekend every weekend. In one case, the project manager had explicitly planed that all developers would be working 80 hours a week in order to achieve the delivery date set by senior management. Obviously, in these situations there are a range of problems that need to be resolved, but at least one of them is the amount of productive time a developer can actually put into a project each week. In the case of the project where the project manager was planning on going 80 hour weeks, as far as I could tell, the developers were being drained; they all seemed exhausted, with no enthusiasm for anything, and weary.

Tired, drained, exhausted developers make mistakes. These are not the sort of developers you want working on an XP project! An XP team should be enthusiastic, full of energy and ready for the challenges facing them. Keeping the amount of time they put in to a limit keeps everyone "fresh and eager" (Beck, 1999). Or to put it another way, developers can only focus on developing code successfully for a certain number of hours a week, beyond this your at best wasting their and your time and at worst helping to introduce problems into the system. The 40-hour rule isn't exactly a 40-hour rule more a guideline as 35 or 45 hours might be appropriate, but 60 to 80 hours every week certainly isn't.

5.4.12 System Metaphor

In XP terms, the system metaphor is a story or view that expresses the overall way in which the system will operate. It is typically less detailed than the architectural design that you may have encountered for example, the system metaphor, if documented explicitly at all, will probably not take more than a few pages of A4 text. In contrast, the system architecture, as described in the Unified Process (Jacobson et al., 1999; Hunt, 2003), may be documented by numerous UML diagrams and extensive supporting literature. However, the system metaphor is intended to fulfil one of the roles of the architecture, that of providing developers with an overview of the core elements and how they fit together. The metaphor might describe the system as being like a "conveyor belt along which information travels and is processed by various units," etc. Overall, the metaphor should help people understand how the system fits together rather than provide a detailed (or very accurate) description.

5.5 What Is So Extreme About Extreme Programming?

When you look at the twelve practises that define Extreme Programming or XP, you will probably notice or at least comment on, the fact that there is very little new here. Many of the practises are, or have been incorporated into, described by, or presented as, parts of various existing software engineering methodologies. So what is so different, so extreme, about Extreme Programming? The answer lies in a number of places:

1. Extreme Programming is very lightweight – it really only focuses on the programming of a software system.
2. Extreme Programming takes the best practises to their ultimate conclusions. Kent Beck says that he pictured each of the practises as a knob on a control board and turned each knob up to maximum and looked at what happened. What happened was XP!

If we consider the second point in more detail, the concept goes as follows:

1. If code reviews are good, then review code all the time (pair programming).
2. If testing is good, everybody will test all the time (unit testing), even customers (acceptance testing).
3. If designing is good, then make it part of what everyone does every day (refactoring).
4. If simplicity is good, then always strive for the simplest effective solution (i.e., the simplest solution that works).
5. If architecture is important, then ensure that everyone is involved in creating and refining the architecture all the time (system metaphor).
6. If integration testing is good, then integration and testing should be an on going (daily or even hourly) thing (continuous integration).
7. If short iterations are good, then make them as short as possible, i.e., hours, or days not weeks and months (the Planning Game).

As you can see from this, each principle has been taken to the Extreme and this is what makes Extreme Programming Extreme!

5.6 Review

It is interesting to note how interrelated all the practises are. Each one on their own can be seen to be (potentially) fatally flawed. For example, allowing anyone in the team to change any aspect of the system at any time could lead to chaos and possibly anarchy! But it is not an isolated thing; rather it is part of the twelve practises of XP. If all twelve are adopted, then allowing such changes by anyone becomes practical. Such an activity is supported by practises such as *Testing, Continuous Integration, Pair Programming*, etc. This is illustrated in Fig. 5.1.

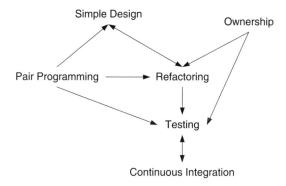

Fig. 5.1 Practises supporting the ability to fix a problem when it is found.

For example, if a problem is noted in one area of the system by John, then:

1. Collective Ownership means that it is John's responsibility to fix it.
2. Pair Programming allows John to work with Steve who is an expert in the problem area.
3. Simple Design means that the solution was already the simplest possible and thus should be clear and easy to understand (relatively).
4. Refactoring allows the change to be made and verified. That is, the revised code can be guaranteed to have been kept as simple as possible and to have not altered the functionality (as it should have passed all the tests).
5. Testing guarantees that the system still functions as before and that we have not broken anything else during the refactoring.
6. Continuous integration ensures that the new code is only integrated once it has passed all the tests, but that it is then immediately part of the evolving solution.

This is at least part of the reason why you can't truly be said to be doing XP unless you have fully adopted all twelve XP practises. That is, the whole is far greater than the sum of the XP parts and you thus get only a stable XP solution if you adopt all twelve practises.

6

Putting XP into Practise

6.1 Introduction

We have already said that XP is not a design method. Indeed, all it actually is in any formal sense is a set of four values that have motivated twelve practises. Some of these practises are more clearly oriented towards a process than others. For example, the planning game practise, as we will see, has a lot to say about itself. Other practises, such as the 40-hour week are rather more like guidelines, than a process. That is, you either over work your developers doing 60–80 hours a week or you don't. There is not a lot to say about how you limit the number of hours worked to 40 (exception management buy in and developer acceptance).

Therefore, at times, XP can seem deceptively simple. When you follow the set of twelve XP practises, you're away. That is, if you follow these twelve practises (which seem fairly straightforward) you will be doing XP. However, this is a deceptively simple approach. I have witnessed projects that claimed to be doing things the XP way and at a first glance they were certainly paying lip service to the XP practises. But, they had failed to really comprehend what XP was all about or truly understand how to implement XP within a software development project.

We will return later in this book to the subject of how you can introduce XP into a larger project methodology for larger applications, or how you can apply a software development process to an XP project. For the moment, we will focus purely on how to implement XP itself. We will not worry about anything outside of what XP offers and will contend ourselves with addressing the issue of how do you make XP work for real.

In this chapter, we will look at how XP projects are planned, we will then consider how developers can adopt a test first coding approach. We will then consider how to make pair programming work. Following on from this, we will discuss refactoring and how to start to refactor. We will then consider how a number of other XP practises can be implemented including how to put into practise continuous integration, employ simple design and produce small releases.

6.2 Planning XP Projects

Planning XP projects – the very idea! It is a common misconception that XP projects do not need to be planned. Even reading the last chapter may or may not have helped this view. This may partly be because the planning aspect of XP is known as "The Planning Game" (ah ha it's a game so not to be taken seriously) but as we said, if this is a problem then consider this as the *Project Planning Workshop* (which to be fair is a rather more accurate description of its purpose). Secondly, however, they may remain un-convinced because the nature of project planning changes. Rather than planning out the whole project in great and fine-grained detail, the overall project plan is left rather vague and high level and detailed plans are only created on an iteration-by-iteration or release-by-release basis. From personal experience, I can vouch that not only does this approach work very well but that it actually involves far more planning, which is more accurate reflecting what is actually happening on the project and is reviewed more often than the traditional approach.

So what is the aim of the game/planning workshop? It is to decide on the scope and priorities of the project and of the releases. It is also to estimate the cost of various features required by the software and to schedule those features into releases. Note that I am using the term feature here as depending on the type of planning being done, we may be dealing with high level user stories, lower level user stories or tasks to implement user stories.

The XP project lifecycle is presented in Figure 6.1. This diagram illustrates the various planning stages and implementation stages within a typical XP project.

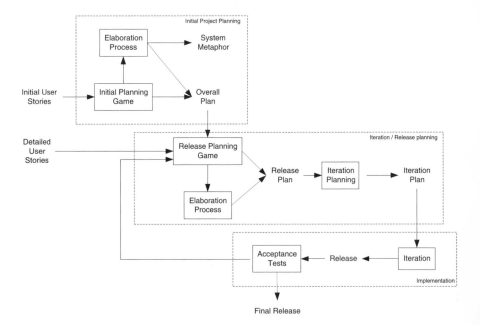

Fig. 6.1 XP project lifecycle.

For example, it starts with an initial project planning process during which the overall plan of the project is roughly sketched out. This is followed by one (and typically more than one) release planning process where the contents of a release is planned and the tasks performed in the iteration to implement the release are also planned. The release is then implemented and the results of this process fed back into the planning for the next iteration.

Note be careful when examining the diagram in Figure 6.1. This diagram may suggest to the un-initiated sequence of events that flow naturally from one point to another. The actuality is rather more incremental, iterative and cyclical than that. For example, if it is realised during an iteration that the project plan and reality are drifting far apart, than an XP project may at any time return to any stage of the planning process to consider what action to take and re-plan the project. Another important point to note is that for those working on an XP project, they may not view life to be ordered as indicated in Figure 6.1. This is partly because it is the iteration step within the implementation that is their main focus and partly as indicated above, real life isn't as ordered as this. However, it makes it easier to consider how an XP project is run by making the process explicit in this way and it is what happens within an XP project but in rather more interactive fashion.

This planning process will be elaborated upon in the rest of this section.

6.2.1 Playing the Planning Game

The planning game has only two conceptual players; these are the "Business" and "Development." The business is formed from those stakeholders who can specify the operation of the system. Development is formed from members of the development team relevant to the features being discussed. The number and size of each "team" may change over time. For example, earlier during initial requirements gathering, there may only be one or two in each team. Here, they are just trying to determine what the system should do at a relatively high level. Later on, when detailed planning is required, both teams may grow in size. For example, all the developers involved in a release may be involved in the planning game for that release.

A key issue, and one which takes time to achieve, is that both sides must trust each other. The Business must trust the Developers to give honest and accurate estimates. The Developers must trust that the Business will give them the information they need and will work with them to create the plan.

The game also has rules that aim to help the two teams work together to produce the plan. These rules can help to gain the mutual trust and respect essential to successful planning (and so often lacking in many projects).

6.2.2 The Goal of the Game

The goal of the planning game is to maximise the value of the software produced by the team.

6.2.3 The Strategy

The main strategy of the game is to invest as little as possible to put the most valuable functionality into production as quickly as possible, but without compromising the required product quality.

The last sentence is worth dissecting a little. Firstly, the strategy is to "invest as little as possible." That is, to get the job done as quickly as possible without incurring unnecessary overheads. For example, the idea of not implementing features today which may or may not be required tomorrow.

Secondly, the aim is to "put the most valuable functionality into production." Few projects have unlimited resources and unlimited time. If they did, then there would be no problem for implementing anything a user might require. Instead, there are usually financial and time constraints on a project. These limit what can effectively be achieved. Thus, we want to use the time and resources available to us to implement those features that will be of most benefit to the end user.

Thirdly, we want to do all this "without compromising the required product quality." Obviously, we want the software we produce to do its job without causing the users any difficulties. But note the use of the phrase "required product quality." Recently, I was involved in two projects that were managed in an agile manner. One was for a UK government office and involved implementing a large piece of client side software to be used over the next several (and possibly many) years. At the same time, we were asked to implement a very small web application that would be used as a placeholder for a much larger system that was to be developed afterwards. It was anticipated that the web application would only have a lifetime of between 1 and 3 months. This raises the question what is the "required product quality" for these two systems. The quality of the first system needed to be high, the quality of the second needed to be acceptable (i.e., not fault ridden but not as fault tolerant as the first system).

6.2.4 The Game Pieces

The pieces used by the two players are the "user stories" described in the last chapter. These are written down on index cards and moved around during the game. Of course you do not necessarily need to use index cards, user stories can be written down on white boards, scrapes of paper, entered into a software system for recording and reference. However, in general, they are put onto things (e.g., index cards) that can be easily placed in piles, written on, thrown away, sorted, etc. Only once they are accepted, as genuine user stories are typically entered into a computer. This is partly as they are harder to view, manipulate, sort, etc. and partly because once something has been entered into an electronic media they are often harder to throw away (then there seems to be more investment into them).

6.2.5 The Players

As mentioned earlier, there are only two players in the game "Business" and "Development." I like to think them as teams, because they are rarely a single person (apart possibly from very early on in the life of the project). The implication of them being teams is that they are a gestalt personality. That is, each team is comprised of the set of personalities of its constituent members. This is important as different people operate in different ways and will have different motivations and it is useful to keep all this in mind when "playing" the game.

As was mentioned earlier, Business is made up of a collection of those individuals (project stakeholders) who can make decisions about what the system should do. In turn, Development consists of those people who will be involved in implementing the system. This includes, but is not limited to, programmers. It may also include database administrators, system support technologists, networking professionals, etc. This may surprise some, as XP (or eXtreme Programming) may seem to be focussed on the programming aspect of a project. However, to ignore the other aspects of a typical modern software system is to invest in future problems. Depending upon the application, non-programmers may be as much part of the team as the programmers and may be as vital to the success of the project as the programmers themselves! How many applications are built today that do not involve at least one of a database, a network, some operating system requirements, low level device drivers, or legacy application. In many cases, systems involve many of these. More than one apparently successful on-going XP project has foundered because of its dependency on the database team who were not geared up to their way of working!

Returning to the two "players." The members of the two teams should be distinct. That is, no one person should be a member of both the Business and the Development. Although this may seem straightforward, these definitions can be blurred. If a software house is building a bespoke system for an external client then it is often very easy to say who should be "Business" and who should be "Development." However, for "off the shelf" shrink wrap products, the "Business" may be the marketing department, internal business analysts or a internal "product owner." These are all people who are internal to the company and may be internal to the department within which the software is being constructed. For systems to be used internally to a company, the development team may find that they are building systems for themselves (or at least for another group of developers). In these cases, "expert customers" need to be identified and kept in this role for the duration of the planning game.

6.2.6 The Moves/Playing the Game

There are three stages to play the game.

1. *Exploration* – Determine new user stories of the system.
2. *Commitment* – Decide which features will be addressed in a particular release.
3. *Steering* – Update the plan as development progresses.

These three phases are iterative and may interact. For example, in the steering phase it may be noticed that some new user stories are required. This may lead to the exploration phase being re-run for the new user stories, followed by the commitment phase, before a revised plan is produced by the steering phase.

Each of the three phases will be discussed in more detail below.

Exploration Phase

Within the exploration phase, the game tries to help the team identify what the system should do. To achieve this, this phase has three steps (or moves). These are:

1. Write a story.
2. Estimate a story.
3. Split a story.

Each of these is elaborated upon below.

Write a story. The Business starts talking about what the system must do. At some point, these descriptions can be written down as user stories (e.g., on index cards). Often initial ideas may best be written on white boards, etc. before being committed to the cards (or electronic media).

Estimate a story. Development then estimates how long it will take to implement a story. If Development cannot estimate the story, then it can ask for clarification or request that the story be split up (to make it easier to consider).

Early on during initial project planning (during the initial planning game) you often are only really trying to get a ballpark figure during estimating. Later (during detailed release planning) you will find that you will need greater detail relating to the user stories.

Split a story. Users are often not good at realising how much work may be involved in a particular system feature. In turn, developers are often not very good at immediately realising what a user wants. As a result, user stories may vary in size and complexity. Typically, user stories require refinement, but large user stories (in terms of complexity or duration) need to be broken down into shorter less complex stories. As a rule of thumb, no single story should be large enough that one programming pair would be unable to complete it within one iteration.

Before we leave the exploration phase, a quick word on Estimating. Estimating how long something will take in software development is notoriously difficult and error prone. XP recommends that you estimate in what Kent Beck calls "Ideal Engineering Time" (Beck, 1999). This form of time is comprised of "Ideal Engineering Days." An Ideal Engineering Day (or IED for short) is the amount of development that could be achieved in a single day by the average developer without any interruptions, where there are no dependencies (you can just get on with what you need to do) and no unforeseen interruptions. Others have used the term "Ideal Engineering Units" (2002) as you will then reconcile the IED with reality during the "Set project velocity" step of the commitment phase. During this step, you say that reality isn't as simple as all that and that it is likely that the developers will get interruptions due to meetings, previous projects, other developers needing help, etc. Thus, the time taken to produce one IED may be anything from one real day to several days, etc. In some cases, an IDE may be matched to one half-person week or more, etc. (thus the reference to a unit). As the project progresses, you may need to revise the mapping between the IED and real time.

Commitment Phase

During this phase of the game, Business must identify what will be in the current iteration and when the next release will be. For their part, Development must commit to the agreed duration and the content of the release. If this situation cannot be met then either the timescale of the release must be changed, the content of the release altered or the number of developers increased.

The steps presented to reach agreement within the game are:

1. Sort by value.
2. Sort by risk.
3. Choose scope.
4. Set project velocity.

These steps are described in a little more detail below:

Sort by value. The user stories are sorted by Business into three piles. These piles represent those stories in the:
1. must have category,
2. should have category, and
3. nice to have category.
This effectively gives each story a relative priority with regard to the three categories. The implication is that, from the Business perspective, the user stories in the "must have" category are more important than those in the "should have" category. In turn, the "should have" category are more important than the "nice to have" category. Thus, an XP project development should focus first on the "must haves" as these will add the greatest value to the Business.

Sort by risk. The user stories are further sorted by Development into piles for:
1. confident estimates,
2. reasonably sure estimates, and
3. cannot estimate.
This is useful because we can then see those user stories that the Business believes are "must haves" and how sure Development is of the estimates given. The result of this is that the planning game may return to the exploration phase to try to clarify any issues relating to the estimation of user stories. Some stories may need to be left for further investigation after the planning game has concluded.

Choose scope. Business must select the final set of user stories that will form the next iteration or release. The only constraint on what comprises a release is that the first release should be complete in terms of end-to-end processing (although very limited in functionality) and that each subsequent release should add something in terms of value to the Business (for it to be considered a release). Note not all iterations may result in a release.

Set velocity. This step maps the Ideal Engineering Unit (IDU) into reality and takes into account the amount of time developers will actually be productive, their experience, etc. It thus provides a way of mapping ideal estimate periods into elapsed actual time.

As can be seen from the above steps, this phase may proceed sequentially, with Business ordering the relative importance of various user stories. Next Development will determine how well they can estimate those stories. Finally, Business will decide on which of the stories will comprise a particular release (or releases). The reality is that this is a far iterative process than that. In general, Business will revise their "piles" as the game proceeds, influenced by Development's estimates, the need to split stories and the discovery of new stories.

Steering Phase

In the real world, plans often change. This may be for a wide variety of reasons including (but by no means limited to):

- changing requirements,
- new requirements,
- changing priorities,
- incorrect estimates,
- changing resources (developers leave and new developers join a project with different skill sets).

All this means that over the lifetime of a project, a plan may require frequent and extensive revision. Indeed, a living project plan should be able to show a history of changes, otherwise it is likely to be out of date and may be of little use. Even within a single XP iteration, these factors may become an issue and certainly across iterations may well be very relevant. The XP planning game explicitly recognises this within its steering phase.

The idea in this phase is that you are helping to steer the project forward. In doing so, you are encouraged to explicitly address the above issues.

The steps in the steering phase are:

1. Iteration planning.
2. Project recovery.
3. Identifying a new story.
4. Project re-estimation.

These four steps are considered in more detail below:

Iteration planning. XP states that you should only plan the current iteration in detail. Therefore, at the start of each iteration (e.g., every 1–3 weeks) Business plans the user stories to be implemented and Development plans the tasks needed to implement those stories. We will discuss iteration planning in more detail later in this chapter.

Project recovery. As the iteration progresses, if Development realises that it is ahead or behind schedule, it can ask Business to help it to re-prioritise the user stories to implement.

Identifying a new story. If a new story is identified and determined to be necessary for the current release then it can be written, estimated and added to the iteration. As a consequence, the remaining user stories will need to be reviewed and some discarded in order to achieve the release.

Project re-estimation. If Development feels that the plan has been shown to bear little reality to the real world, then the whole iteration can be re-planned, user stories re-estimated, the project velocity reset and the implications for the project timetable considered.

As you can see from the description of these steps, they are at a very different level to the steps focussed on user stories of the exploration and commitment phases. This phase is also likely to happen at some point during (or at the end) of an iteration. Whereas, the first two phases occur at the start of an iteration. Thus, the planning game as an XP practise is broken into various parts that are performed at different points in the lifetime of the project.

6.2.7 Planning Your XP Project

So how do you use the planning game to plan you XP project? What do you do when and how? In this section, I will look at how the various types of planning game fit together to help you plan your XP project.

There are actually two forms of the planning game:

1. The initial planning game, and
2. The release planning game.

In general, there is also another step between these, which is called variously the "Elaboration" phase, and the "Exploration" process. To avoid confusion with what has already been described, we will call it the "Elaboration" process. The elaboration process allows clarification of user stories to take place outside the constraints of the game. Thus, a typical XP project might be planned in the following manner:

1.   An initial planning game (aims to get overall view of project);
2.   Initial elaboration process (focusing on high level user stories);
3.   Release 1 planning game;
4.   Release 1 elaboration process (if required);
5.   Plan iteration 1;
6.   .... Release 1 iteration/implementation ...;
7.   Release 2 planning game;
8.   Release 2 elaboration process (if required);
9.   Plan iteration 2;
10. ... Release 2 iteration/implementation ...;

11. ...
12. Release *n* Planning game;
13. Release *n* Elaboration process (if required);
14. Plan iteration *n*;
15. ... Release *n* iteration/implementation.

The Initial Planning Game

The initial planning game focuses on what the system as a whole should do. It considers all user stories that are in scope (and indeed what that scope is). It happens at the start of the project and may reconvene at various points throughout the lifetime of the project to review the scope of the system, the set of user stories, their relative priorities, etc.

The Release Planning Game

The release planning game focuses on the contents of a release or iteration. It has the same steps as the initial planning game but the level of detail that needs to be considered is much greater. During the initial planning game, the overall plan for the project should have been roughly planned out. At the start of a release, the details of what will be done in that release need to be determined. This means that:

1. User stories need to be fleshed out and may need to be broken down into finer grained stories (in order that they can be implemented).
2. Detailed estimates of the stories need to be obtained.
3. The user stories to be implemented as part of the release need to be confirmed, revised or modified as required.
4. The project velocity may need to be revised. For example, as the development team become more experienced in XP and the application in which you may find development speeds up.

On completion of the release planning game it may be necessary to explore some of the user stories (or the knockons of the user stories) further. This can happen during the elaboration process. Once this is completed, the iteration tasks will be planned in detail during the iteration planning process.

The Elaboration Process

The elaboration process follows the initial planning game, and typically on a smaller scale, a release planning game. During this phase, research is carried out to clarify user stories in order to estimate, clarify requirements, or technical issues. The aim of this is to:

- Lower the risk of bad estimates,
- Experiment/prototype different solutions,

- Improve the development teams to understand the domain/technology,
- Ensure procedures and processes required are in place.

Between the initial planning game and the first release planning game, the elaboration process may last anywhere from a day to a month to several months, depending on the development teams level of expertise in the domain in question, in the technologies being applied and in the methods being used. Between releases, the elaboration process is likely to be shorter, typically in terms of days.

Iteration Planning

There are two issues to consider when planning an iteration. These are (1) determining the size of an iteration; (2) determining what should be done within an iteration to implement the user stories.

Size of an iteration. Ho do you determine how big an iteration should be? How long is a piece of string? The answer is that an iteration needs to be big enough to allow either a new release to be created that adds value to the business or large enough that you are able to make significant progress. However, it should also be small enough that the development does not move on too far without being reviewed (by another release planning game, etc.). The classic length of time for an XP iteration ranges from 1 to 3 weeks. Generally, XP projects are quiet small involving between 2 and 6 and generally at most 10 developers. This limits the amount of work that can be done within 2–3 weeks. For example, if you have a team of six and your iteration is of 2 weeks duration, then at most you have 12 person weeks to play with.

Planning the iteration. If the release planning game identifies what new features should be added to the evolving system in the current iteration, then the iteration plan defines how those features will be achieved.

During the planning of an iteration, user stories are converted into tasks which will result in the story being implemented. One user story may be implemented by a single task or by many tasks. One task may support several stories; in turn one story may be implemented as one or more tasks. Some tasks may not directly relate to any user story, such as a task to move to the latest version of Java.

Iteration planning usually incorporates the following phases:

1. Evaluation of the last iterations lessons learned, changes to be made, etc.
2. Review of user stories to incorporate into the iteration.
3. Task exploration during which tasks are written for user stories. These tasks may be broken down into smaller tasks to help with planning and estimating. This generally happens when a developer volunteers to break a user story down into one or more tasks. They may offer to do this because they believe they know how to address that task. To break the user story down, they should find at least one other developer (pair-programming style) to help with the

analysis. As this step progresses, they may or may not need input from the customer or other developers. Therefore, the on-site customer can be vital to the success of the iteration planning process.

4. Task commitment during which tasks are estimated, load factors determined and balancing takes place.
5. Finally, the iteration plan is verified.

The whole process should take not more than 1 or 2 days (and may take considerably less). The end result is that a series of tasks is identified, prioritised and ordered. Pair programmers can then address these tasks during the iteration. The idea is that developers select their own tasks to do by selecting the highest-level priority tasks first and start on them. There are two approaches to this, one is the "Select one task at a time" and the other is known as "Fill your bag." In the first approach, a developer only selects a single task to address. When they have completed that task they will select another task and so on until either there are no tasks left or the iteration is completed. With the "Fill your bag" approach, a kind of round robin task selection process takes place. During this, each developer selects one or more tasks that they would like to do. In general, the developers get first call on the tasks that they identified, analysed and estimated. This process continues until there are no tasks left or the estimates match the duration of the iteration. Each developer then knows the set of tasks that have been nominally allocated to him/her for the current iteration. This may change as the iteration progresses as some developers may become bogged down in a particular task while others may complete their tasks faster than expected.

Summary

Thus, the project first outlines the whole scope of the system and then outlines the iterations and releases. The team then elaborates on the user stories (focussing on the ones they don't know how to estimate). They then plan an iteration and implement it. Within an iteration, it is the tasks that implement a user story that are considered in detail.

6.3 Test First Coding

If anyone reading this does not believe that it is good to do unit tests before releasing it to your colleagues for integrating into the current build, please put this book down and pick up a first year undergraduate text on software development and start there instead!

You may well wonder why I have just put that sentence here, well, at least one project I know used the "if I compile then you can release it into the current build" rule as sufficient evidence of testing – with obvious and predictably disastrous results. So, unit testing all code before releasing it, is not a universal truth!

However, it should be! When you have written some code that is to be used by the rest of the project, you should be sure that it works. Making these unit tests part of what you release into the central source code repository of your project also means that if anything changes anyone can re-run your unit tests and check that your code still works (even if you are not around). Again, this may seem self-evident but the inclusion of unit test code within your version control system is a trick that all too often seems to be overlooked.

At this point, hopefully, we are all agreed that when you write code you should also write the unit tests that go with it to verify that code. The next step towards test first coding is therefore not a huge one. That is, you should write the tests before you write the code. This may/will seem strange at first, but over time it does become second nature. Indeed, from my own personal experience, it can become quiet liberating, allowing you to clearly focus on what the code needs to do before determining how it will be done (indeed I continue to use this practise whether I am involved in an XP project or not). Test first coding also ensures, of course, that all code produced does have a relevant set of unit tests available for it.

In many ways, the unit test first approach is an obvious extension of an approach I have been pushing within Java for years. I used to say that you should write the Javadoc (the comments picked up by the Java Javadoc tool) for your Java classes, interfaces and methods before you write the implementation. If you couldn't write the Javadoc (i.e., can't explain what the class, interface or method does), then you shouldn't write the code. The reason for this is that you clearly did not know what the method should do and thus couldn't write it. By extending this to the unit test, we have something that is both executable and verifiable.

6.3.1 How to Write Tests First?

So how do you move to an approach in which you write the test first? There is no hard and fast answer, as this question is a bit like "so how do you decide what to program first." But the following points try to give a flavour of how I (and many others) try to go about test first coding.

1. Think about what the code should do and try to ignore, for the moment, how it will do it. This can be very difficult for programmers to get to grips with, not least because in general their focus has always been on "how." It can feel like a leap of faith, or a bit like wandering around in the dark (with your eyes closed!). However, if you persevere with it, you will see that in order to do the "how," you really need not think about the "what" first anyway. One way to do this is to write down, for example as Javadoc, what the test or tests will do. This removes the need for the moment for code and classes, interfaces and methods that don't yet exist.

2. Now write a test that will use the classes and methods you haven't yet implemented! This will also seem strange at first. How can you write a test using code that doesn't yet exist! It is possible. If you can determine what the classes involved will be called, what the method signatures should be, what parameter values should be involved then you can write the test case. This test case will not compile (obviously) but it should at a later date. If you use tools such

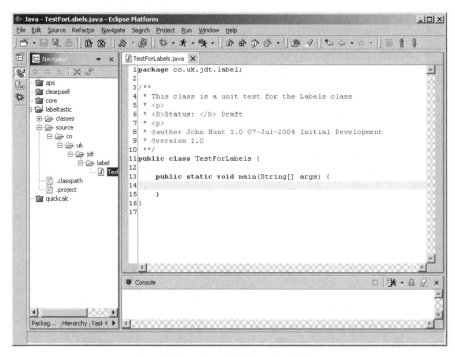

Fig. 6.2 Creating a simple test in Eclipse.

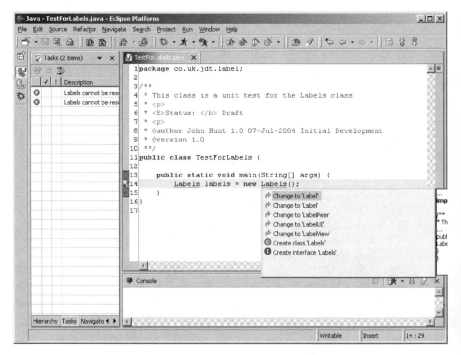

Fig. 6.3 Eclipse offers to create an as-yet undefined class.

as Eclipse, this can be made much easier. For example, in Figure 6.2, I have started to create a simple test class called *TestForLabels* using Eclipse. At this point, there is no behaviour defined for the main method in the test case (note I am purposely not using a framework such as JUnit here as I want to keep things as simple as possible for this example).

In Figure 6.3, I have added a statement that creates an instance of a class that I have yet to define. Eclipse notices this and prompts me with a set of options. Two of these options allow me to either create an interface or a class. In this case *Labels* is a class that I want to instantiate (and interfaces cannot be instantiated). Thus, I will select the option allowing me to create the Labels class (at the click of a mouse button!).

Figure 6.4 illustrates the class creation dialogue presented by Eclipse to allow me to create a new class Labels. It allows me to select the parent class, interfaces to implement and whether I want any abstract methods to be implemented and constructors provided. Using this feature, I can quickly create many of the stubs I would need for a new class.

Figure 6.5 illustrates what the (very simple) resulting class looks like in Eclipse. At the moment, this class will compile but has no methods (as I am keeping things simple).

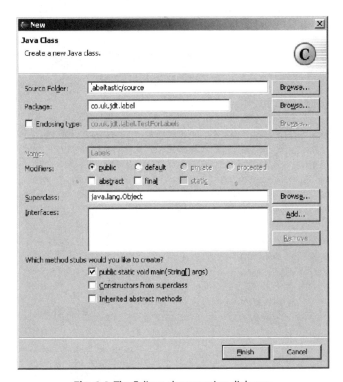

Fig. 6.4 The Eclipse class creation dialogue.

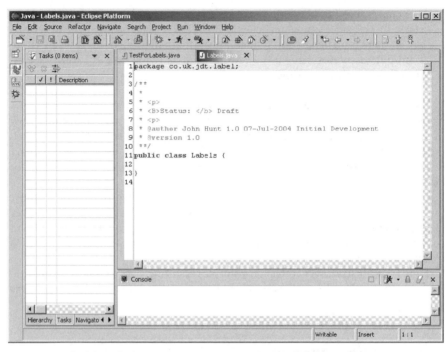

Fig. 6.5 The initial "implementation" class with no methods.

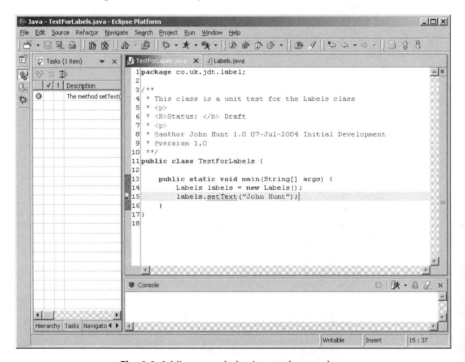

Fig. 6.6 Adding some behaviour to the test class.

I can now return to my test case and add some more to it. In Figure 6.6, I have added the following statement:

```
labels.setText("John Hunt");
```

This calls the method *setText* on the newly created object referenced by the local variable *labels*. But *setText* does not yet exist. I have just referenced it within the test harness.

Again Eclipse notices this and prompts me to allow it to create this method for me. This is illustrated in Figure 6.7. It even gives me a preview of what it would generate in a box to the side of the editor.

The result of Eclipse auto-creating the *setText* method is presented in Figure 6.8. This method takes a string as a parameter and does nothing with it. But that's okay; it is enough to allow the test harness to compile. We can take this further by entering another method into the test case example requiring the text to be returned for the label, using a *getText* method. The result of Eclipse auto-creating this method is presented in Figure 6.9. Note that this method returns a value, thus a default value is defined in the return statement. This will not be correct in all situations (and indeed should not be correct in all situations). This is fine, as it is enough to allow us to compile the test class.

The key thing here to notice is that we have focussed on the class and the methods it should provide and used those to build our test harness. We have allowed Eclipse to create these stub classes and methods for us along the way.

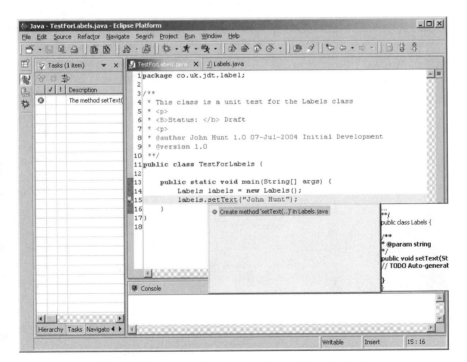

Fig. 6.7 Eclipse prompting to create the undefined method.

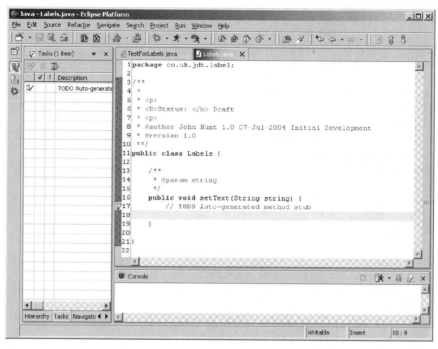

Fig. 6.8 The method auto-created by Eclipse.

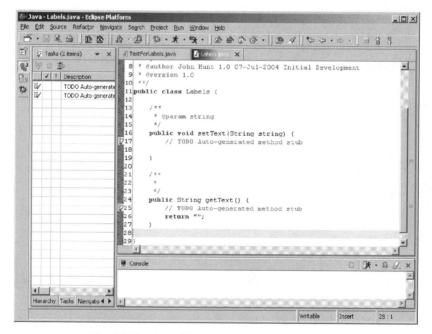

Fig. 6.9 The class with two auto-created stub methods.

Eclipse has kindly placed stub code within the methods that allow everything to compile (but not more). Thus, by doing this, you can design and generate the framework of the code being tested as you create the unit test itself!

3. If you haven't already done so, then write the stub code for the class(es) being tested. As mentioned above, tools such as Eclipse may do this for you, however, if you are using tools such as Emacs you will have to do it yourself.
4. Now put the code you have created for the test into whatever project code repository you are using. This includes your test code. If you are using a framework such as JUnit then add your test to that as well.
5. Now run your newly created test against the stub code. It should fail but that's okay – you haven't implemented the methods you are testing yet! This is actually an important step (although at this point you may think it redundant). It does two things, firstly it validates that the test will run and secondly it ensures that the test will fail. If the test passes then something is likely to be missing from your test. For example, if your test only ever checked that the result returned from the Labels class was a null string, then that would not be a very good test. It would be better to check that the value set for the text was the value returned by the get method!
6. Now you are in a position to actually write the implementation of the methods being tested. This may lead to creating additional supporting methods but that's okay. However, your focus should be on writing only enough code required to pass the test. This firstly focuses your efforts on exactly what is needed; ignoring additional bells and whistles that you think might be useful in the future. It also helps you to produce the simplest code that meets all the requirements. After all, if it passes all the tests then it meets its requirements no matter how simple the code is.
7. Re-run your tests against the newly implemented methods. If all the tests pass, then continue. If not returned to step 6 and revise your code as necessary.
8. Now re-run the tests for the entire system. If all tests pass, then add the changes in your current test suite and implementation to your code repository (your tests may have needed revision as you implemented the classes and methods). Now you can continue. If one or more of the tests fail then you must return to step 6 and revise your code as necessary (as it must have been your changes that caused any tests to fail).
9. Refactor your code for clarity and to remove any duplication. Return to step 7 if you are sure that no refactoring is required, then you have finished the current test. Return to step 1 for the next test.

You may notice that you are repeatedly encouraged to re-run your tests during the above steps. This may seem like overkill, but stick with it. You should try to move to a position where you naturally "make a change/run a test" as your normal mode of operation. This ensures that you never move far from any problem and that you are moving in small but perfectly formed steps.

An additional benefit of test first programming is the confidence it installs in developers. This is because at any one time, the latest version of their code will have passed all previous tests and it is only the changes they are making now which may cause a test to fail.

6.3.2 What to Test?

Okay so testing is good and writing tests first is better. Great, but what should I test? Should every single method in every class in my application have a test written for it? Probably not! Should I only write tests for major subsystems – again probably not! So, what should I test?

As with many things in software, there are no hard and fast rules for what you should test, but here are some XP-oriented guidelines:

1. Write tests for any tasks being implemented.
2. Write tests for any classes or combinations of classes that are non-trivial and could easily be broken. For example, if one particular class implements a complex algorithm to find sneak circuits within electronic relays, then write tests for that class even though it may only be one element of a larger module.
3. Avoid writing tests for methods that just call another method, e.g. delegate methods, if the called method already has a test written for it.
4. Assume that more tests are better then less and that no one will complain about having too many tests, but that people will complain if an important test is missing.
5. Write tests that instil confidence in the system. For example, if one area of the system is invoked by many others (such as a data access management subsystem), then having a set of tests for that area adds to the confidence of those using it.
6. Add tests that will help cover areas of the system being modified. If you are refactoring some code, and feel that one or more tests are missing then add them.
7. If you happen to notice that a suite of tests for a particular module, subsystem or class appears to be missing in one or more tests, then add them.

As you will notice from the above, testing is not expected to be perfect first time around and that the suite of tests you have are expected to grow over time as new tests emerge and your ability to identify tests grows (as your experience with XP, the application, the domain, the technology, etc. increases).

Note that an important point to remember is that once you have identified a test and defined it you must run it. If the test fails, then either the test is wrong, so fix it or the implementation has a bug in it, so fix it. This is true even if the test you have added is for some class that you were merely examining and hadn't originally planned to work on!

Finally, remember that even poor tests are better than no tests at all and that over time the test suite will improve (i.e., from iteration to iteration).

6.3.3 Confidence in the Test Suite

The developers must have confidence in the test suite created. Not only is this important for their belief in the system but it is also particularly important for two other importance practises, namely:

1. your ability to refactor and prove that you have not changed the functionality of the system;
2. the guarantee that if you code in a test first manner, that you have produced the simplest code that covers the requirements.

However, you should not get hung up on the quality of the tests, just do the best you can. It is very unlikely that you will never miss out some test condition – that's life but that is what refactoring is for (so you can improve the code to deal with some missed functionality) and why everyone is responsible for all the code (collective ownership). If you have missed something out, then at some point someone should notice this and come back and add a new test. If the code now fails that test, then it should be "improved" such that it passes the test. This is a normal XP practise and should not elicit any response such as "I found a bug in your code AGAIN!!" If it does then it indicates that there is a problem within the XP team far more than that there was a problem with your work.

6.4 Making Pair Programming Work

The idea behind pair programming is of course very simple, essentially it comes done to "two heads are better than one" most of the time. In addition, in pair programming all code is always reviewed by at least one other person who is focussed on what the code needs to do.

Okay, but how does it work in practise? How do you get two developers to pair program, particularly when most programmers like to work on their own, have often been trained primarily to work on their own, indeed where some programmers seem sometimes to be incapable of relating to other human beings, let alone working in a pair!

Okay let us be honest here – pair programming isn't easy, actually its quite hard. This is not what you often hear, but it is a fact! Most programmers have been trained to work alone, to change the habit of a lifetime is never easy. In addition, few people can just pair program straight off, most need to learn (or be trained) how to pair program.

Knowing how to work in pairs is hard because it is not only a different way of working, it involves inter-personal skills, pair dynamics, communication, tolerance and trust.

For example, when people think of pair programming, they think of two people working on the same code. Fine, but it is not possible for two people to actually program at the same time. In pair programming, one developer takes hands on control of the keyboard and mouse, while the other monitors what the "driver" is doing (often referred to as the "navigator"). This requires active participation from both sides. But this is not how most programmers have been trained to work. Most programmers expect to be the "driver," they are not attuned to being the "navigator."

Being the driver is what programmers traditionally have been. In pair programming situations, many programmers will initially fall straight into this role. However, they must communicate with their navigator (not necessarily an easy exercise). In turn, the navigator should participate in the development by considering what the driver is doing, how they might test it, what other options there might be, etc.

However, it is all too easy for the navigator to just sit back and enjoy the ride. Note that this is not pair programming! Taking the analogy of the driver and the navigator for a moment. Consider what would happen if the pair were actually in a car on the M25 (the orbital motorway around London). The driver is focussed on manoeuvring through the throng of traffic, road works, traffic cones, speed restrictions, and police speed cameras, etc. that are typical of the M25. If the navigator sits back and "enjoys the ride," then the driver might miss the turn for the M4. They would then carry on round towards the M42 or M1. At some point, the driver might realise his mistake and at worst be completely lost and at best need to take a major detour to get back on his route. Having a programming partner who is just along for the ride is a bit like this. Both developers must be engaged in the effort if it is to succeed.

Whilst there are no hard and fast rules to how to do this, there are things that can help:

1. *Engage in a dialogue.* The "driver" should try and explain what they are doing. The "navigator" should ask questions in order to understand what is being done. This is not as simple as it sounds. For example, the next time you are in your car and driving, try telling an imaginary passenger what you are doing, what you are considering and what concerns you have about the road ahead (it helps if the passenger is imaginary so that none of your friends think you are mad!).
2. *Listen to each other.* If one member of the pair is doing all the talking then it is probably isn't working. The one who isn't saying much might not be clear on what is being done. Try swapping roles, or have a break, or take time out to review where you are.
3. *Take frequent breaks.* Pair programming is intensive. It is intensive in terms of the little grey cells and also in terms of inter-personal communications and dynamics. Have regular breaks, talk about other things, see how others are getting on, catch up on the news, etc. Don't take a break and discuss the code!
4. *Don't be a back seat driver.* Nothing can be quiet as annoying as a back seat driver (particularly if its your mother in law!). One of the common problems, particular if the "navigator" is more experienced relative to the current task than the "driver" is the back seat driver syndrome. If you are the navigator and you find yourself telling the driver what to do all the time try and stop yourself. It is not only really annoying but it is not pair programming. You are not performing the role of the navigator. You are acting as the virtual driver and using someone else's fingers to type the code in! You can either swap roles, or better stop and discuss your proposed solution with the driver and then let them run with it. They will learn a lot more.
5. *Make pair programming practical.* Providing enough space to allow a pair to work together comfortably isn't essential but it can help. This may only go as far as having desks that are big enough for two developers to sit next to each other, or it may involve special double size workstation environments.

6. *Use a common environment.* Developers tend to have their own personal favourite development environment. For Java this might be JCreator, JBuilder, NetBeans, Eclipse or even Emacs, etc. However, having different development environments makes pair programming harder. Selecting one development environment to be used by all makes life a lot easier. However, developers are notoriously difficult to get to change environments (partly because they have invested time and effort in learning the tools they use to the extent where the tool does not interrupt their thought processes). Selecting a single environment and enforcing this can therefore cause friction and so must be handled with care (for example, by proposing an initial tool selection process before the project starts and getting developers to work with different tools, etc.).

7. *Shared language and vocabulary.* Developers who have a shared vocabulary of design and programming concepts tend to work together better. This is partly because it avoids the "what do you mean by *Factory Method*?" type question. This is not as easy as it may seem. As an analogy, consider the following question that I was once asked when buying some fast food while visiting the USA:

    "Would you like that on a biscuit?"

    To me this was somewhat surprising as what I pictured at this point was what I would call a Digestive biscuit. Which is a type of edible item I would normally "dunk" in my coffee. It turned out that what I was being offered was something I thought of as a scone, and when I explained my confusion to the person serving, I had to describe a Digestive as being a bit like a very thin cookie.

    Thus, having the same vocabulary means understanding what each other is saying as well as having the same terminology. This also helps to build trust and confidence in each other. Having a shared understanding of the domain and application specific terms helps. Equally (and possibly more importantly) having a shared understanding of technical vocabulary is invaluable. One very good starting point for this is the so-called *Gang of Four*[1] Patterns book (Gamma et al., 1995). These patterns have been translated into Java (and extended upon) in Grand (1999, 2001, 2002). Two further patterns books are Buschmann et al. (1996) (which represents the progression and evolution of the pattern approach into a system capable of describing and documenting large scale applications) and Fowler (1997) which considers how patterns can be used for analysis to help build reusable object models. Others books worth of consideration include Larman (2001), and Metsker (2002). In addition to the papers mentioned earlier in this book, there is also a web page dedicated to the patterns movement (which includes many of the papers referenced as well as tutorials and example patterns).

8. *Allowing non-pair time.* There are some situations where allowing a pair to work alone can be beneficial. This may be a little controversial for some in the XP community, as they will argue that it is *always* between to work in pairs. However, in the following situations, flying solo may be an alternative (but it should be the rare exception to pair programming):

---

[1] The Gang of Four are Erich Gamma, Richard Helm, Ralph Johnson and John Vlissides.

    a. Exploring completing alternative solutions,

    b. Following multiple competing lines of investigation during debugging (but not bug fixing).

9. *Change partners often.* Pairs should not be permanent. Instead, pairs should change as and when required. The typical point at which to change is at the start of a new task. However, if a task ranges over a number of areas, then a "driver" developer may pair with several "navigators" in order to benefit from their different areas of expertise.

Pair programming takes practise. Ideally, in any pair, one of the pair should be an experienced pair programmer. In many situations, this is not possible, so the above points should be borne in mind by all members of an XP team. The key thing is to stick with it.

    The typical pair programming workflow is illustrated in Figure 6.10. It illustrates a number of important features of pair programming. Firstly, pairs are not

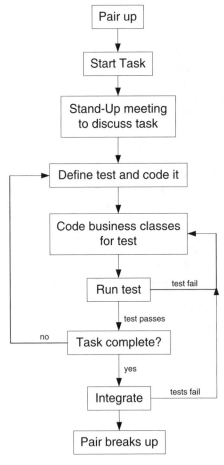

Fig. 6.10 Pair-programming workflow.

permanent (and indeed should be changed regularly). A pair forms to carry out a particular task. At the start of the task, they have a brief meeting to discuss what it is they are about to do and how they might approach it, what the options are, etc. This helps to ensure that no one is along just for the ride. They then work on the code in a test first manner, proposing a test, implementing the business classes that will meet the requirements of that test and then running the test. If the test is passed, then they move onto the next test. If the test fails, then they review the code and determine what is wrong. Once the tests are completed, they integrate the code with the current build. If this causes any tests for the whole system to fail, they must revise the code and determine why the test failed, etc. They can only finish integrating once all the tests have passed. The task is then completed and the pair breaks up.

In some cases, developers really object to pair programming. They then need to be educated in the benefits of pair programming and helped to fit into the pair-programming framework. If they cannot adapt then it is likely that they will have a bright future on a non-XP project elsewhere.

6.5 Refactoring

It would be possible to dedicate a whole book on refactoring code (and indeed people have, an excellent text on refactoring is Fowler (1999)). Here, I will try merely to give some guidance on the *when*, *how* and *when not* of refactoring.

6.5.1 The Very Idea

In many ways, refactoring is an obvious idea but one that is hard to put into practise. To some extent this can be due to the old maxim "if it ain't broke, don't fix it." That is, if the code is working at the moment then you don't need to change it. This can be particularly true if management do not see the benefit in refactoring and believe that code that is already written and working should be left as it is and that to do otherwise is a waste of time, effort and money. They presume that you have done it once, so why re-do it. When faced with this approach, many developers will merely opt for the path of least resistance (partly due to management pressure and partly due to their own fear of breaking something that is working). One of the first things that needs to happen for refactoring to be effective is for management to show that they understand the benefits in refactoring (and indeed in the case of XP, its intrinsic part in the development process).

Actually, the old maxim "if it ain't broke, don't fix it" still applies to refactoring within an XP project. That is, if code isn't broken in some way then you shouldn't refactor it. Thus, you don't refactor just for the sake of it, you refactor with a purpose. For example, if the code you are examining does not comply with XP practises, then it is broken relative to the XP goals and should be refactored.

An interesting way to look at it is that there are three stages to any software development effort, these are:

1. making the software work,
2. making the software right,
3. making the software efficient.

That is, the first aim of the programmer is to make the software work correctly. In many cases, that's where the process ends, but not in XP. Although, this may be the initial emphasis (particularly given the use of test first coding), later on you may find that the subsequent tasks introduce, for example, duplication into the code. This is when you make it right. It is at this point that refactoring first enters the frame. You now need to alter existing code to remove the duplication, but leave the behaviour unaltered. The third stage follows the idea that you should first make your software work, and then you can tidy it up so that it is as clear and as simple as possible. You are then in a position to make it efficient. By clarifying your code in stage 2, you should be in a better position to make it efficient. Such optimisation is a form of "improving" the software and is therefore a type of refactoring. Remember an optimisation might improve the performance of the system but should not affect its behaviour (this is exactly what refactoring is about).

6.5.2 When to Refactor?

In general, there are two situations when you should consider refactoring code. These are:

1. Before you implement new code.
2. After you implement new code.

These two situations are important points in the development of the system. At the first point, you are considering how to implement a new feature in the system. You are therefore considering the existing system with respect to this new, previously unimplemented requirement. The existing code should not have taken this requirement into consideration when it was being implemented (as this would have broken the rules of XP). Thus, this is a good opportunity to consider the existing code and review whether it can be improved upon (for example, by simplifying it). In doing so, even if you do not actually do the refactoring, you will gain valuable insight into the code that will help when you implement the new requirement. Of course, if you do any refactoring, then you should make sure that the system still passes all its tests before you actually start working on the new requirement.

The second point at which you should consider refactoring is once you have implemented the new code. This gives you a better opportunity to consider how your new (and now working) code and the existing code base fit together. For example, at this point you may notice that two similar classes have essentially duplicate code. You may be able to eradicate this duplication either by using a pluggable component or by creating a common abstract class and moving the duplicate code into that abstract class.

Personally, I find that the most common points at which I find I need to refactor are:

1. when I examine existing code to understand how it works (for example, to work out how to add a new feature),
2. after implementing a new feature and examining related code new similarities or relationships suddenly become apparent.

Note that the above is as true for bug fixes as it is for implementing a completely new feature.

6.5.3 How to Refactor?

How you should go about refactoring is a large topic (which is covered in detail by Fowler (1999)). However, the general issues to consider when you start to refactor are:

1. Make sure that the code you want to refactor has a complete test suite available for it.
2. Make sure you know how to improve the code.
3. Make sure what you have done has improved the code.
4. Make sure all tests are still passed, plus any new ones you have identified have also passed.
5. Make use of tool support wherever possible.

Of these, the two most important points are:

1. know what you are doing,
2. and test, test, test.

What do these mean? Firstly, if you find some code that you believe requires refactoring, then you should make sure you are clear about what your refactoring will be. For example, just because an algorithm looks complex and convoluted does not mean that re-writing it will improve on it. You may well end up with an algorithm that is equally as complex and convoluted, just different. This has not necessarily improved the code! Secondly, when refactoring, testing should be your constant companion. If you make a change, then test it immediately. It is only through testing that you can have any confidence to refactor.

6.5.4 When Not to Refactor?

When should you not refactor? Well an implication of our earlier discussion means that you shouldn't refactor when:

> "You haven't got a clear plan of how you will improve the code."

This is because, if you don't know how to improve it, then you are unlikely to succeed in improving the code!

Another situation where you don't want to refactor is within bug fixing. You may refactor before or after fixing a bug, but bug fixing itself is not part of refactoring. Thus, you should only refactor correctly functioning code.

Finally, you don't want to refactor just for the sake of it. There has to be a reason to refactor. There are those who will say that you can never refactor too much. But few projects have the luxury of unlimited time and/or resources. And remember, at the end of the day, the aim is to produce working software that is of value to the user. Refactoring code may help with this aim, but refactoring for refactorings' own sake does not.

6.6 Keeping on Track

6.6.1 Small Releases

It can come as a surprise, but keeping releases small can actually be a difficult challenge. This can be because organisations are used to larger releases and try to focus on these, customers expect fully functional releases and so want larger releases or because the practicalities of releasing software to an end user may make it difficult to do regularly.

On one recent project I led, we could not make many small releases to the actual end users, because they were working with an earlier version of the software in the "real" world. They were not particularly computer literate and would require training on any new features. There were over 250 users so doing this at very regular intervals was not an option. Instead, representatives from regional user groups throughout the UK were selected from regular release meetings. At each meeting, they were given the new release and the new features in the release were worked through. These sample users would then use the new release for a period of time to allow a range of users to provide representative feedback. This feedback would then be used to guide following releases. This allowed regular monthly releases to be created without interrupting the actual work being done by the majority of users.

6.6.2 Simple Design

So XP states that you should keep your designs as simple as possible, but still implement the functionality required. Well that's easy then! Well actually no, creating simple design is not easy! For a start what is "Simple Design." Is it a basic design? and when can you say that a design is simple? As before there are no hard and fast rules, but the simplest design, that does what you need it to do, is one which:

1.   Runs all the tests cases. If it doesn't it is not yet complete.
2.   Contains no duplicate code.

3. Makes it clear to another programmer, what the original programmers intended the code to mean. This is a very important point and one that often mitigates against naïve, obscure or basic designs.
4. Contains the fewest possible classes and methods.
5. Doesn't include any unused features.

This doesn't mean that all designs implemented are small and trivial. If the problem being addressed is a complex one, then the design to solve that problem may well be complex relative to other parts of the system. However, our aim should still be to produce the simplest design possible, that implements the required functionality, passes all the tests and is as clear as possible to someone reading the code. To me this last point, clarity in the code, is very important. Many times over the years, I have chosen a solution which I believe to be clearer to someone reading the code compared to another solution which may use less code or initially appear in some way better. My argument is always the same, if it is clearer to me now, it is likely to be clearer to someone else later on (when I may not be around).

Even given the above guidance, finding a simple design can be hard and may not be achieved on the first attempt. This is where brainstorming on a white board with other developers can be invaluable for refining and simplifying something that at first seems to be incredibly complex. More than once I have been in such meetings, outlining my plan of attack for some feature, and someone else in the room, possibly with less experience or less familiar with the issues will say something like "I may be missing something here, but why don't you ...." At which point, I usually stare at the white board, try to find a reason to counter what now seems to be "blindingly obvious" and typically fail. The end result is that I have been able to produce a simpler implementation and my colleague has felt good about the help they have given.

So what else can we do to try to help ourselves find the "simplest" design? Here are some other nuggets that have been found useful:

1. Be driven by the tests. This helps to focus on what is actually required and not on what you think may be required.
2. Although experience is invaluable, try to apply it sparingly. I mean by this, that just because you have seen a similar problem before, does not mean that the solution you identified last time should be used wholesale in the new application. Rather, it should allow you to gain insight into the problem, and thus to determine what the best current solution should be.
3. Start with simplifying assumptions. This makes things easier to understand initially.
4. As your understanding grows, retract one simplifying assumption at a time and refine your design.
5. Consider what is missing from your simple solution (relative to any new tests identified) and plan the simplest way to introduce it that maintains the clarity of the solution.
6. Involve your programming partner – don't take them along for the ride.
7. Use your head. Ask yourself, "is this the simplest, clearest, most obvious way to do this." For example, soon after starting with Java, I noticed it didn't have

a case statement that could support testing on objects. Initially, I started to use a map object to mimic a "case" statements behaviour. In time it became clear that although the end result looked quite clever (and indeed I felt quite smug at the invention) the resulting code was far less clear that it should have been. I have since resorted to multiple "if" statements that are much clearer to read.
8.   Use refactoring to refine the design as the project progresses (this is part of the purpose of refactoring).

Another thing that can help your design is not to forget some basic object oriented design guidelines. Such as:

Naming Classes. The naming of a class is extremely important. The class is the core element in any object-oriented program and its name has huge semantic meaning that can greatly affect the clarity of the program. Examples of Java system classes include:

```
HashTable
FileInputStream
SecurityManager
```

The above names are good examples of how a name can describe a class. The name of a class is used by most developers to indicate its purpose or intent. This is partly due to the fact that it is the class name that is used when searching for appropriate classes (for example, by using the documentation generated by Javadoc).

You should, therefore, use descriptive class names; classes with names such as *MyClass* or *ProjectClass1* are of little use. However, class names should not be so specific that they make it appear that the class is unlikely to be of use except in one specific situation (unless, of course this is the case). For example, in an application that records details about university lecturers, a class with a name such as *ComputerScienceDepartmentLecturer* is probably not appropriate, unless it really does relate only to lecturers in the Computer Science Department. If this is the case, you need to ask yourself in what way computer science lecturers are different from other lecturers.

The role of a class. A subclass or class should accomplish one specific purpose; that is, it should capture only one idea. If more than one idea is encapsulated in a class, you should break the class down into its constituent parts. This guideline leads to small classes (in terms of methods, instance variables and code). Breaking a class down, costs little but may produce major gains in reusability and flexibility.

A subclass should only be used to modify the behaviour of its parent class. This modification should be a refinement of the class and should therefore extend the behaviour of the class in some way. For example, a subclass may redefine one or more of the methods, add methods that use the inherited behaviour, or add class or instance variables. Therefore, a subclass which does not do at least one of these is inappropriate.

Creating new data structure classes. When working with data structures, there is always the question of whether to create a new data structure class to hold your data or whether to define a class which holds the data within one of its instance variables and then provide methods which access that variable.

For example, let us assume that we wish to define a new class, called *Account*, which holds information on deposits and withdrawals. We believe that we should use a hash table to hold the actual data, but should *Account* be a subclass of *HashTable* or of something else (for example, *Object*, with an instance variable holding an instance of *HashTable*)? Of course, it depends on what you are going to do with the `Account` class. If it provides a new data structure class (in some way), even if it is only for your application, then you should consider making it a subclass of *HashTable*. However, if you need to provide a functionally complex class that just happens to contain a hash table, then it is almost certainly better to make it a subclass of *Object*.

There is another point to consider: if `Account` is a subclass of *HashTable*, then any instance of *Account* responds to the whole of the *HashTable* protocol. You should ask yourself whether this is what you want, or whether a more limited protocol (one appropriate to an account object) is more suitable.

Class comments. Every class, whether abstract or concrete, should have a class comment. This comment is the basic documentation for the class. It should, therefore, tell a developer creating a subclass from the class, or a user of the class, what they need to know.

Using a class or an instance. In situations where only a single instance of a class is required, it is better style to define a class which is instantiated once, than to provide the required behaviour in class-side methods. Using a class instead of an instance is very poor style, breaks the rules of object orientation and may have implications for the future maintenance of the system.

6.6.3 Continuous Integration

The aim when trying to implement "continuous integration" it not to integrate every 5 min, but between one and several times per day. The aim is to avoid the problems encountered with big bang integrations. Big bang integrations happen when a period of time (typically days or weeks rather than hours) has elapsed. In many situations, the act of integrating all the code can take days in itself. In one project that I witnessed, the integration took a week just to get to the point that all the code compiled (it had yet to be tested!). One developer in particular seemed to have gone off on their own causing chaos.

Big bang integrations slow development projects down and can help to create a culture of blame. The reason for regular integration (every few hours) is to help you find out:

1. Have you broken anything?
2. Has anyone broken anything you have done with his or her changes?

To "implement" continuous integration you need to try and adopt a development model where you code for a while, and then integrate before continuing coding. This may be as frequently as every hour or may be a couple of times a day. If you go for too long without integrating you may be storing up problems for yourself. If you find that others have been integrating and you haven't, then you should try to integrate as you may be storing up problems when you come to try and integrate your own code. By regularly integrating your code with the current build, you should also have everyone else's latest code (give or take an hour or two).

How can this work? Certainly in the past, there was the idea what developers should only integrate their code into the current build, once the task they were working was completed, fully tested and possibly reviewed and signed off.

The key to continuous integration is that pair programmers should work in small steps and that these small steps can be integrated. Remember the way in which pair programmers should work:

1. Write a test.
2. Write the code stubs.
3. Make sure everything compiles so far.
4. Run the test – it should fail. That's okay.
5. Implement stubs.
6. Make sure the test is passed before continuing.
7. Make sure all tests can pass before continuing further.
8. Integrate the now working code into the current build.
9. Return to step 1 until complete.

Thus, each step taken is a relatively small one (defined by a single test case). Any one task may involve many such tests but you address one test at a time. You implement just enough behaviour to pass the test and then integrate the result once everything is shown to be working. Within this framework, continuous integration becomes part of the way you work, as natural as writing tests for your code. It is surprising how soon it becomes unthinkable not to integrate your code regularly in this way.

Note incorrect, incompatible, buggy code should never be integrated into the current build.

Another aid to make continuous integration happen is to have a specific integration machine. This machine is used for integrating code into the current build. The use of a specific integration machine, set up within the project office, workspace or similar, is that:

1. Everyone can see who is integrating at the moment. The people at the integration machine are the ones integrating right now.
2. Only one pair can integrate at any one time. This avoids the situation where two or more pairs are trying to integrate. If this happens, you can find that one pair start to step on the toes of the other pair as they try to fix problems introduced by their particular integrations. Another way round this is to have some form of token that integration builders must possess in order to integrate. At one point we had a rather strange hat, that some of the developers

liked to ware which was labelled "Build Hat."[2] If you had the build hat you could integrate your code. If you didn't have it, then you couldn't build it.

3. The use of the integration machine makes it clear that integration is a separate, deliberate step in the development process.
4. The integration machine can be a nice big powerful machine able to run all the tests quickly and compile all the code, etc.

The actual integration process itself, should follow these basic steps:

1. Retrieve the current build and re-run all the tests. This makes sure that every-thing is okay before you start. It should be, as the last pair to integrate should have left the system in a state where all tests are passed. However, life just isn't always as simple as that so it is often best to make sure. If not all the tests have passed then the last pair to integrate needs to fix the problems (and have a bit of a telling off !).
2. Next the pair should add their new code to the integration build.
3. The pairs are now ready to rebuild the system. In the case of Java, this will involve "javac-ing" the code and creating one or more Jars, Wars or Ears, etc. Tools such as ANT can greatly simplify this.
4. Now the pairs are ready to re-run all the tests. If all the tests have been passed, a new build is released and the rest of the team informed of the successful build. This allows other developers to update their source code base, obtain the new build, etc.
5. If one or more tests failed, then the pair must fix the problem before contin-uing. If the problem is too big to fix quickly on the integration machine, then they should remove their changes from the build machine and return to their own area to carry on with resolving the problem.

6.6.4 Making Collective Ownership Happen

Getting programmers to give up personal ownership of code and to take collective ownership is actually not that difficult to do. Often the problem is steering away from lack of ownership. The "oh! if its not my code then I am not responsible for it" attitude. Actually, the attitude is "all the code is my code."

To make it work, you need a few things to happen. First of all you need devel-opers to:

1. Let us go of their egos. There should be no prima donnas, no gurus whose work no one will touch. Everyone is in the same boat, everyone is trying to do the best they can for the project and most importantly of all everyone, and I do mean everyone can make a mistake. The sooner everyone realises these points and stops trying to score points over each other, the quicker collective ownership can happen. I have personally found one of the best ways to help this along is to try and be the best proponent of myself. That way, less

---

[2] This "hat" was actually the remains of a white cardboard box, cut-out to make a hat!

experienced members of the team hopefully follow my example. I do say I try to do this because I am just as human as anyone else and can sometimes be too protective as well, but that also shows everyone that nobody is perfect (well not me anyway!).

2. Let go of the software once it is integrated. It is now the property of the project and everyone owns it. Therefore, everyone has the right (indeed the duty) to improve it if they can see how (and have a reason to do so). This can be tricky, but with pair programming, this means that there are two people who created it (so its not yours alone anyway) and that there may be another two refactoring it.

Next you need software support that can make this happen. One of the most important support tools available to any XP project is a reliable version control system. Later in this book, we will talk about CVS (Continuous Version control System others include subversion). This will allow the project to recover from any unfortunate instances and to examine who made what changes when.

6.6.5 Getting an On-Site Customer

You need to try and get an "on-site customer" as part of your team – to do this try asking your client for one. They may be very happy to give you one. They may be surprised by the request as no one may ever have made such a request before, but they may see that it makes sense. If they don't then try to educate them, explaining to them the great benefits that an on-site customer can bring to a project. You can even point out that you will probably not need them all the time once the project gets started and thus they can still do some of their normal work, just from a desk within the project team. Depending on the type of client, they may or may not be able to do this. If you don't succeed in getting an on-site customer, then try and get an "always available" one. This often works just as well. On a recent project, we were working with a government department in London and our office is based in Bath over an hour train journey away. As the project was expected to run for some time, no one from the London office wished to effectively relocate to Bath for any period of time. Instead, we had an always-available customer using the phone, email and video conferencing and who was an on-site customer when we really needed her. Overall, this worked out really well and the project did not suffer in the slightest.

6.6.6 Stand-Up Meetings

A common practise within an XP project is the stand-up meeting. This is a meeting, which as its name indicates, is held with everyone standing up. The idea is that the meeting will be short, everyone will be focussed on the purpose of the meeting, and no one will be sliding down in his/her seat snoozing quietly and not contributing. Such meetings might be held at the start of the day to review where everyone is and to allocate pairs, tasks to pairs, discuss any concerns, etc. A pair may also use stand-up meetings during a task when they wish to discuss some issue or concern with other members of the team, etc. Stand-up meeting should be short, concise and focussed (and this is really the point) with a particular goal. Once the goal is met, then the meeting should be adjourned.

6.7 Summary

As you can see from this chapter, actually implementing XP is a non-trivial task and it takes time and practise to get it right. In answer to the question, how best to introduce XP into a project, the simplest answer is to get an experienced XP expert in to act as an XP coach and ideally have a couple of experienced XP programmers who can help to smooth the introduction. As this is often not an option, then you need to give XP time and to introduce a bit of it at a time, but understand you will not get the full benefit of XP until you introduce all twelve practises.

7

Agile Modelling and XP

7.1 Introduction

Over the last four chapters, we have considered in detail both Agile Modelling (AM) and eXtreme Programming (XP). Both are from the agile movement and both are motivated by the desire to produce better software faster. But how do they relate (if at all)? What is the relationship between Agile Modelling and XP? Are they complementary or contradictory? In this Chapter, we will consider exactly this issue and look at how Agile Modelling can actually enhance an XP project.

7.2 The Fit

In actual fact, many of the Agile Modelling practises fit straight into XP. In many cases, they are the modelling equivalent of the XP programming-oriented practises. However, Agile Modelling's emphasis is obviously modelling and XP's emphasis is programing, so there are differences and there are practises that are only relevant to one of the methods or the other.

The question therefore is, "Do the Agile Modelling practises add any value to the XP practises?" Here we mean, "Do they add value in terms of helping to produce the end product, that is, the software?" If they don't actually help to produce a better piece of software or to speed up the process of creating that software, then they don't add value.

It is also important to consider whether Agile Modelling actually fits in with the philosophy of XP at all. At first sight, there may be a fundamental conflict. That is, XP does not encourage big up-front modelling and Agile Modelling is obviously about modelling, therefore, they are at odds. Except that, Agile Modelling is more of a philosophy than a hard and fast approach. Indeed, Agile Modelling needs to be applied with some other development methodology to be of any real benefit. As such, it brings a suite of agile techniques to the process of modelling. XP does do modelling, although this may come as a shock to some alleged XP practitioners. However, it does not do "big up-front modelling." Instead, modelling is performed as and when required during the lifetime of an XP project. It is at these points that Agile Modelling practises can become not only relevant but also extremely useful.

Table 7.1 Common practises between Agile Modelling and eXtreme Programming

Agile Modelling	eXtreme Programming
Collective ownership	Collective ownership
Create simple content/depict models simply	Simple design
Model with others	Pair programming
Apply modelling standards	Use coding standards
Active stakeholder participation	On-site customer

7.3 Common Practises

So both Agile Modelling and XP are part of the agile movement so what practises do they have in common. Actually, they have quite a few practises in common (although the names may differ from one approach to the other). To illustrate this, consider Table 7.1. This table pairs up various Agile Modelling practises with their equivalent (or near-equivalent) XP practises.

Note that as the emphasis on the two approaches differs, there is bound to be a slight variation in emphasis within common practises. For example, "Model with Others" is matched to "Pair Programming" because the intention in both cases is that everything produced is examined and thought about by two or more people. Some differences are more obvious; in Agile Modelling we use modelling standards while in eXtreme Programming we use coding standards but again the intention is the same.

Other Agile Modelling practises have potentially less obvious parallels within XP practises. But again if they are examined, it can be seen that they represent the same or similar intention but from the modelling perspective. These are illustrated in Table 7.2.

For example, in Table 7.2 when performing Agile Modelling you should consider how what you are modelling might be tested? How you can model to facilitate testing? (and by implication what those tests are). This can be then fed into the test-first coding style of XP (this is discussed in more detail later in this Chapter). In turn, the practise of displaying models publicly (for example, on a modelling wall) is akin to the open communication promoted by XP. Agile Modelling also encourages modellers to work in "small increments" that is similar to XP's practise of defining a single test, implementing what is needed for that test, before continuing with the next test. Finally, one way of validating models created in Agile Modelling is to prove those models by implementing them. This is akin to requiring code to pass an individual test before continuing. It also fits

Table 7.2 Parallel practises between Agile Modelling and eXtreme Programming.

Agile Modelling	eXtreme Programming
Consider testability	Testing (test-first coding)
Display models publicly	Open communication
Model in small increments	Implement a test at a time
Prove it with code	Pass a test before continuing

in very well with XP, in that you may model a little bit, then implement it before continuing with modelling which is a very XP-like approach.

7.4 Modelling Specific Practises

There are some Agile Modelling practises that may, at first at least, appear to have no place within XP at all. These practises include:

- model with a purpose,
- using multiple models and
- know your models.

This is partly as they are very clearly specific to the act of modelling. It is also partly because XP does not have much to say about the act of modelling or of the models that might be created. The only thing that tends to be discussed is the use of stand-up modelling meetings during which existing code is analysed or new code explored through the use of diagrams (which are a form of model). The resulting XP "models" are often thrown away as soon as they are no longer needed (as they may only exist for a short time on white boards, note pads or index cards and are never translated into a design tool).

In the remainder of this section, we will look at each of the three practises listed above and consider whether they actually do have a role within XP.

7.4.1 Model with a Purpose

As many XP practitioners may see no place for modelling at all, this point may, to them, seem self-defeating. That is, there is no purpose to modelling within an XP project! However, this can be very wrong. There are a number of purposes to modelling which can be very relevant to XP. For example, the motivational category within Agile Modelling that includes the practises "Model to Understand" and "Model to Communicate." These two practises are considered in more detail below.

Model to understand the software. This is relevant because, before you refactor or extend your code you must understand it. Individual methods or classes may be understandable merely by considering them in isolation. However, due to the nature of object-oriented systems, such as those implemented in languages such as Java, it is often necessary to consider a group of cooperating classes together. This may involve reviewing how the instances of the classes are created, interacted and are discarded. Personally, I found doing this much easier using diagrams and pictures than by purely examining the source code (although the diagrams and pictures may be derived from that very source code). When confronted with a new area of a system, I will usually find it necessary to produce a structural class diagram and one or more sequence diagrams to help me understand the code. This may be in a modelling tool or it might be through the modelling generation capabilities of a tool such as Together

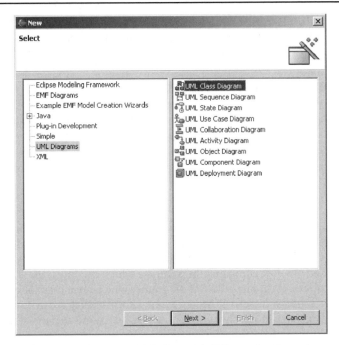

Fig. 7.1 Creating a new UML diagram in Eclipse using Omondo.

or Eclipse. For example, when looking at part of the implementation of the ClearSpell spell checker developed by a colleague, I need to become familiar with the structure of the main spell-checking engine. To do this, I have decided to use the Omondo plug-in for Eclipse to generate a class diagram for myself. This is done within Eclipse by creating a new UML diagram as illustrated in Figure 7.1. Once this is done, Omondo finds out which classes and interfaces are in the selected package. It then presents a selection dialog to the user, which allows them to select which classes and interfaces they actually want to include in the diagram and what type of relationships to show. This is illustrated in Figure 7.2.

Having done this, Omondo then creates the class diagram displayed in Figure 7.3. Although I must still determine what the various elements of this package now do, I have a much better feel for the structure of this package, then I would have got just by looking at what the package contains (as illustrated in Figure 7.4).

Of course, I do not need to use a tool such as Eclipse or Together at all. I might find that merely drawing out the structure on a white board is more than sufficient (as illustrated in Figure 7.5).

Model to communicate. Source code is the end result that we all are trying to produce (it is not a model which will be delivered as an executable after all). However, it is not the best way to explain your ideas to one or more other people. Within XP, if a new piece of code is to be implemented, a programmer may call a quick "stand-up" meeting to run through their ideas with their pair-programming

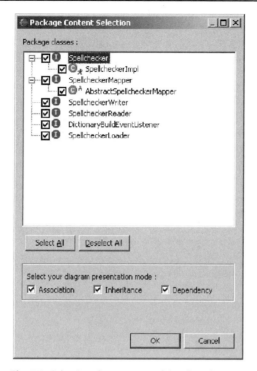

Fig. 7.2 Selecting the contents of the class diagram.

partner (and a few other people with relevant knowledge or experience). At such a meeting, models may well be the best form of communication. Of course, this does not necessarily imply the use of a modelling tool. It may involve white boards, post-it notes, index cards, etc. But then, that is exactly what Agile Modelling encourages you to use (if they are appropriate).

The key to both of these issues: "Model to understand" and "Model to communicate," is the need for a "valid purpose." Stating that XP does not explicitly include modelling is **not** a valid reason for not to do modelling. Even in XP, there can be "valid reasons" to model!

7.4.2 Multiple Models

If XP is all about programming, then I don't want to get bogged down in modelling, let alone end up having to create multiple models! Do I? However, the problem with this argument is that by only using a single model is a bit like only ever looking at works of art on a 15″ black and white monitor or TV – you will fail to see the whole picture let along understand the many subtleties and textures of the work being scrutinised.

In just the same way, if you wish to fully understand your application, then you may well need to consider a class diagram (for the system structure), a sequence

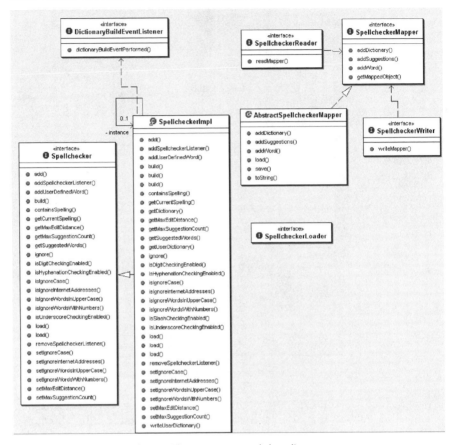

Fig. 7.3 The auto-generated class diagram.

Fig. 7.4 Listing the package contents.

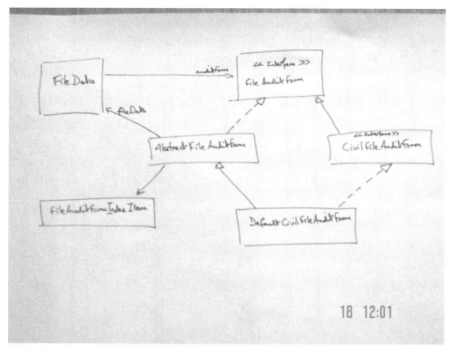

Fig. 7.5 Hand drawn class diagram.

diagram (for its behaviour), a data diagram (for the database representation), etc. This is still as true for XP as it is for Agile Modelling! You should then switch between the different models as and when required.

7.4.3 Know Your Models

Whether you are an Agile modeller or an XP developer you need to know the tools available to you. Even for those working on an XP project, modelling is relevant (as has already been said). Thus, XP developers need to understand the models available to them just as much as an Agile modeller should. That is, they should understand the strengths and weaknesses of different types of models. This will help them to keep models as simple as possible, as well as helps to apply appropriate models which will help them to understand the systems under consideration.

7.5 XP Objections to Agile Modelling

Other arguments raised by XP practitioners against Agile Modelling include:

- *Modelling is all about big up-front design* (the so called BMUF – Big Modelling Up-Front syndrome). Agile Modelling clearly does not promote this. This is illustrated by the Agile Modelling practises such as "Model in Small Increments" and "Prove it with Code."

- *All models are permanent documents* that must be updated when any changes are made. This is clearly not what Agile Modelling says. For example, the practises "Discard temporary models," "Use the simplest tools" and "Update only when it hurts" contradict this view.
- *You need to use a complex modelling tool,* such as Rational Rose to carry out any modelling activity. However, as Agile Modelling explicitly debunks that myth, stating you should use whatever modelling medium is appropriate, which may include modelling tools such as Rational Rose, but also white boards, index cards, post-it notes, etc.
- *You need to know, and use, UML to create models.* Agile Modelling does say that you should know how to apply whatever representation you are using in your models and that UML is one example of this. But it does not mandate any particular type of representation and indeed Agile modellers know that something like UML does not cover all the modelling situations you might want. In addition, an Agile modeller will not worry about creating a precise and complete UML diagram. Instead, they will focus on the audience of what they are creating and make sure that it is comprehensible to that audience.
- *XP does not encourage modelling.* Actually this is wrong. XP does promote the creation and use of models. The use of index cards for user stories and classes is a form of modelling. XP practitioners will also often draw diagrams on white boards while trying to consider how to address a problem of refactor code, etc. These are again forms of models.
- *XP does not create any documentation* and models are a form of unnecessary documentation. XP promotes code as the core form of documentation for a system as only code is in sync with code. However, documentation needs to be appropriate for the reader of that documentation. Source code may be a good source of reference for programmers, but it is unlikely to be appropriate for end users, non-programmers, support personnel, etc. In some cases, models may be a very useful form of documentation for some of these audiences. For example, a UML deployment diagram may be very useful for understanding how the system will be installed over a network.

7.6 Agile Modelling and Planning XP Projects

In this section, we will consider how and where Agile Modelling fits into the project-planning aspects of an XP project. An XP project is planned at a number of levels and at various points during an XP projects lifetime (see Figure 7.6). This means that Agile Modelling practises may be more or less relevant at different stages during this process. In the following, we will consider the planning process and where Agile Modelling can be exploited to the benefit of XP.

7.6.1 Initial Project Planning

There are two primary steps within the initial project-planning phase; these are the initial planning game and the elaboration process.

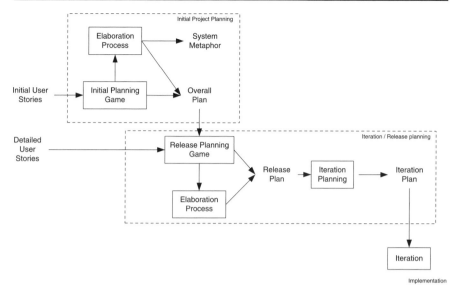

Fig. 7.6 The planning aspects of an XP project lifecycle.

Initial planning game. During this process, business and development may resort to modelling to help them clarify the user stories. By applying Agile Modelling practises, this modelling can be controlled and focused. An example of where they might do this is when a User Interface mock up might be created, with some simple flow charts to prototype system behaviour as a way of elaborating a user story. For example, Figure 7.7 illustrates a possible user interface design for a membership web site. This is a diagram drawn on a white board to consider what fields are needed and what will happen when a user selects the submit option. The flow diagram presented in Figure 7.8 expresses what happens when the submit button is pressed. Again, this is a diagram drawn on a white board. The eventual application will be implemented as a Java 2 Enterprise Edition-based web application and is presented in Figure 7.9.

Elaboration process. During the elaboration process, various models may be created to help the developers understand what will be required of the system. This will help to produce better estimates, etc. Again Agile Modelling practises can be of great help here.

7.6.2 Iteration/Release Planning

During the iteration/release planning stages, modelling is again important.

Release planning game. As with the initial planning game, Agile Modelling practises can help focus the modelling activities used to clarify user requirements.

Elaboration process. Although this is typically a shorter process than for the initial project planning phase, some modelling often still takes place and Agile Modelling can be applied to ensure that modelling does not become a burden.

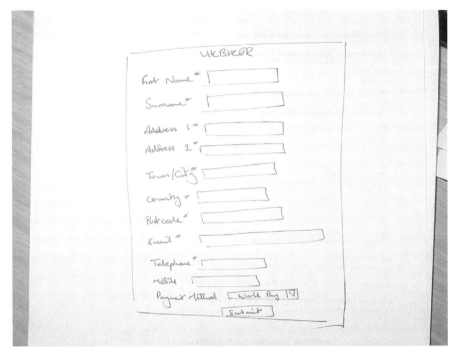

Fig. 7.7 User interface design.

Iteration planning. In order to break down user stories into tasks, it may be necessary to model how the user stories might be implemented. This might involve initial class structures, behaviour, etc. This can allow tasks to be identified, clarified or split up. Note that this is not large up-front design, as the models may be discarded and may only be intended to help elaborate the tasks.

7.7 XP Implementation Phase

This is where the code actually gets written within an XP project. There are therefore various points at which a model may be relevant and therefore Agile Modelling practises may be applied. For example, in helping to understand code in order to refactor it, etc. We will now look at how Agile Modelling can complement several of the implementation-oriented practises of XP. By implementation-oriented practises, I mean practises such as "Test-first coding," and "Refactoring," rather than the more process-oriented ones such as, "The Planning Game" or the "40 hour week rule."

The practises to be looked at in this section are:

- refactoring,
- test-first coding,

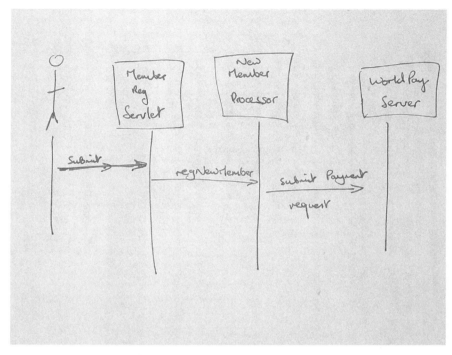

Fig. 7.8 Basic member creation workflow.

- simple design and
- pair programming.

Each of these will be discussed in more detail below.

7.7.1 Refactoring

Refactoring is primarily a code improvement technique, so is it compatible with a modelling activity? Is modelling and Agile Modelling in particular, relevant to refactoring? The answer of course is "yes," as we have already indicated earlier in this chapter. In the last chapter, some of the issues to consider when refactoring were given as:

- Make sure you know how to improve the code.
- Make sure what you have done has improved the code.

That is, "know what you are doing!" It was also stressed that you should not refactor:

"When you haven't got a clear plan of how you will improve the code."

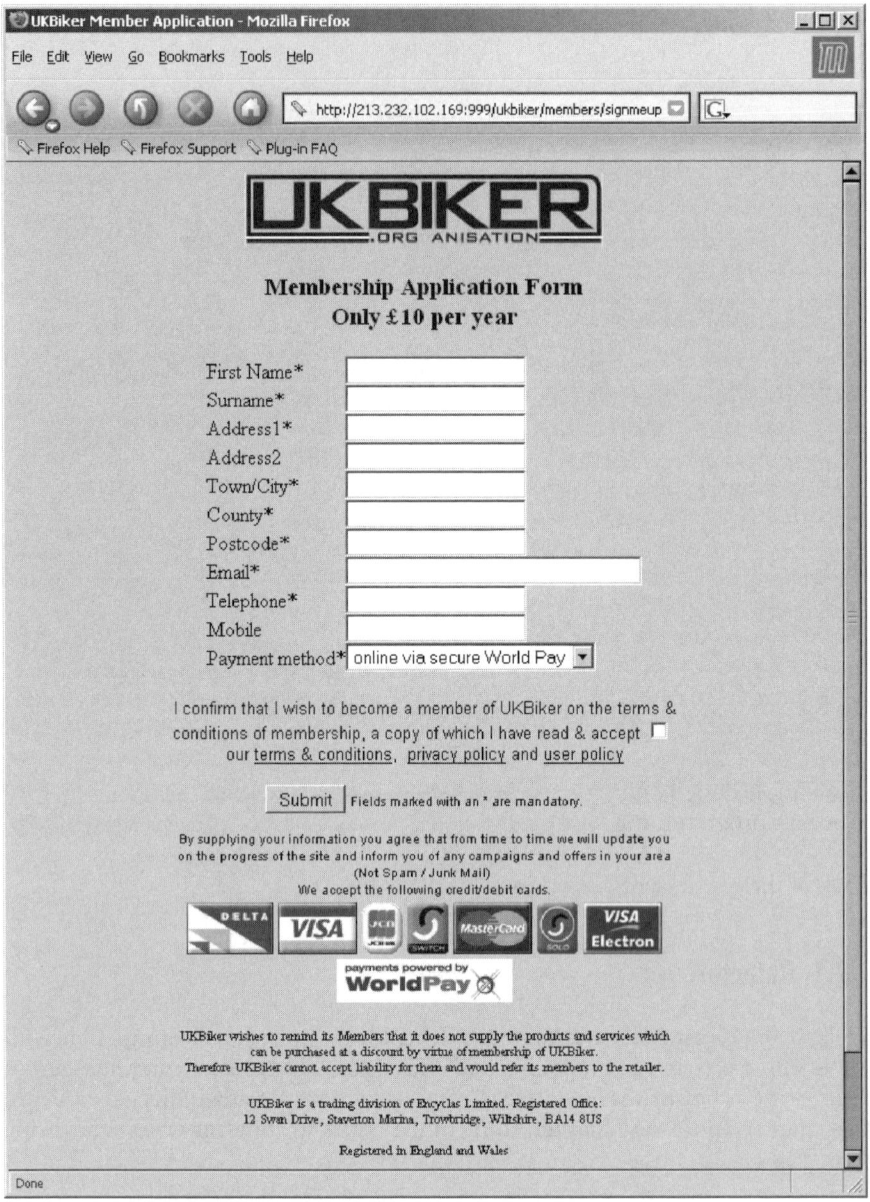

Fig. 7.9 The membership web site implementation.

Agile Modelling can be used to help with all three issues. By modelling various aspects of the system, you may gain a better understanding of what it does. By modifying the model, you can evaluate how you might refactor it and whether it appears to have benefited from the refactoring. This is a lot cheaper than actually coding the changes and then considering the results. It may also be a better medium through which to convey your ideas to your pair-programming partner or to others; thus allowing improved communication of ideas.

If the project you are working has moved to XP since its inception, there may also already be system models available. When you refactor, you may need to think about updating these models as well. By applying Agile Modelling practises, you can determine if they do actually need to be revised or not. For example, by considering the following two Agile Modelling practises:

- Update only when it hurts not to do so.
- Discard temporary models.

You might decide not to update the existing models until absolutely necessary. Even then, I find it better to wait until someone shouts for the models and update them at that point (in Just-In-Time fashion) as an XP project may refactor the code several times before the point at which someone wants to reference the documentation. This would lead to unnecessary model revisions taking place.

Finally, tools that provide "in sync" modelling can really help Agile Modelling during refactoring (such as the Eclipse tool with the Omondo plug-in as was seen earlier in this chapter). Using such tools minimises the extra work required to produce the models but maximises the benefits from having the models. For example, the models can be created at the click of a few buttons (including sequence diagram style models) and any changes subsequently made to the source code are immediately reflected in the models. Personally, I certainly find that I refactor structurally using models, behaviourally across objects using models and internally to methods using the course code editor. This helps me because it fits with the way I think (it also tends to be much quicker to do things this way if you have tools such as Together and Eclipse). For example, moving a class into a new package and changing all references to that class to the new package can be as simple as dragging and dropping the class into a new package!

7.7.2 Test-First Coding

At first sight, with respect to test-first coding, modelling may seem at best superfluous and at worst contradictory. This is because, in test-first coding, you essentially follow this cycle:

1. Write a test.
2. Write the code to be tested.
3. Run the test/get the code to work.
4. If the test has passed, then return to step 1 until finished.

So where does Agile Modelling fit into this cycle? It may fit in at a couple of points. You may have decided to carry out a small amount of modelling at the start of the current task in order to understand what you need to do. If you have taken into account the "Design for Testability" Agile Modelling practise, then it may have helped to identify the tests to be implemented. Another point at which Agile

Modelling may be relevant is once a test has been written and you need to consider how to implement the business code. A short "stand up" design session with your pair-programming partner can be invaluable. It can help to clarify any number of issues and help to make sure that they (and you) are engaged in what is being done and that no one is just along for the ride. This also fits with the Agile Modelling practise "Prove it with Code."

Thus, if you modify the test-first coding cycle to the following, then you are maximising this XP practise, as well as, supporting the Agile Modelling principle of rapid feedback:

1. Write a test.
2. Model the solution.
3. Implement the solution.
4. Run the test/get the code to work.
5. Discard temporary models.
6. If the test has passed, then return to step 1 until finished.

7.7.3 Simple Design

The XP practise of simple design aims to promote the simplest implementation that will:

1. Run all the tests.
2. Has no duplicate code.
3. Makes it clear to anyone reading the code what it is meant to do.
4. Have the fewest possible classes and methods.

For many within the XP circles, this pushes against what they think models promote. It has been thought that "Implement for today, design for tomorrow" means that you model for tomorrow and that is not what XP is all about. But of course this is also not what Agile Modelling is about. Indeed, Agile Modelling is about designing for today and leaving tomorrow to tomorrow.

There are in fact a variety of Agile Modelling practises that also promote simplicity within modelling. These are:

1. Create simple content.
2. Depict models simply.
3. Apply patterns gently.
4. Formalise contract models.

Each of these practises helps promote the simplest designs that meet your needs. However, they also promote simplicity in the design process. For example, the first practise essentially exhorts you not to get hung up on representation but focus on the content and the meaning. In turn, the "Depict Models Simply" practise is complementary to this, promoting how you present your models.

One common problem for Java and object-oriented developers in general, brought up in the late 1990s and after is actually something that was intended to help in object-oriented design – "Design Patterns." Don't get me wrong, I am a great believer in Design Patterns, they help you re-use proven design knowledge in new applications, they provide a common design vocabulary and they promote the whole design process when used effectively and appropriately. However, it is this last point that is often the problem – "appropriately." It is not uncommon to apply design patterns very early on in the design process just because they are a good technique (and I am just as guilty of doing this as the next designer). However, in many situations, a design pattern may provide a solution to engineers with significant flexibility and extendibility that isn't required yet. XP requires us to go for the simplest solution that solves the problem today, rather than engineer in features for tomorrow. In addition, pattern-based solutions may be more complex than is currently required, may take longer time to develop and may actually make it harder for others to extend or refactor as they incorporate additional meta knowledge. The end result is that we do not have the simplest design required for the job. At this point, you may argue "yes, but once other features are added, it will be the simplest solution." The Agile Modelling and XP answer to this is "yes, but those features may never be added or may never be added in the way you anticipate."

For example, in 2003, I was asked to develop a proof of concept resource management and planning tool for another company that already had a project-planning tool. The resource management tool was to sit along side the project-planning tool that was generating a lot of interest from clients. They wished to see how they could handle both project planning and resource planning within a single tool. There was however, not enough time (or budget) available to create the real thing, so a "smoke and mirrors" demonstrator was to be built. The intention of this tool was that it could be used to illustrate to potential customers what could be done and if enough clients signed up to the tool it could be created for real. However, rather than waste what would be done, the idea was that the demonstrator would evolve and be integrated into the main tool at a later date. Due to this last "aim," I decided that I would create the demonstrator in the right way.

The demonstrator I built made extensive use of design patterns, it applied the Model—View–Controller pattern (known as the MVC pattern), used the Factory method and Singleton patterns extensively and the Mediator pattern for inter-MVC triad communications. Finally, it used an object pool for handling memory efficiency that would be an issue in the final system. The intention of the MVC pattern is the separation of the user display, from the control of user input, from the underlying information model. The Factory method pattern provides a pattern that describes the use of a factory class for constructing objects. The Singleton pattern describes a class that can only have one object constructed for it. The Mediator pattern is one that promotes the loose coupling of a set of communicating objects. Finally, the object pool pattern manages the reuse of objects when a type of object is expensive to create or only a limited number can be created. For more detail on these and other patterns see the Gang of Four Patterns book (Gamma et al., 1995; Grand, 1999; Hunt, 2003).

In the demonstration system, all these patterns were implemented and integrated along with the demonstrator's own code. Behind the basic user interface code, the application even made use of XML files to hold data, process this data and store the results (rather than use the main system). This allowed an XML editor to be used to configure the data for various client demonstrations (without the need to hard code anything into that data). This prototype worked very well and generated a lot of interaction with the clients and the company involved with many new leads being generated. However, when it came to "integrate" the prototype, many of the initial ideas had changed so that the tool would require extensive re-working. It addition, the main tool had gone through a new release (due in part to customer feedback) and so the assumptions made about how we would integrate the tools together no longer held. Finally, the tool vendor company decided to take back the creation of the resource management and planning tool in-house. The internal developers were not familiar with design patterns. The end result was that virtually all the prototype code was dumped and the whole lot was started again! In the end, I wished that I had gone for a simpler implementation that would have done the job just as well!

In this case, the best thing would have been to apply a design pattern when the code indicated that it was really needed and not just because I could. This is of course exactly what Agile Modelling encourages you to do. Thus, it helps you to produce as simple an implementation as is required to meet the requirements.

The final Agile Modelling practise, we will look at in this section, is the "Formalise Contract Models" practise. This practise is intended to help the interface between the project and external technical groups (such as database teams, those maintaining legacy applications, external service suppliers, etc.). In many (most?) cases, these groups will not have adopted an agile methodology, and trying to work in an agile manner with them can be problematic. This is particularly true for XP projects. Agile Modelling encourages you to define the interface between such systems and yourselves formally. This makes it easier later on when working in an XP manner to determine how to use the external groups systems. Producing the contract model can take time, but can be part of the XP elaboration process and can be controlled using Agile Modelling practises (to avoid the creation of excessive documentation and extensive up-front design).

7.7.4 Pair Programming

Pair programming, as we know, involves two developers working together at a single machine. Within the pair, one developer controls the mouse and keyboard (the driver) while the other essentially monitors what the first is doing (the navigator). It is essentially that the pair communicates and understands what they are trying to achieve. It is also important that the navigator understands how the driver is intended to achieve their goals. There are situations when these goals can be achieved merely by discussing what is to be done while sitting at the terminal. However, from experience, I have found that it is generally far better to engage in a modelling session to help analyse the current software, consider alternative solutions and review how we should proceed. In the last chapter, we presented a

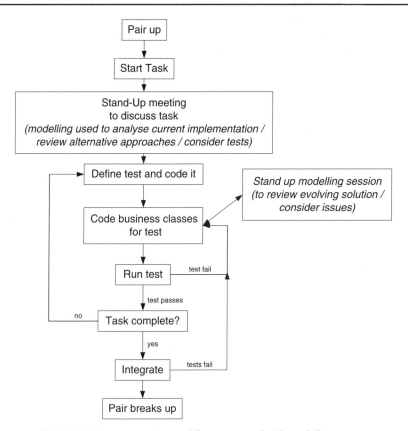

Fig. 7.10 Pair-programming workflow annotated with modelling steps.

flow chart style diagram outlining the workflow that occurs during pair programming. In this chapter, I have annotated it with the point at which modelling is relevant within pair programming (Figure 7.10). Using Agile Modelling practises help ensure that these points are handled in an appropriately agile manner.

7.8 Focus on XP

You may wonder why the focus in this Chapter has been on how Agile Modelling practises can help an XP project. The reason we have taken in this focus is that at the end of the day, modelling in any form, is merely an aid to the production of the software. From an agile perspective, it is the production of the software that is the central aim. Anything else must either contribute to this goal or is unnecessary. Therefore, as the primary focus of eXtreme Programming is on the production of the software used by the end users/clients, Agile Modelling must be an aid to that. The other way around makes little sense (from an agile perspective). That is, if you have created wonderful models in an agile manner, you still do not have any software to deliver to the clients. You have not, as yet, added value. Any method that helps you to create the actual software could do this, but XP is the approach we have considered from the agile portfolio. Thus, having a programming step is essential (and therefore not an optional one) whereas modelling may be considered an optional step from an XP perspective.

There is also a second reason for this focus. From my own perspective, I strongly believe that whether you are doing XP or another form of agile development, you will still need to perform some form of modelling at some stage. Applying the practises defined by Agile Modelling is essential to ensure that the modelling you do fits in with the agile development process used. This is not less true for XP than for any other agile method. Indeed, I would go as far as to state that if you only apply XP and ignore Agile Modelling then you are not being truly agile (on anything other than very simple projects), because you are not appropriately using all the agile tools available to you!

8

Agile Modelling and XP Reviewed

8.1 Introduction

In this chapter, we will consider what experiences teams developing with XP and Agile Modelling methods have had. It considers what issues have been found and how they have been overcome. It does reach some contentious conclusions about some aspects of XP and also considers what happens when XP is applied to larger software projects.

The remainder of this chapter is structured in the following manner. Section 8.2 reviews the twelve XP practices given the current experiences. Section 8.3 considers other factors such as scalability and the use of daily meetings. Section 8.4 addresses the issue of the need for a core software architecture around which to build the software. Section 8.5 addresses the uses of XP on larger projects, while Section 8.6 considers where XP tends to be applied most successfully.

8.2 Review of XP/AM Practices

8.2.1 The Planning Game

One of the biggest benefits of the planning game is that it requires a great deal of interaction between the developers and the customers. It thus helps to breakdown barriers and open the two sides of the project up to each other. Post-planning game, people know each other by name, can put a face to that name and are able to work together more effectively.

It is also typically important to capture performance and quality expectations at this stage as well as user stories. Not all requirements can easily be expressed (or at least are best expressed) as user stories.

8.2.2 Small Releases

The definition of a small release turns out to be relative. A small release does allow for the fastest possible return on investment and for greater customer visibility of the project and its progress. However, on a large 2-year project, a small release may well be after 3 months rather than after 2 weeks. This may still be a very radical step for an organisation if it normally creates releases every 12 to 24 months. Compared to 1–2 years, a 3-month delivery cycle is both radical and challenging. However, on such a project, a 3-month cycle still gives ample opportunity to reduce risk, respond to changes, to be agile!

8.2.3 Simple Design

Simple design is a lot easier to agree to and to aim for than to achieve. What is a simple design to one person may not be a simple design to another. On large projects, what is a simple design may actually be quite complex. However, striving for the goal of "simple design" is important in the long-run as it helps overall project velocity. However, interestingly and possibly perversely, it can slowdown development in the short-term. If a programming pair develop a piece of software and realise on completion that they could have done a better, and simpler job, a different way than by following XP principles, they are duty bound to simplify it. However, they are taking the code that they have just made work and essentially refactoring it immediately. Thus, in the short-term, they are taking longer time to complete the task – this can be a difficult practice to embrace whole-heartedly (both for developers and managers). However, if the design is simplified, then in the future when this area of the system is returned to it should be easier to evolve!

8.2.4 Testing

Automated testing of the application (using a test framework such as JUnit) can be one of the most useful features and techniques learned on an XP project. However, it may result in a blind belief in the automated tests – the "if it passes all the tests then it is fine" approach.

One problem with these unit tests is that it is exactly what they are – unit tests – they typically fail to test overall system behaviour. In particular, writing unit tests for interactive applications (such as a Swing desktop application) are notoriously difficult. In my own case, I have tended to write unit tests for the business logic behind the GUI classes but test the GUI classes manually. This is far from ideal, but without reference to a sophisticated Swing-based testing tool, it is the best I currently have to offer. However, to help this, the user interface classes are broken up into the controller, view and model classes such that all the actual operational behaviour is in the model. However, this still fails to capture what happens when the user clicks on this option, followed by this button and then Ctrl-S!

Another problem with unit tests is that they are only as good as the people who write them. The idea in XP is that as the project evolves, if you as a developer notice a test is missing, then you should add it. The code should then be tested against the new test and if it fails, corrected. Once it passes the new test, it can be released by the central repository and a new build created. However, what often happens is that once a series of tests are created, few new tests are added for existing code. Developers come to believe that the tests are all there and no new ones needed.

Then at some (far) later stage, a problem is identified which is the result of one or more missing tests.

Even when a large test suite has been created, problems can arise. As a test suite grows, changes in the system can result in many of the tests needing to be modified to deal with the system changes. This can be time consuming to fix and the problem can be that as a project progresses, the existing unit tests are abandoned as too much effort to maintain!

XP talks a great deal about Test-first coding. This is an excellent idea, as it requires the developer to write the test before the code is to be tested. There is then no bias in the test and the code should only do what is required to pass the test(s). The end result is independent tests, but it is easier to write the tests after the code – so the temptation is to do just that! So teams need to be careful to stick to the test-first coding philosophy.

It is also important not to forget that black box testing (which is what the test first coding produces) is not the only form of unit testing. It is still useful to carry out white box testing (that is examine the code to determine all paths through the code and to ensure that it doesn't do something it shouldn't).

Although unit testing is given a very high prominence within XP, it is still necessary to carryout System testing, User testing, "destruction" testing and Acceptance testing, etc. Indeed, Acceptance tests must be defined upfront at the same time (or at least just after) the user stories are captured. It is easy for these to slip and be left until the end. In addition, although in an ideal world the business should write the acceptance tests, they may need help in formulating them in a way that is understandable to both the sides.

8.2.5 Refactoring

Experience with XP projects has lead to things being recognized about refactoring, these are:

1. It is easy to ignore.
2. Refactoring effort is not flat.

We will take each of these points in turn. First, it is easy to ignore refactoring. This is because refactoring is not about fixing bugs or adding functionality, it is about improving existing code such that it behaves in exactly the same way as it did, only its implementation is better. Thus, from an external perspective, the 2 days spent refactoring those classes has not altered the system in any way at all – it behaves exactly as it always did. So why refactor it! Of course the reasons for refactoring have already been given and so will not be reproduced here, but the point is still a valid one. If I am examining some code (which works and passes all its tests) and I think I could (probably) improve this – what is the motivation to do so? No one else in the team is looking at the code with me and even if they are, unless I tell them I can improve it, who will know (unless they are mind readers they won't know). If we add in that I have deadlines of my own to meet on my current task, the delivery date is looming and its 3:30 on Friday – let us not bother refactoring this code! This is probably not that uncommon a scenario – when you add to this the value judgement involved in "improving working code" the ease with which refactoring can be ignored becomes apparent.

Second, the refactoring effort is not flat (Bowers et al., 2002). That is, that experience suggests that code requires more and more refactoring later in a projects life cycle than early on. This should not actually be a surprise as we have been saying that we expect the quality of the code, its functionality and its scope to evolve as the project progress and that developers should not worry about what might be done next only what they are doing now. As more and more features are added to a software system, so the simplifying assumptions of yesterday need more and more refactoring! However, later on in a projects lifecycle, pressures tends to be greater than early on, with tighter timescales and more riding on successful deliveries – which again means that refactoring might be put off. If the tendency for management to want to keep the changes to the code base to a minimum late on in a projects development are also applied, later refactoring may effective grind to a halt! Actually, this may not be a bad thing I know of at least two instances where late refactoring resulted in significant problems in the software that almost progressed through to delivery. These problems were invariably related to feature interactions that the refactoring had helped introduce (or at least made worse). Interestingly, these problems were not picked up by unit tests due to their cross system nature. The general feeling was that due to time pressures, the code had been refactored too quickly and the overall application not retested sufficiently at the system and user levels.

The key thing on refactoring is that it appears to be very helpful to have someone coordinating refactoring efforts and monitoring what refactoring is being carried out. This is particularly true of larger projects where rather than refactoring immediately, refactoring requests may be placed on a whiteboard and coordinated within the project. For example, late on in an iteration, it may be felt that rather than refactor now, it would be better to leave some of the refactoring until the start of the next iteration so that there is less pressure and more time to evaluate the results of the refactoring.

8.2.6 Pair Programming

This is of course the thing that most people think of when they think of XP. So how well does it work in practice?

Well, it is certainly a very good way of transferring skills, including but not limited to XP skills, between experienced and less-experienced developers. In addition, research has shown that a pair programming team can produce higher quality code in about half the time as a solo programming (Williams, 2000; Williams et al., 2000; Williams and Erdogmus, 2002; Williams and Kessler, 2003). So we should all be pair programming all the time?

Life of course is not always as simple as we would like. Pair programming is a good example for this. The concept is great, get two people to work on the same problem. Thereby having two minds producing a solution which should be no worse and potentially, better than if only one of them had addressed a problem alone – the old "two heads are better than one" adage. In addition, the idea is that code is always being reviewed, and is being reviewed by someone who actually is taking the trouble to think about the problem in hand (rather than making sure that all coding styles have been adhered too). But, and this is a big BUT, this does not take into account human dynamics!

In many cases, pair programming is promoted to sceptical management, as a way of transferring skills from experienced senior software engineers to more junior developers. And indeed, it can be very effective as a tool for this. However, it is important that the senior developer work at the pace of the junior developer so that they can absorb what is being done, and don't just sit there watching the cursor fly across the screen in bemused wonder. Of course, all developers will agree to this, actually making it work is harder, senior developers are not necessarily natural mentors and little of the experience they have typically gained is aimed at them acquiring such mentoring skills.

As was stated earlier in this book, developers are not trained to work together. Indeed, most graduate courses at best encourage separate work (and at worst actively discourage collaborative work) on the majority of projects (not least as it makes marking those projects easier!). In addition, many of those attracted to software development like the fact that they can often focus on a programming task without the need to communicate with another human. Forcing these people to work in pairs can be a difficult and problematic process.

This means that the success or otherwise of pair programming often comes down to the people involved. For example, you need to match personalities as well as align developers with tasks, based on knowledge and experience. This would seem to go against what XP tells you. In XP, two developers will pair up to address a problem. The task owner will select an appropriate pair to work with based on their knowledge and experience and away they will go. XP also recommends that pairs be changed regularly to spread the experience and the knowledge. This is great in theory but often doesn't work in practice. Some years ago, I worked in a team in which one particular developer was brilliant but socially inept and convinced of their own abilities (which were extremely good). However, no one wanted to work with him, and numerous colleagues forced to work with him asked to leave his team. He was blissfully unaware of the problems, and the management were either not skilled enough to deal with him or willing to accept his behaviour due to the perceived quality of his work (this was not in an XP context mind you). Such a person would probably have a disastrous affect if thrown into an XP pair-programming environment without any training or introduction to the approach. Given the appropriate backup, he might well prosper but not without some intervention. However, even given his social issues, there were still some people who found that they could work with him well, so even here there was potential.

The issue is that there needs to be some form of team leader to coordinate pair programming teams and to "deal" with any issues that arise. Pair programming takes time to get right and takes effort to maintain – so it needs a certain level of management and mentoring itself. All of this is true for larger projects only doubly so!

8.2.7 Collective Ownership

Although it is common to find developers agreeing to the concept of Collective Ownership, in reality, you will often find that some developers keep a watchful eye over "their" code. This may not necessarily be because they wish to protect it from attack by other developers (although this can certainly be a reason), but it may be because they don't want any bugs found in their code! This may be due to a lack of confidence in their own abilities or it may be a misplaced (and long held acceptance of) blame culture. If developers have worked in an environment in which a culture of blame has been prevalent and then move to an XP environment, it can be hard to give up "the old ways." In some cases, they seem to find it easier to give up such a culture with reference to others, but not with reference to themselves. For example, they will be magnanimous if they find a problem in "someone else's code" but become very defensive if anyone finds a bug in their code. Although at first sight, it may seem that they are being kind to other developers, it illustrates a deep-seated problem that will undermine the collective ownership concept – they still believe in "my code" and the "code of others." Why might this be a problem? because collective ownership is fundamental to the ability to refactor code, to fix problems when you encounter them to work in an agile manner? In such situations, it requires a mind shift to move to the new way of thinking (not just working) and that can take time.

8.2.8 Continuous Integration

Having tools that help to do this can be a great help. For example, tools such as Eclipse can be integrated with version control systems such as CVS to simplify the process of submitting code into the central repository.

However, submitting code to the central version control system does not necessarily mean that it forms part of the build immediately. It is necessary to extract all the current code from the version control system, re-build the application and run all unit tests. This can be automated using tools such as ANT. This can greatly simplify the whole process.

Other tools can be used to check for changes in the version control system and to initiate the build process automatically. An example of such a tool is *CruiseControl* available from Source Forge (http://cruisecontrol.sourceforge.net).

However, this approach may not work for larger projects in which it may be necessary to create regular builds at certain milestones or once certain features are completed. In such situations, the build process needs to be controlled and is unlikely to be hourly or even daily.

8.2.9 On-Site Customer

The concept of an on-site customer is extremely important (actually I would suggest for the success of any software development project). However, it is the concept of the on-site customer that is important rather than their physical presence. What I mean by that is that they need to be accessible by the development team at (almost) any moment to answer questions, clarify issues and generally provide the detailed application and domain knowledge required. However, they don't actually need to be physically located with the team (although if they are, that's great but life is often not like that).

If the "on-site" customer is available during normal working hours via a combination of email, phone, possibly video link, etc., then this is often as good. On numerous occasions, I have sent something to my "on-site" customer by email and then talked to them by phone to work through whatever was needed. This is often good enough. On occasions where it is not, then a meeting either "on-site" or at the customers' office can usually be quickly arranged. This is certainly helped by the planning game that helps to create a working relationship between the "on-site" customer and the team before they move "off-site."

The key is that the "on-site" customer can (1) answer the questions you may put to them and (2) deal with any unresolved issues either using their own authority or quickly by dealing with other members of the business. This tends to mean that the on-site customer must be senior enough to have the experience of the domain (and application) required and influential enough to make things happen, but not too senior so that they are available when you need them!

8.2.10 Coding Standards

Coding standards are essential in my opinion for making it easier for developers to move between pairs, to work on each other's code and to understand what is going on. However, in general, it is the most obvious coding standards that are the most useful, such as naming conventions, the use of title case and modified title case in a standard manner, etc. One such convention for "case" use in Java classes and interfaces is presented in Table 8.1.

Equally, in Java, variable names such as `t1`, `i`, `j`, or `temp` should rarely be used. Variable names should be descriptive (semantic variables) or should indicate the type of object that the variable holds (typed variables).

However, even simple things such as having a spelling convention can make life easier. If you are from the US, this is not an issue; however, if you are from the UK or one of the countries that follow the UK form of English, then this is a major issue. In order to maintain consistency with the core Java classes (and the

Table 8.1 Naming conventions.

Type	Convention
Constant class variable containing an object	Modified title case
Constant class variable containing a fundamental type (e.g. int)	Upper case (multiple words separated by underscores)
Interface names	Title case
Class names	Title case
Temporary variables	Modified title case
Class (static) variables	Modified title case
Instance variables	Modified title case
Method names	Modified title case

majority of the world), it is recommended that US spellings are adopted for all names in your system (including classes, variables and methods). For example:

```
Color not Colour
Center not Centre
Editor.initialize() not Editor.initialise()
```

These sorts of conventions are the things that make life easier. Issues such as how many characters on a line, how many spaces to leave when starting a nested statement or event where to place the curly brackets are much less important and can get in the way of the real issues.

In addition, standards should be applied to models (as have been discussed) and to how code is reused. Developers should understand the different ways in which they can, for example, reuse code. For example, as well as pushing reusable code up the class hierarchy, they can also use Java interfaces to create pluggable components that work in a simple client–server style. By having conventions relating to how this is done, developers will be more familiar with the structures in place when they examine code for the first time.

8.2.11 40-hour Week

Even taking into account that this is really more of a guideline to say you "shouldn't work too much all the time" rather than a hard and fast rule, there are some observations that can be made about this.

First, in organisations where it has been the norm to work long hours for extended periods of time, it can take a while to overcome that mentality. I know of one particular organisation that tried to make the 40-hour week the norm and overcome its previous corporate culture "of long hours." However, 2 years after the new policy was instigated, people would still say to someone leaving at 6 pm (who had been at their desk since 8:30 am) "oh so you are a part timer then" or "see you are skipping off early." Obviously, this didn't help the move to the new culture (this was actually made worse when a manager was given a monthly award for working 80 hour weeks)! So moving from the long hours culture to a 40-hour week culture is hard (for management as well as for the team players).

However, a more worrying trend can be seen (often in larger software projects) where the 40-hour limit is adhered to during the early parts of the project and/or iteration. But then, as pressure begins to mount and progress is required, the number of hours worked increases. This may again seem at odds with an agile approach as agile philosophy would suggest that the correct thing to do would be to drop some of the features of the system from the current release (to be implemented in the next release). First, life is not always that easy as the features being worked on may be fundamental to provide a working system for the users and second, there is (in reality) often management and business pressure to produce certain things in "the next release" whether that is an iteration release or not. Thus, the pressure mounts to complete the work. Finally, developers often apply pressure to themselves to complete a task, because they were asked to do so, even though it ends up taking longer than anyone expected. A few years ago, I had one developer who started doing exactly that. It only happened two or three times, but in each case, he did not come to me, I noticed the pattern that was developing and tried to rein it in. However, this was on a project of just five people and so was reasonably easy to spot; in a project of 30 it would be much harder.

8.2.12 System Metaphor

The concept of a system metaphor is probably the least used practice within XP. Invariably, even when XP teams have defined a system metaphor, they have not really used it. This is in part because the role of the system metaphor is not understood very well and in part (possibly) a reflection on the size of the projects being undertaken. In larger projects, where a System Metaphor has been used, if that "metaphor" is examined, it would look a lot more like a traditional software architecture description than the metaphor concept proposed in XP. For more on the idea of using an architecture, see the section on architecture later in this chapter.

8.3 Other Factors

8.3.1 Scalability

More than one XP project has been scuppered because scalability problems were encountered later on. XP promotes dealing with the issues of today and leaving whatever is required for tomorrow to tomorrow. However, some issues such as scalability and performance may need earlier consideration. Some XP projects have found that scalability can be a real headache. For example, one project I know of worked fine when it supported a single user in iteration 1, however by six iterations later when it had to support hundreds of users, it could not scale. The basic architecture had not taken into account the needs of hundreds of users. This may have been down to poor design, poor coding or lack of thought on the developers side; however, they were told not to worry about multiple users, as that wasn't in the initial iterations!

Personally, I have found that you do need to take into account scalability issues, performance requirements and, if relevant, multiple process access. That is not to say that you have to radically change the way you implement the code, but make sure that you don't create software that won't scale if it is assumed that eventually it should support hundreds of users.

This is really very hard to do, as you are not trying to support hundreds of users yet, and in fact XP takes the view it may never support hundreds of users. So what do you do? Your best! If you keep it in mind from the beginning, you may still have problems but at least you tried. Notably, it is an issue that often dominates larger software development projects that adopt XP!

8.3.2 Post Project Review

Although this has been mentioned earlier in this book, I am going to re-iterate it here, as it has been one of the most useful practices I have adopted on numerous projects. That is, the post-iteration/release review. Ideally, the review should involve all project stakeholders including developers, clients, support teams, etc. This can be carried out within a single meeting, or if you wish to deal with the non-developers and developers separately, then in two meetings. However, in either case, the idea is to conduct a retrospective review of the iteration/project to pinpoint lessons learned, review processes, see how things can be improved for the next iteration/release. It is often surprising what surfaces and how this can make future relations within the project much better.

8.3.3 Environment

The software development environment seems to be quite important to the success of XP. By environment, I mean the physical environment, rather than a suit of software tools (although those too can be important). This is not to say that a "poor" environment will not let an XP project succeed, rather that the right environment can make it much easier to succeed with XP.

Auer and Miller (2002) propose the concept of "Caves" and "Common" rooms. This layout has common areas for meetings, discussions, pair programming but caves for privacy when needed. This acknowledges the need for even XP hardened pair programmers to get away and have a space to think on their own. This may be to consider some problem from one particular angle and then to return to compare solutions with their pair programmer. Or it may have a space to relax in, check email, view the latest news bulletin on the web, etc. This is actually very important as pair programming is rather intense and programmers need periods where they can come up for air and have a breather.

8.3.4 Daily Meeting

If possible (i.e., if the project size isn't too big), having a daily meeting of everyone as part of the normal operation of the XP project is extremely beneficial. It really does promote communication within the team and the sharing of experiences and knowledge. It also helps ensure that the lines of communication are kept to a minimum and that team leaders actually know what is happening. Such a meeting often occurs first thing in the morning before everyone gets going and may be held as a stand-up meeting to keep it brief (although this is by no means compulsory!). However, the meeting can happen at any point in the day, on one recent project, we would hold the meeting just before lunch. The desire to get to lunch ensured the meeting stayed short, but having it later in the day allowed those working flexitime to arrive in the office first!

8.4 Architecture

Having an architecture is not a recognized element within an XP project. Indeed, many will take that having an "Architecture" implies a Big Up Front Design (BUFD) and that is not what XP is about. Indeed, it is not even what Agile

Modelling is about. However, some experience suggests that XP projects should only be used where you know what the system architecture is. That is, you should only build an XP application where you are building the *n*th application in the same domain – and thus implicitly know what you need to do where, when and how.

This is a controversial idea for XP as it is more typically promoted for green-field applications where the applications requirements are subject to frequent change or are relatively poorly understood. However, the point is most often made about larger XP projects, where larger teams are working on longer-lived development projects. Having an architecture to work within is one way of mitigating the problems associated with larger XP projects (known as the boundaries and interfaces).

In this section, we will look at why an XP project (if appropriate) might consider creating an architecture to work within.

8.4.1 Why Have an Architecture

Why have an architecture? This is a very valid and important question, not only because XP essentially dismisses the idea of having an architecture – the closest it gets is having a System Metaphor.

Let us consider what role requirements (and in this case user stories) have. They help identify what the system should do, that is, its functionality. They do not state anything about how that functionality should be provided. In some cases, non-functional requirements may also be identified which may impose restrictions on the realization of the system, but even these say very little about how the system should be structured or designed.

However, XP takes the *requirements* of a system (i.e., its required functionality) and uses them as its *sole starting point* in producing a design and implementation of a software system. In some (many) cases, this has been successful and in others it has not be so successful. I would argue the size of the project and the domain knowledge of those involved in the development have been the critical issues in whether the projects have succeeded without an architecture. However, if this is the first time you have produced a system to these requirements (and the system is large), it is likely to be fraught with danger.

Consider the equivalent case within the domain of the built environment (i.e., buildings). If you were to construct a simple *garden shed*, you may well start of by thinking about what you need to do with it. For example, "store the grass mower," "store shovels and forks," "keep dangerous liquids away from children." You might then produce a design that exactly matches these requirements. This end result could be a simple 5 × 6 × 7 foot shed or it could be a smaller 5 × 4 × 6 foot construction. It could be made out of wood, etc. You might also add other functional requirements such as "must be high enough to walk into" and "must have light for germinating plants." This might direct you towards a higher shed and one with a window in it. You might well produce a design in your head with minimal paper work and go along to your local wood merchants and purchase the required amount of materials. You can then fabricate the shed at your convenience. Such an approach is satisfactory because most of us have witnessed a garden shed at some time or another and have a reasonable idea of what it should look like. In addition, the requirements are fairly basic and can easily be realized.

However, let us now consider constructing a house from just its functions having never seen a house (merely hearing from someone else what they want it to do). The list of functions might be:

- Park car securely inside.
- Have a place to cook food and do the clothes washing.
- Be able to sleep inside.
- Have amenities to allow relaxation including music and television.

What might be the end result of providing these functions be? This list of functions says nothing about the relationships between them. Indeed, some bright aspiring young designer might note that the car will be inside the house. The car might reasonably have a stereo. If the car could be upgraded to include a television, well then this would be the ideal place to provide relaxation. Thus, the "car secure inside" function and the "relaxation with music and television" could be achieved together by placing the car in the middle of the house and requiring the users to sit inside the car!

If you think this example seems a little absurd then have a think about some of the software systems you or others have "endured" and see if you can make a connection – I certainly can!

What is required is something that expresses the overall relationship between the elements that will satisfy the required functions. In the case of a house, it is the architectural blue prints. These describe where everything should go; they present different views for different contractors (i.e., those presenting the heating system, those presenting the wiring, those presenting the physical structure of the walls, floors and ceilings, etc.). In the case of automobiles, there are equivalent diagrams (e.g., the wiring harness, the suspension). In fact, in almost every example of large-scale engineering endeavour, there are architectural blue prints. Software engineering really is no exception and thus the software architecture represents the blue prints for the software system.

You might at this point argue that you have built a number of systems without the need to resort to an architecture. However, ask yourself the question "did I have an implicit architecture in mind?" Often with simple systems, people have an architecture that they have adopted sub-conscientiously. They often argue that it's the obvious way to structure the system. That may well be so, but it is obvious either because the system is straightforward or because they have seen similar systems before. This is really why the shed example was okay – we had a mental model/architecture of the shed. With the house, as we had never seen a house before, we had no mental model or architecture to follow.

It should also be fairly clear to you now that if your system is straight forward (in that you already know how to approach the problem or it is relatively simple), you may not need to produce an explicit architecture – but that doesn't mean you don't have one – just that it is not being made explicit!

We need an architecture to:

- Understand the system.
- Organize development.
- Promote reuse.
- Promote continued development.

One very useful analogy for the architecture is that the architecture is like a space station. Within the core element of the space station, all the conduits and connections have been put in place for future modules to be plugged into. Then, as new modules for the space station are designed and developed, they can be plugged into this core and will work safely with the rest of the system. In addition, Java facilities such as interfaces can be used to provide "air locks." These act as fire doors between different parts of the space station, so that if one part of the architecture (space station) fails or needs to be redesigned, an air lock protects the remainder of the architecture from being affected. This is illustrated in Figure 8.1.

The architecture provides the context within which the more detailed design decisions, made for example by pair programmers working on a task, can be framed. For more information on software architectures, see Bass et al. (1998), Buschmann et al. (1996), Hofmeister et al. (1999), Kruchten (1995) and Rechtin and Maier (1997).

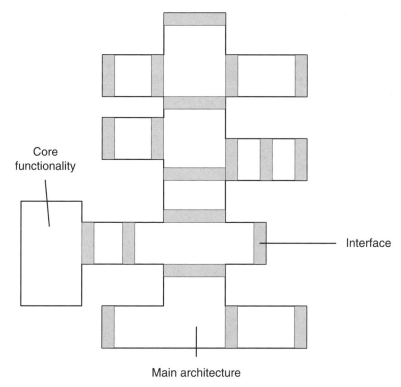

Fig. 8.1 Conceptualising an architecture.

8.4.2 Characteristics of a Good Architecture

It is easier to specify what makes a good architecture than to actually produce a good architecture, and in many cases, it is not possible to maximise all of the following. However, we present the guiding characteristics which all software architects should bear in mind when developing an architecture:

- *Resilient.* The architecture should be resilient to change. That is, changes in functionality or additional functionality should have a minimal effect on the architecture (although they may have a major effect on the design). Thus subsystems should have clear and specific interfaces. Indeed it is almost true to say that the very first thing an architect should do is to identify the interfaces which will be used within the architecture and then identify the subsystems which will realize the interfaces, etc.
- *Simple.* The architecture should be simple. Remember as a rule of thumb the architecture should only be about 10% the size of the overall design and is supposed to be comprehensible on its own and in its entirety. Avoid making the architecture complex just for the sake of it.
- *Clarity of presentation.* As the architecture will be used not only as the base reference for the remainder of the design but also for future iterations of the system, it should be easily accessible and devoid of ambiguity (this is a biggy!) and avoid assuming current project knowledge.
- *Clear separation of concerns.* The architecture should clearly separate out different aspects of the system. For example, in the case of the house, the plumber probably doesn't want to know about the wiring of the house except where it might impinge on what they are doing. Therefore, the plumbers plans should not have a great deal of detail about the wiring harness for the house.
- *Balanced distribution of responsibilities.* The responsibilities of the subsystems should be appropriate and balanced. That is, if a subsystem is identified for dealing with general application security don't then make it also responsible for user login. Instead provide a user login subsystem (which may well make use of the security subsystem).
- *Balances economic and technological constraints.* The architecture may well need to justify why one approach was adopted over another – partly to explain the overall choices to those working within different aspects of the design. This is important as it may impose restrictions on what elements of the design can and cannot do (or technologies or solutions they may adopt).

8.4.3 So What is an Architecture?

Let us now go back to the question of what a software architecture actually is. In essence, it is a number of things, earlier discussions have indicated that it is more than just a set of diagrams; here, we will consider that in more detail:

- *An architecture baseline.* The software architecture contains an architectural baseline that will provide both a proof of concept and the basic skeleton of the system. This is a "small, skinny" system that captures the essential functionality of the final system. It is a working prototype that proves the concepts and the architectural structure. In many ways, it might be considered to be the results of the iteration 1 release of an XP project. The only real difference is that its primary aim is to provide the core architecture as well as the simplest fully functional system possible. So still no big design upfront, but more of an eye the future than purest XPers might like.

- *An architecture description.* This is a detailed description of the architecture containing information on the systems, subsystems, classes and interfaces that comprise the architecture. It should also contain discussions of architectural design decisions, constraints, required behaviour, etc. Indeed, everything that is necessary to understand the architecture. Indeed, the information should be sufficient to guide the whole development team throughout the lifetime of the system. As has already been said, this description may evolve over time. But what form should this description take, it might be in the form of descriptions on a whiteboard, diagrams pined up on a model board or a (lightweight) document. Remember, we still want to travel light, but with a road map in our pockets!

8.4.4 Architecture Can Make XP Work

We will talk more about architectures in Chapter 9, but it is the role of the architecture as the road map of the application that helps us to travel light. I have been involved in a couple of large agile projects; in each case, once we got the basic architecture in place, the remaining iterations flowed around it. This is not to say that the architecture did not require modification – it did. We are still trying to be agile and to travel light, so the architecture does not try to offer everything, instead it provides a little more of a nod to the future than we might otherwise provide and it provides the infrastructure for future data communication, organisation of modules, etc. Note that if you are working on an XP project using EJBs, then you already have an architecture that you are working within, that of the EJB framework. Thus, the architecture may be imposed by the technology you are using just as much as from the project itself.

The final thing to remember is that, in an agile project, the architecture does just enough to stop you falling over yourself and provide the basis of the development and no more. It should not be a leviathan that takes over the whole project (if it does you aren't being agile!).

8.5 XP on Large Projects

Is it possible to apply XP to large-scale project? Certainly, the published material on XP implies that you can – although interestingly most of the examples of XP projects cited in the literature appear to refer to smaller projects of less than 10 developers on projects lasting less than 6 months. What happens if you consider applying XP to larger projects lasting for a couple of years, with dozens of developers?

We have already raised a number of issues relating to larger projects in this chapter. However, there are a number of issues relating specifically to larger projects. These are discussed below:

1. *Pair programming.* In large teams, pair programming may or may not always be necessary, effective or even possible. In large teams, different developers may not be available due to the varied nature of the tasks being carried out. In determining whether a task should be pair programmed, it is useful to consider the experience of the developers involved, the significance of the feature being implemented and the knowledge required for that feature. This implies the need to have someone coordinating task allocation and resource to task allocation. That is, some form of team leader or project manager who coordinates task and pair assignments. These people can then be held ultimately accountable for the results of any decisions made (rather than the developers themselves who may wish to always, or indeed never, pair program). The team leader can also make sure that pairs do not stick and that they are changed when appropriate. This sort of management (with a small "m") should not be a surprise for a larger project as it is akin to having a conductor organising an orchestra and is at the heart of what people project management should (but often isn't) about.

2. *Small releases.* A small release may be on that occurs in 4, 6, 8, 12 or more week cycles. Iterations may be of different sizes ranging from 1, 2, 3 or more months. The key is that key features are not broken up. That is, an iteration should not be made artificially small just for the sake of it. If key features of the iteration will take 2 months to implement (given the current team), then so be it. The iteration will take 2 months. However, if previous cycles have been every 1 or 2 years, then this is a major change and greatly increases the feedback cycle.

3. *Reviews and testing.* In large projects, with a number of different facets (such as web interfaces, Java Servlets, JSps and EJBs, and relational databases), formal code reviews can compliment pair programming. A review involving several colleagues from different areas of the project can help identify deficiencies in a body of code that a pair may miss. For example, if a particular database feature will speed up the search time in a JDBC based application, and the developers are unaware of it (as it has only recently been introduced), then a formal review may uncover this if a representative of the database team is present.

4. *Architecture and simple design.* XP does not of course promote Big Up Front Design, but larger projects may greatly benefit from an architectural design and implementation (possibly as the first iteration). This lets the developers understand the space within which they are working. It may also help the team to understand feature interactions that may otherwise be missed – this is particularly true of larger more complex systems.

5. *Refactoring.* On larger projects being able to refactor at any time may not be desirable. In these cases, it is still useful to identify refactoring situations. These can be listed on a public "refactoring wish list" board. These

refactoring requirements can be considered during the daily meetings, etc. This thus allows the team leader or project manager to coordinate refactoring efforts, at appropriate times and gives it the same scrutiny as the main feature development process.

6. *On-site customer.* Probably even more important for a large project than for smaller projects!

8.6 Where XP Works Best

Given all of what has been said above, what can we say about where XP and Agile Modelling should be applied? There are actually a number of rules of thumb that can be identified. Note that these are rules of thumb and are not hard and fast rules. For example, XP can be and has been applied successfully to larger projects. However, it is more difficult and there is a greater potential for failure, particularly for those inexperienced in agile approaches.

The rules of thumb that have emerged (and some are quite contentious) include:

1. *Smaller projects of typically less than 10 people.* The larger the project, the harder it is to manage as a pure XP project. The XP approach, that is to a large extent self-organising, becomes difficult with 20 or 30 developers involved. Of course, the team can be broken down into smaller groups and treated as smaller XP projects, but then that's what you have, smaller XP projects interacting.
2. *Known domain/applications.* For larger projects, XP projects work best where the domain and the type of application are well understood.
3. *Well-established architectures.* This point is related to rule 2 in that the reason that XP works well in well-understood applications is that there is a (possibly) implicit architecture. The developers know what they should do where, when and how. If this is not the case, then an architecture needs to be established within which the XP project can operate.
4. *Scalability not an issue.* If scalability is an issue, it must be considered early on in the project so that it does not become an issue later on. This is typically a problem in larger, longer-lived projects where it is difficult to see the scalability issues early on. Again, an architecture may help.

8.7 Summary

In this chapter, we have examined what experience has taught us about XP and Agile Modelling. We have considered how refactoring works in practice, we have addressed the issue of the need for an architecture within which to frame an XP project and we have discussed pair programming in practice. This chapter is not intended to indicate that agile methodologies are not practical. Far from it, instead it is intended to bring some important perspective to the subject and to make sure that you are aware of the potential pitfalls associated with these approaches.

It is worth noting that we have been careful to talk here of using XP and Agile Modelling in isolation and have not discussed how they may be incorporated into other methodologies. This is because applying XP and Agile modelling with other approaches can overcome some or all of the above issues. Indeed, in the next three chapters, we will consider exactly these issues.

9
Feature-Driven Development

9.1 Introduction

Planning, managing and monitoring projects that are agile, adaptive and incremental can be very difficult. As was illustrated in the last chapter, although many of the ideas behind methods such as XP can, and indeed have been very successfully applied, it does not mean that it is easy or that they are particularly scalable (particularly for those new to XP).

So, what do you do if you want to acknowledge that the real world is an uncertain and changing place. If you want to adopt an agile and adaptive method, but you don't want to lose control of the project. That is, you don't want to sacrifice the project on the altar of agility!

This is no trivial matter. Adaptive, iterative projects are more complex to control, and to plan, than more traditional, linear, waterfall models (partly because they reflect reality but more on this later). In the linear model, life is simpler, no design starts until all analysis has been completed, in turn no implementation starts until all the design is finished. Thus, at any one time, it should be very clear what is being done, by whom and why. In addition, the requirements are fixed back at the start of the whole project, making things a lot simpler for the poor developer. Of course, the reality is, that not only may the requirements have been wrong in the first place or they may have missed some important behaviour, but the world may change over the 2 years that the system is being implemented and the end result may be of less use to the end user than they had hoped. But from the perspective of managing the project, many of the variables have been removed in a linear project, so it is easier to plan (initially at least, the project may need re-planning at a later stage when it is realised that creating a persistence layer for Java takes longer than 2 days – I quote from a project plan I once saw!).

The additional complexity facing the project manager of an agile, adaptive and incremental project is an inevitable consequence of the acknowledge that the real world has many variables in it that can change. It is also a consequence of the parallel nature and dependencies between multiple iterations.

One solution to control the complexity inherent in agile, incremental projects is to apply a feature-centric process. A feature-centric process is one that tries to provide a way for management to handle questions such as:

- What must we do next to add value to the client?
- How are we progressing against time and budgets?
- What issues and risks does the project face?
- How can the issues and risks be addressed or mitigated?
- What should we do next?

Feature-centric processes do this while retaining the motivations behind the agile movement such as:

1. Individuals and interactions over processes and tools.
2. Working software over comprehensive documentation.
3. Customer collaboration over contract negotiation.
4. Responding to change over following a plan.

With the key aims being:

1. To satisfy the customer.
2. Deliver working software that adds value to the customer.
3. Working software is the primary measure of progress.
4. Promote sustainable development.
5. Keep any process as simple as is reasonably possible.

The term feature-centric refers to development processes that attempt to focus on combining the units of requirements, with the units of planning and the units of work. This allows:

- the things users want,
- to be planned for and monitored,
- and to be used as the basis of work allocation.

Feature-driven development (FDD) is an example of a feature-centric process which we will look at in more detail in this chapter. However, FDD is not the only feature-centric process available. The development process EVO is feature-centric (Glib 1997, 2002) as to some extent is DSDM, with its requirements catalogue (Stapleton, 1997).

In the remainder of this chapter, we first consider the incremental software development process as a whole and contrast it with the more traditional waterfall model. We then explain the need for a feature-centric approach in order to control the planning and management processes within an iterative approach (this is necessary as such an approach can increase the complexity of the management process). Following this, we explain the benefit in defining a timebox for each iteration so that their duration is known (even if their content is not). The section is completed by a discussion on planning an iterative project and planning each iteration.

9.2 Incremental Software Development

Let us review what happens during an incremental software development project. An incremental software development process is one that does not try to complete the whole design task in one go. This is in contrast to the more traditional waterfall model of software development.

One of the features of the waterfall model of software engineering used by many design methods (see Figure 9.1) is that it primarily assumes that you will complete the requirements analysis before you start the design phase. In turn, you will complete the design phase before you start the implementation phase, and so on. It does accept that there may be some feedback of information from one phase to any preceding phases and that this feedback may impact upon the products of the preceding phases. However, this is a secondary issue and the assumption is that you will be able to complete the vast majority of one phase before ever considering the next phase. This may be true if this is the fifth or sixth system you have built in the same domain for the same type of application. It is unlikely to be the case with your first application in a new domain (such as your first e-commerce project!).

When applying some form of iterative approach, the intention is that each iteration adds something to the evolving system. Some iterations may lead to a release of the software system, while others may not. Each iteration:

1. Determines what will be done during the iteration.
2. Designs and implements the required functionality.
3. Tests the new functionality.
4. (Optionally) Creates a new release.
5. Reviews what has been done before moving to the next iteration.

Figure 9.2 depicts the spiral nature of this approach to software development. Note that in effect, each iteration around the spiral is a mini-software development project.

The end result is that you incrementally produce the system being designed. While you do this, you explicitly identify the risks to your design/system upfront and deal with them early on. Note that this neither means that you are hacking the

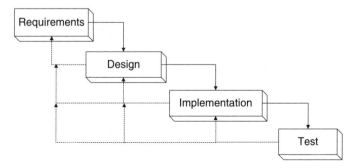

Fig. 9.1 The waterfall model.

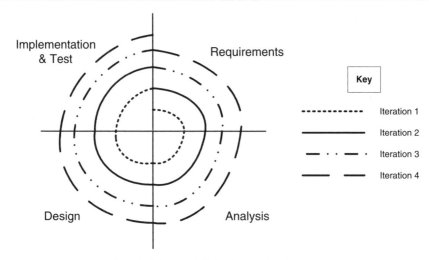

Fig. 9.2 Spiral model of software development.

system together nor carrying out some form of rapid prototyping (you are not!). However, it does mean that a great deal of planning is required, both upfront and as the design develops.

At this point, you may be wondering why I am making so much of this approach as it is not a million miles away from what we looked at during the chapters on XP. However, the iterations within XP projects tend to be between 1 and 3 weeks, with new releases at the end of most iterations. This works best, I believe, for smaller projects with requirements that are subject to rapid and frequent change (as discussed in the last chapter). What if, your project is not a small one, but a larger one in which requirements may still be subject to change but in a more controlled manner (for example, business rules may change but they have to be filtered through a complex organisational structure before they affect you). An iterative approach may still be relevant, but the iterations may be in terms of months rather than weeks. How do you manage such a project in an agile manner? This is where feature-driven development will come-in.

9.3 Regaining Control: The Motivation Behind FDD

An important aspect to address at this point is the potential explosion in planning effort that may be required to deal with the iterative lifecycle model that is being described here. It is certainly more complex than a linear waterfall lifecycle to plan and manage. However, given that our goal is to simplify the lifecycle in order that we can deal with the risks and complexities as well as uncertainties of the development process, we need to regain some control of the planning and management aspects of such a project. A key strategy for this is feature-centric planning. This is discussed in the next section. Feature-centric is not the only aspect of regaining control of an iterative project; another feature is that of timeboxing each iteration. The final aspect is being adaptive.

Thus, to regain control of an iterative project the guidelines are:

- The process should be *feature-centric*. This means that the units of requirements (e.g., use cases, user stories) should be unified with the units of planning (e.g., work packages and tasks).
- Project planning should be based around *timeboxes* (rather than phases) so that the length of each iteration is known.
- The project plan should be *adaptive* that is responsive to the changing risks and benefits of the system and business environment.

Each of these concepts is discussed in the remainder of this section.

9.3.1 Feature-Centric Development

The term feature-centric is used to refer to development processes that combine the expression of requirements with the units of activity for planning purposes. A feature in such a process can be viewed as a unit of "plannable functionality." Feature-driven development (FDD) uses features in this way. Note that features are closely related to use cases and to the realisation of use cases in the standard Unified Process.

A feature is a schedulable piece of functionality, something that delivers value to the user. Note the emphasis on schedulable. That is, a feature is derived from a planning perspective rather than from the user perspective or indeed the requirements perspective. This is an important distinction and why features differ from requirements, user stories or use cases (even if they are derived from them).

To aid in planning, features go further, they must also be associated with:

- a priority (so that they can be ordered),
- a cost (so that they can be accounted for),
- resources (so that they can be scheduled).

Costs and resources can be determined by examining the number of person days taken to accomplish the feature. Priority can be harder to determine but should take into account:

- Architectural importance of the feature.
- Utility to the user.
- Risk involved.
- Requirements of the system/use cases.

With consideration given to each in obtaining the priority.

To illustrate what I mean by a feature, consider the requirement "Add a New File" to an application. This might be described by a user story that explains how the user might add a new file to a file auditing system. The user story describes this activity from the perspective of the user (obviously) and without reference to resource or costs (although user stories do have a relative priority). From this we can extract one or more system features that will be needed to implement this requirement. For example, these might be:

1. "New File Dialog" feature.
2. Java business objects for new file creation feature.
3. New file details XML writer.

In some cases, a user story or requirement might relate directly to a single feature, or to many features. In turn, a feature might relate to a single requirement. However, it is also possible for a feature to support many requirements (such as an object persistence layer feature or features).

So are features only driven from user stories/requirements/use cases? Not necessarily! There are other sources of information which can lead to features including (but not limited to):

- Bug fixes.
- Maintenance enhancements (for example, due to changing to a new version of a language or operating system).
- General tidying operations.

These can all lead to features being added to a feature list without associated requirements or user stories.

Another issue is how big should a feature be? As before with these sorts of questions, there is no simple answer.

A feature could take just a couple of days (any smaller and the feature may be too trivial to consider on its own).

A feature could take a couple of weeks (much larger and it is a candidate for decomposition into smaller features as these may make monitoring and planning easier).

The exact size depends on the size of the project, the nature of the work and the size of the team. For example, earlier on in the lifecycle of a software development project, the feature may be larger and more fundamental (such as those associated with creating the underlying object persistence layer, etc.). Later on they may have a higher user profile, but may be smaller in terms of implementation time (such as adding additional running totals to some spreadsheet). The approach taken by some of those working with feature-driven development is to apply the "Feature per fortnight" rule (Carmichael and Haywood, 2002).

9.3.2 Timeboxing Iterations

The emphasis in most formal development processes is on the phases a project goes through and then on the steps within the phases that may or may not be carried out iteratively. This is true of modern processes such as the standard Unified Process as much as of more traditional processes such as the waterfall process.

However, with iterative processes, although the details of the current iteration may be known, details of the next or subsequent iterations are less clear. Indeed, as the aim of this approach is to allow an iteration to be planned, at the start of the iteration, the time taken for an iteration may only become clear at the start of that iteration. This is not very good for budget planning, for release planning or indeed for management of the project. It certainly has issues with fixed release dates.

There is therefore a conflict between the flexible and responsive nature of an iterative approach and the constraints of budgets and timescales.

This is where timeboxing comes in. Rather than defining each iteration by the features it will implement, it is possible to define an iteration in terms of the time period it will take and the ordered list of features that will be attempted during the time period. Features that are lower down the priority list will only be attempted if time allows, otherwise they will be relegated to a later iteration.

Timeboxing iteration has a number of benefits including the ability to:

- schedule and plan for incremental releases of the software,
- schedule and implement features,
- manage budgets,
- monitor progress within fixed time constraints.

All within a flexible and responsive process.

What this also means is that regular reviews (typically on a weekly basis) are required to consider how features and tasks are progressing, which (if any) are behind schedule and why. It is also necessary to consider what the impact on the project will be, both from a technical and a business point of view. This may then lead to modification of the work packages and features to be included in the current iteration. Note this does not necessarily mean that the plan is revised weekly, rather that the implications are considered and appropriate action taken if necessary.

9.3.3 Being Adaptive but Managed

What is required is a management process that is flexible enough to deal with the changing requirements of the business and users, and to deal with the emerging uncertainties. It also needs to be one in which we can still monitor progress, determine resources, ensure quality and guarantee delivery. Most traditional management styles set out what will be done when and for how long right at the start of a project and well before detailed design and implementation has begun. The project is then measured against these estimates with little or no room for change. However, an iterative project explicitly acknowledges the need for change and the need for ongoing management.

To this end, an iterative project is effectively planned and re-planned at each stage of the spiral presented back in Figure 9.2. There is an overall planning activity before the whole process starts and then there are planning activities at the start of each iteration. In addition, regular (weekly) reviews may also affect the current plan for an iteration.

In terms of management monitoring of project activity, person days for tasks should be monitored (on a weekly basis) and fed into the project plan to determine how the project is progressing relative to the planned effort. However, due to issues such as holidays, sick leave, etc. It is also necessary to compare the current progress in elapsed time with the project plan.

9.4 Planning an Iterative Project

Before any project embarks on an iteration development process there are a number of steps that should be followed. These steps are:

- Identify and prioritise features (the feature list should be continually revised throughout the project).
- Roughly identify iterations and allocate features.
- Timebox iterations/calculate costs.
- For each iteration
  - Plan iterations (which should be continually revised during lifetime of project).
  - Identify tasks required to implement features.
  - Allocate tasks to resources (that is, allocate tasks to project members).
  - Implement iteration.

The key here is that iterations are based on "timeboxes" so that their length is known and can be managed. Iterations are also based on tasks constructed around features so that they can be responsive to user feedback and to changing business requirements. Note that depending upon the size and complexity of the tasks, I have at times grouped related tasks together to form packages of work that make high level project planning easier. However, for smaller features, I have tended to always work directly at the task level.

9.4.1 Iterations, Timeboxes and Releases

The next section will describe how a single iteration is planned, but first let us review the overall project planning process. This is illustrated in Figure 9.3. We will discuss this figure in more detail below.

At the start of the project, the project team along with various project stakeholders create a prioritised feature list. Note that this cannot be done without the collaboration of those project stakeholders who can state what the priorities of the features should be. Thus, as with XP, the "business" is an essential part of this process.

I have found that in general giving features priorities such as High, Medium and Low is enough (certainly at this stage). Associated with the features at this stage is a cost. A cost is related to how many person days it will take to implement the feature. I say related as we are only roughly estimating at this point, and typically we use a "Three-Point" estimation approach (which is discussed later on), but essentially

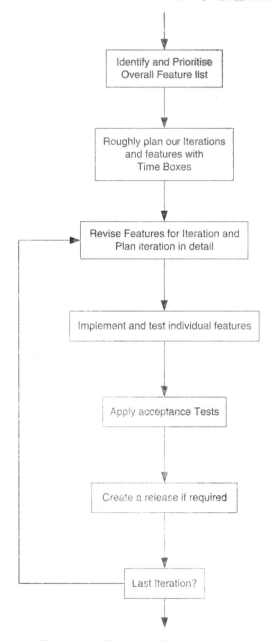

Fig. 9.3 Overall structure of an FDD project.

this requires a best estimate, an average estimate and a worst-case estimate to be given. The overall cost is derived from these three estimates. Finally, the number of software engineers involved with the feature is also estimated. We now have our initial feature list.

Next, we try to determine how many iterations we expect to have, how long the iterations will last and which features will be in the iterations. This can only be done with the involvement of those business representatives who have the knowledge and authority to agree to the timescales being discussed. In general, we have found that this usually involves a series of meetings with the client representatives, during which exact timescales for timeboxes, features for iterations, etc. are agreed. In general, timeboxes should not change, but the features implemented within the iterations defined by the timeboxes may.

From this, we emerge with an outline plan for what will be done when and at what point we will be completing various iterations of the end system.

As an example, consider the following iteration plan, taken from an actual project of a few years ago. There are five iterations in total for a legal advice expert system. The first iteration aimed to explore the problem domain and to produce a prototype expert system based on a combination of a simple Case-Based Reasoning system and a Rule-Based Reasoning system. The second iteration aimed to fill out this prototype with a larger amount of domain knowledge to confirm the viability of the approach. Iteration 3 then aimed to produce a commercial quality version of the initial prototype. Iteration 4 introduced a variety of management information system aspects to the system to review results, advice given, problems not dealt with, etc. The final iteration would address user feedback and any deployment issues encountered earlier in the project.

The timing for the iterations were

Iteration 1: Analyse and Prototype
  58 person days. April 2003 – end of June 2003
Iteration 2: Prototype II
  119 person days. July 2003 – start of December 2003
Iteration 3: Pilot and Develop
  55 person days. December 2003 – end of February 2004
Iteration 4: Develop II
  41 person days. March 2004 – April 2004
Iteration 5: Final Release
  16 person days. End of April 2004 – mid May 2004.

ID	Task Name	Start	End	Duration	Q2 03 Apr May Jun	Q3 03 Jul Aug Sep	Q4 03 Oct Nov Dec	Q1 04 Jan Feb Mar	Q2 04 Apr May
1	Analyse and Prototype	07/04/2003	25/06/2003	58d					
2	Prototype II	26/06/2003	09/12/2003	119d					
3	Pilot and Develop	10/12/2003	24/02/2004	55d					
4	Develop II	25/02/2004	21/04/2004	41d					
5	Final Release	22/04/2004	13/05/2004	16d					

Having produced the overall iteration plan, we must now focus on planning the first iteration in detail. Note, we only plan an iteration in detail as we are about to start it (and not before). This topic is considered in the next section.

9.4.2 Planning an Iteration

Each iteration will be comprised of a similar set of steps. These steps are presented graphically in Figure 9.4.

The key steps in any iteration are:

1. *Iteration initiation meeting.* The length of the iteration should already have been determined but may be revised at this point. The features to be addressed in this iteration should be revised and confirmed along with the resources to be applied, etc. This meeting should involve all stakeholders in the project.

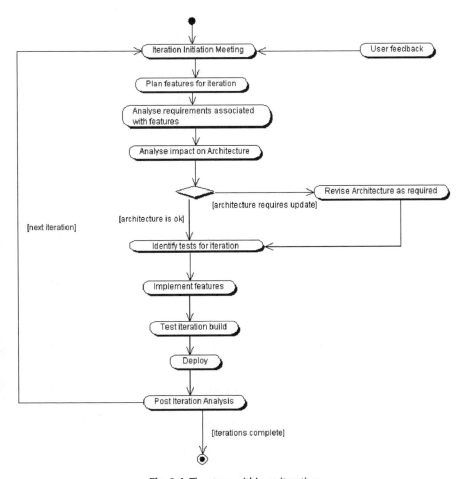

Fig. 9.4 The steps within an iteration.

2. *Plan features for iteration.* Having agreed the features to be addressed, a detailed plan should be produced mapping features to work packages and work packages to tasks. The tasks in turn should be allocated to actual resources, etc. This plan must be accepted by the key stakeholders (including the clients).

3. *Analyse the requirements associated with the features.* This may involve writing or revising a use case document, designing new GUI displays, determining the user interaction sequence, etc. The acceptance criteria for this iteration should also be identified and agreed.

4. *Analyse impact on the architecture.* The architecture is the backbone upon which the iterative process operates, therefore the next step to perform is to examine the impact any new features are likely to have on the architecture. It may also involve identifying new architecturally significant entities that feed into the next step.

5. *(Optionally) Revise architecture as required.* This step involves revisiting and amending the application architecture in response to the features required by this implementation. Note that this may mean that some of the design and analysis work associated with core features may be performed at this stage to determine their architectural impact.

6. Next a *new acceptance test plan and specification* should be written for this iteration. Note this document may not include all tests as some features may only be implemented if time allows. The specification of the tests for these features should be considered to be a task within the work package that will address that feature. Also, note the difference here between the iteration test specification and the JUnit tests that might be written as part of a feature. The test specification is oriented towards the system as a whole (its overall operation) where as JUnit tests tend to be oriented towards individual class, subsystems or systems. There is therefore a major difference of focus – both are required.

7. The next step involves *implementing the features.* The features are actually implemented via tasks that should be monitored as normal (although reference should be made to the timebox of the iteration). It is recommended that each feature should have a set of associated unit tests that must be passed before the feature is taken to have been completed. These unit tests should be part of the code released for the feature and ideally should be added to a unit test framework (such as JUnit) that can easily be re-run at regular intervals (such as every time a new build of the system occurs).

8. Once the features are implemented, the new *system should be tested* (this includes the generation of a test report). This includes unit tests and acceptance tests. All tests should pass before the iteration is allowed to proceed. If any tests fail, then the release cannot be deployed and the problems must be corrected. If earlier steps have been adhered to, the unit tests should pass and thus it should only be the acceptance tests that cause a problem. At this point, the project needs to determine why the system/acceptance tests have failed. If this is because of some features that have been moved to a subsequent iteration, then the acceptance tests need to be changed. If it is due to some missing or erroneous functionality then this functionality needs

to be removed (in order to release on time) or if it must be included then the problems must be addressed. In general, time should be allocated to this process to allow for such unforeseen problems (as with the best will in the world they will occur).

9. The new application should then be *deployed* to the client who should then perform any agreed user acceptance tests. This may lead to the revision of the deployed system, if and when deficiencies are identified.

10. A *post iteration meeting* should review the progress made during the iteration, it should consider any issues that arose and re-prioritise any features that were not addressed. Again, this should involve all project stakeholders.

11. At this point, a decision should also be made regarding the *validity of the next* iteration and whether any further iterations are required.

One outstanding issue for this iterative approach is what comprises the acceptance tests at the end of an iteration. This cannot be carved in stone upfront as the iteration may have changed once started (as features may have been moved due to changing business or user requirements). This is an area that requires careful management and understanding between the various stakeholders in the project. Typically it means that the "features" implemented must be tested and that the acceptance tests must be based on these features. However, as the features may change, the acceptance tests need to be flexible enough to take this into account.

9.4.3 An Aside on Planning within an FDD Project

I have probably been involved in more work managed using feature-driven development (FDD) than any of the agile methods. And one comment made by one of the clients sticks out in my mind. We had worked on a system over a couple of years, with at least six iterations developed and successfully released. Near the end of this project, she commented to me one day, that the thing that had surprised her the most was the amount of planning we had done on the project. We had planned the iterations, and then at the start of each iteration we planned the details of that iteration and reviewed the plans as we progressed and had moved features into other iterations as required. She had thought that an iterative and incremental approach would have less planning in it! How wrong she had been? However, she also commented that ours had been the only project during her time with her employer that had delivered on time and within budget!

9.4.4 Estimating the Cost of a Feature

The approach I have taken over the last few years towards estimating the cost of features is heavily influenced by the approach described by Carmichael and Haywood (2002). This approach involves applying three-point estimating. Three-point estimating involves producing three estimates of the effort that will be required to implement a feature. These are:

	A	B	C	D	E	F
1						
2						
3	Feature	Priority	Best Case	Likely Case	Worst Case	Estimate (person days)
4	Assessment summary page	H	1	2	4	2.17
5	Management of Not Audsitable Files	H	3	4	7	4.33
6	Remove account manager field	H	1	1	2	1.17
7	Copy / cut / paste on screens	H	1	2	5	2.33
8	Order of summary trends	H	3	5	10	5.50
9	Formatting of text	L	3	5	11	5.67
10	Lock cross reference key	H	1	3	4	2.83
11	Support for London Weighting	M	2	4	5	3.83
12	Summary report modifications	L	2	3.5	6	3.67
13						
14		Person days	17	29.5	54	31.50

Fig. 9.5 Three-point estimating for a list of features.

- *The best-case scenario.* This represents the situations where everything goes as well as it could and there are absolutely no surprises or problems encountered.
- *The best guess at what it will really take.* This represents the situation where mostly everything goes okay, but one or two unexpected situations occur which take a little longer than originally expected to handle.
- *The worst-case scenario.* This represents the situation where major issues were overlooked (because they were not obvious until implementation started).

Why have these three estimates. Partly it acknowledges the difficulty of estimating how long something will take to implement before you actually implement it. It also reflects the fact that some people are more optimistic and some more pessimistic than others. And, thus a range of estimates can capture their different views.

A table illustrating this style of estimating for a list of features is illustrated in Figure 9.5. The table illustrates the feature, its priority and the three estimates for best, most likely and worst-case scenarios.

The overall estimate for each feature is derived by applying a formula in the underlying spreadsheet. There are various formulas that could be applied; in this case we have applied the following formula:

$$(\text{Best case} + (4 \times \text{likely case}) + \text{worst case})/6$$

This formula gives weight to the most likely case but also takes into account the range from the best and worst cases. It is possible to take this further and use a pseudo standard deviation to gain an estimate of how reliable the numbers are. However, care needs to be used here as these are still estimates and performing further numerical analysis on them to produce some pseudo levels of probability is likely to end up providing a false sense of security rather than any illumination on the likelihood of completing the project on time!

Finally, the other technique I have used to help with producing reasonable estimates is to involve the best and most experienced developers, designers, managers working on the project (if the project is small enough, then all those involved can help) as well as gaining input from the end users.

9.5 Architecture Centric

Feature-driven development or feature-centric development (FCD) is only feasible (and successful) if there is a solid architecture on which each iteration can be built. This section examines what is meant by an architecture and why it is central to a successful iterative process.

9.5.1 Why Architecture Centric?

One problem with an iterative and incremental approach is that if no order or structure was defined for the application it could (would?) grow more and more unwieldy and more and more dis-organised as each iteration progressed. To ensure that all the various parts fit together, there needs to be something. That something is the architecture. The architecture is the skeleton on which the muscles (function-ality) and skin (the user interface) of the system will be hung. A good architecture will be resilient to change and to the evolving design and implementation. The Unified Process explicitly acknowledges the need for this architecture by being architecture centric. It describes how you identify what should be the part of the architecture and how you go about designing and implementing the architecture. The remainder of the Unified Process then refers back to that architecture.

Obviously, the generation of this architecture is both critical and difficult. Many people think therefore that the architecture must be defined in its entirety upfront, at the start of the whole process. While this might make life easier (if you could really do it), in general you won't know all the details of the architecture until the end. Therefore, even the Unified Process prescribes the successive refinement of the executable architecture during each iteration, thereby attempting to ensure that the architecture remains relevant. With an adaptive, agile approach, this is even true.

As the architectural aspects of any system developed with an iterative process are so important, the remainder of this section will discuss the role of the architecture.

9.5.2 Architecture Defined

In this section, we will try to define what we mean by an architecture. A software architecture encompasses

- *the overall plan for the structure of the system.* That is, it is the blueprint for the system. It should be possible to read the architecture and gain an appreciation for how the system was structured (without needing to know the details of the structural elements).
- *the key structural elements and their interfaces.* That is what with which elements make up the system, their interfaces and how they are plugged together.
- *how those elements interact (at the top level).* That is, when the various elements of the architecture interface, what do they do and why do they do it.

- *how these elements form subsystems and systems.* This is a very important aspect of the architecture. Early identification of the core systems and subsystem of the design not only helps organise future design (and implementation) work, it helps promote reuse and the comprehensibility of the system.
- *architectural style* that guides this project.

The intention is that within this architecture, designers are then free to work in the "spaces" left for them by the architecture. However, this is not the end of the story, the software architecture also involves:

- How the system will be used?
- What the functionality of the final system is expected to be?
- Any performance issues that need to be addressed (these may involve more detailed development of the software architecture's implementation to assess performance constraints).
- Resilience to further development.
- Economic and technology constraints and tradeoffs. The architecture can consider different solutions to the same problem, allowing different technological solutions to be aired and the most appropriate adopted (for example, CGI scripts versus Java servlets on a web server).

9.5.3 Why Have an Architecture?

Let us review the argument being made about why an architecture is a critical element of the object-oriented design process. We need an architecture to

- *understand the system.* Software systems can be large, complex and must meet conflicting requirements. An architecture provides a convenient blueprint or model of the system to be produced. It abstracts out much of the implementation detail, but "positions" the elements that must meet the various functional requirements.
- *organise development.* It helps organise "plumbers" and "electricians." That is, it helps firstly to separate out different concerns so that those involved in the "plumbing" of the system only need to worry about plumbing issues. However, it also identifies how they are related, so that the points at which different concerns intersect, are well documented and clearly specified (for example, in the central heating boiler).
- *promote reuse.* The problem with writing reusable code is that you need to identify that what you are producing is reusable. I have personally been in situations where two people on one project are reproducing the same solution but from different aspects. In at least one case, they were sitting opposite to each other. It is certainly easier to produce reusable code the second, third or even fourth time you are designing and implementing a system than the first. Indeed, in many systems, the only form of reuse that occurs is at the class level, i.e. at a very detailed level and is identified by the coder during implementation. However, an architecture can help at a much higher level by

identifying critical systems and subsystems early on. Common subsystems can then be made reusable.

- *promote continued development.* Few systems of any size or consequence are produced and never altered. Instead, it is much more common for a system to evolve over time with new requirements being identified and new functionality added or existing functionality modified. The original architecture can be essential in helping to control the evolution of the system over time (both within a single release and between releases of a system). Indeed, a good architecture need change little over the lifecycle of a system but can be instrumental to the success of future releases. This is because it provides the overall structure into which the new additions or modifications must be fitted. Often, the actual design of the system is too detailed to allow an overview to be gained, and thus, future designers and implementers may misinterpret part of a design or (worse) ignore it. The architecture can help to minimise such problems.

9.5.4 Architecture Myths

At this point, let us stop and stand back and consider some of the myths that surround the concept of an architecture. For a start, it is important to realise that the architecture and the design are not the same thing (indeed we hinted at that in the last paragraph) but it is important to re-iterate this. The architecture highlights the most significant elements of the design. These include the major systems and subsystems, their interfaces, how the system will be deployed, etc. It does not include many details of the systems and subsystems and how they are implemented – that is the job of the design. It is useful to picture the level of detail in the architecture and the level of detail in the final design as bar charts as is done in Figure 9.6. As can be seen from this diagram, the architecture leaves much out, while the design must address many more aspects in detail.

Another myth to be debunked is that the architecture and the infrastructure are the same thing. This is an easy mistake to make (not least given what we have said about the role of the architecture). However, it is important to remember

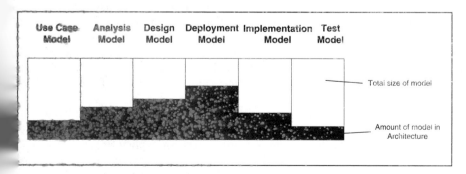

Fig. 9.6 Relationship between design and architecture.

that the architecture only captures those elements of the design that are necessary to provide an understanding of the overall design of the system. In fact, Jacobson et al. (1999) state that only about 10% of all the classes in a design are architecturally significant. The remaining 90% may well be functionally significant but are not key to understand the overall structure of the system. However, for the infrastructure of the system, i.e. the essential functionality of the system, it is likely that many more classes will be needed (indeed it is likely that at least 50% of the classes in the design will make up the infrastructure).

9.5.5 Plan Incremental Build of Software

Once you have put an architecture in place, you are in a position to plan an incremental, feature-centric approach to further implementation and extension. The development of the architecture should have helped to identify the appropriate subsystems, active classes, interfaces, etc. which can be used as the starting point for further iterations of a development process.

Of course, this is where approaches such as FDD come-in. They provide the managed, incremental development necessary. While the architecture provides the backbone on which each iteration can be grown.

It should also be noted that the architecture does not try to be all encompassing and incorporate hooks for all possible required features. Rather, it should represent the core features and provide all those hooks for architecturally significant features or those features that are most likely to be incorporated.

9.6 FDD and XP

One thing you may have noticed in this chapter is that we have focussed almost exclusively on planning an iterative project and how FDD can help with this. But what about modelling your solution or implementing that solution? This is where agile methods such as Agile Modelling and eXtreme Programming come-in. Feature-driven development provides a way of controlling the iterative and incremental nature of agile projects. It does not really have anything to say about how you implement those features.

Features can be implemented in a variety of different ways using a variety of techniques. However, taking an agile approach means that applying the techniques we have discussed so far in this book can work extremely well.

Within a development model in which FDD is used to plan the details of iterations and in which features are treated as the tasks to be performed, then applying Agile Modelling and XP practices can result in a workflow resembling that presented in Figure 9.7.

Note that within this approach, we are using Agile Modelling to allow any modelling activities to take place and XP practices to implement the required behaviour. Also, note that we are assuming here an explicit analysis step that involves some design and/or modelling work in order to determine how the feature should be implemented or broken down into tasks. This reflects the higher focus

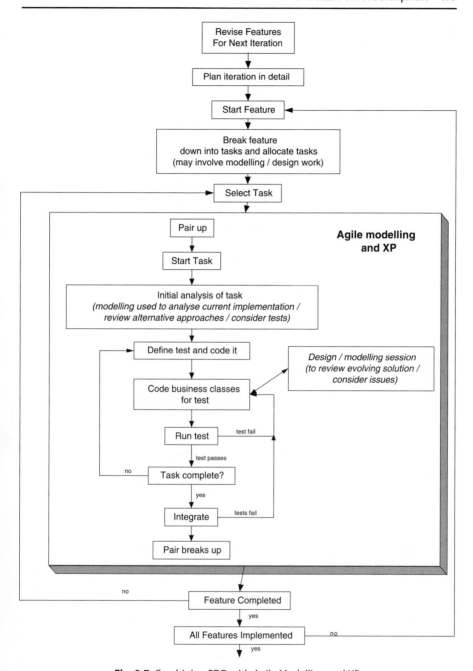

Fig. 9.7 Combining FDD with Agile Medelling and XP.

in this chapter on analysis and design than may have been the case in previous chapters. Note we are still not trying to promote a large up-front design, merely acknowledging that in larger software systems you need to know where you are going in order to try and minimise the problems that may be caused by un-guarded or un-informed development work (which is much easier in a big software system).

An important point to note, and one that might mean that hardened XP de-velopers will say that we are not doing XP is that we are not (explicitly at least) applying the planning game. This is because the planning game is effectively subsumed by the role played by the feature-driven development process itself. I personally do not have a problem with this and in fact recognise it as a benefit of the FDD – there is a greater emphasis on planning. That is not to say that the planning game has nothing to offer FDD, and in many ways, the planning activi-ties I have used within the FDD process have been influenced by ideas within the planning game. Indeed, they have many of the same motivations including the full cooperation and involvement of the "business" representatives in feature-oriented planning.

A final point I would make with regard to the application of XP practices is that the remaining XP practices are still relevant and still applicable within an FDD planned project. Whether you apply them or not is to some extent an issue for the particular project at hand.

For example, one of the most visible features of an XP project is the use of pair programming. Indeed, it is often the one thing that everyone who has heard about XP is aware of. However, as was discussed in the last chapter, it is not always practical. FDD certainly does not mandate pair programming, and thus, it is up to you whether you apply it within an FDD project or not. FDD aims at controlling adaptive, agile and iterative projects that may or may not be XP based. In my own case (and this may be taken as sacrilege by the XP community), I have often applied it more in some parts of a project and less in others. This is often influenced by the resources available and other practicalities at that time. My general rules of thumb regarding whether to employ pair programming or not, include questions such as:

- How experienced are those involved?
- How complex or problematic is this area of code being worked on?
- What impact might a problem within this area have?

The end result might be that I am not employing XP per se, but I am exploiting many of the features of XP, Agile Modelling and feature-driven development.

9.7 Summary

In this chapter, we have examined an agile approach to manage the complexity and concurrency inherent in (larger) iterative software development projects.

This approach, called feature-driven development, manages the issues involved by being:

1. Feature-centric.
2. Timebox focussed.
3. Adaptive to changing requirements.

It does not prescribe how the features should be implemented and approaches based on Agile Modelling and XP practices fit extremely well with FDD. In the next chapter, we will explore how one such FDD project was planned.

10

Planning a Sample FDD Project

10.1 Introduction

In this chapter, we will look at how a project was planned using the ideas presented in the last chapter on Feature-Driven Development. As you will remember, an FDD project is based on the identification of features, their implementation as tasks (possibly grouped into packages of work) implemented within a fixed time box for each iteration.

Note that, in the context of this chapter, it is not important that you fully understand what each feature represents (indeed with a detailed explanation of the application and the associated business processes they would not be clear, and such topics are outside the scope of this chapter) but rather that you see how such a project planning process evolves and how the different aspects of the process relate.

The remainder of this chapter is structured in the following manner. In Section 10.2, we will consider how this project started off. In Section 10.3, we will discuss the overall project plan. Section 10.4 describes how the first iteration was planned. Section 10.5 then briefly addresses what happened post iteration 1 delivery.

10.2 Initiating the Project

The particular project being considered is a real system (with names changed to protect the innocent). One interesting aspect of this system was that it was based on an earlier system that we had implemented for the clients. The previous system had been implemented some time before in a non-agile manner. The resulting software worked, but by now the client's requirements had moved on. The new project was proposed as an agile development in order that emerging and future requirements could be incorporated into the software in a more natural way. In retrospect, I believe that one of the reasons that the client was willing to do this was that we had already proved to them that we could deliver the goods, and thus we had already built up a significant level of trust with them prior to moving to an agile way of working!

Another very important feature of the project was that the client agreed to provide a "virtual" on-site customer representative (whom we will call SM for short). SM was a senior Business Analyst with the client, who not only knew the existing business set up inside out, but also worked closely with the business to determine exactly what their new requirements would be. SM was thus in an ideal position to act as the "on-site client." Although SM was not on-site all the time, SM was available on the phone or via email and would always answer any question we threw at her.

At the start of the project, SM and the team sat down to work out what features were required of the system (by the end of the project, SM started to present new features to us in a form that was essential to a user-requirement set-up for entry as a feature!). Each requirement was allocated a priority and one or more resources. It was then estimated to obtain a cost. Where features seemed too big, they were broken down into smaller features. Where priorities were not clear, SM returned to the business to resolve any of the issues and help produce a stronger understanding of what was required. In general, over a number of days, a detailed feel for the highest priority features was obtained and all features had a priority.

In consultation with the business (and taking into account the activities of the business throughout the year), a timetable for iterations was also derived. Using the features, costs, resource estimates and priorities, features were then allocated to iterations. This was done on the basis of what could be expected within the fixed time boxes allocated to the iterations.

The resulting proposed project plan was then returned to the business for sign off. Interestingly, the business side of the project was run using the Prince 2 methodology that may at first seem too inflexible to accommodate an agile development process. However, the two approaches glued perfectly together (with a little goodwill on both the sides).

10.3 The Overall Project Plan

The end result of the initial project meetings was a document summarising the features to be implemented, their priority, cost and resources required, framed within the context of a set of fixed time iterations. This last feature proved important to the business in a number of ways. Firstly, it specified the maximum cost for an iteration (as they knew the cost of each feature in terms of person days as well as how many elapsed months the iteration would take).

At this point the budget for the project was accepted and the project plan signed off.

The resulting project had the following time boxed iterations (Figure 10.1):

The individual iterations are presented below. The overall plan for the civil audit extensions is also presented below.

Iteration 1: File Review Audit.
   This iteration will modify the core architecture of the application to support a new type of audit (the file review audit) and provide business and GUI logic for the execution of a File Review Audit. Note that this first iteration is limited to conduct the file review audit on a single machine.

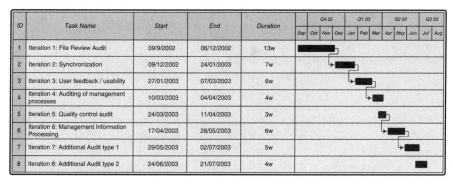

ID	Task Name	Start	End	Duration	Q4 02			Q1 03			Q2 03			Q3 03	
					Sep	Oct	Nov	Dec	Jan	Feb	Mar	Apr	May	Jun	Jul	Aug
1	Iteration 1: File Review Audit	09/9/2002	06/12/2002	13w												
2	Iteration 2: Synchronization	09/12/2002	24/01/2003	7w												
3	Iteration 3: User feedback / usability	27/01/2003	07/03/2003	6w												
4	Iteration 4: Auditing of management processes	10/03/2003	04/04/2003	4w												
5	Iteration 5: Quality control audit	24/03/2003	11/04/2003	3w												
6	Iteration 6: Management Information Processing	17/04/2003	28/05/2003	6w												
7	Iteration 7: Additional Audit type 1	29/05/2003	02/07/2003	5w												
8	Iteration 8: Additional Audit type 2	24/06/2003	21/07/2003	4w												

Fig. 10.1 Proposed iterations.

Iteration 2: Synchronization support.

This iteration will extend the software so that the file review audit can be conducted concurrently by a number of users on separate machines. This will involve synchronization of results as well as exchange of information for the validation of selected files for audit, etc.

Iteration 3: User feedback and usability changes.

This iteration will respond to the feedback provided by actual users from their experiences of using the software produced from iteration 1.

Iteration 4: Auditing of management processes.

This iteration will introduce a new type of audit to review management processes.

Iteration 5: Quality control audit.

This iteration will introduce a new type of audit that will measure the quality of the material produced by each file associated with a file reviewed in iteration 1.

Iteration 6: Management Information Processing.

This iteration will look at generating management summary information across audits.

Iteration 7: Additional Audit Type 1.

The aim of this iteration is to extend the software system to additional types of audit.

Iteration 8: Additional Audit Type 2.

The aim of this iteration is to extend the software system to additional types of audit.

The time boxes for each iteration were set at:

Iteration 1: File Review Audit.

230 person days. September 2002–End of November 2002 (elapsed duration 13 weeks).

Iteration 2: Synchronization support.

113 person days. December 2002–Mid Janurary 2003 (elapsed duration 7 weeks to include Christmas).

Iteration 3: User feedback and usability changes.
113 person days. Mid January 2003–Early March 2003 (elapsed duration 6 weeks).
Iteration 4: Auditing of management processes.
46 person days. Early March 2003–End of March 2003 (elapsed duration 4 weeks).
Iteration 5: Quality control audit.
17 person days. Mid March 2003–Early April 2003 (to run concurrently with the end of Man iteration 1) (elapsed duration 3 weeks).
Iteration 6: Management Information Processing.
113 person days: Early April 2003–Mid May 2003 (elapsed duration 6 weeks).
Iteration 7: Additional Audit Type 1.
70 person days. Late May 2003–Late June 2003 (elapsed duration 5 weeks to include Easter).
Iteration 8: Additional Audit Type 2.
20 person days. Mid June 2003–Late July 2003 (elapsed duration 4 weeks).

An important point to note is that only the first iteration was firmly planned. That is, the remaining iterations were speculative and each iteration would be (and indeed was) planned in detail at the start of that iteration. Thus, the actual content of iteration 4 changed significantly by the time we got there, and focussed on a new type of audit altogether – however, we did still do 46 person days of work at that point!

10.4 Planning the First Iteration

10.4.1 Selecting Features for Iteration 1

Features are selected based on a number of criteria:

1. Importance to the business
2. Level of risk
3. Application requirement

Of course, the priority allocated to the feature is the primary source of this information, but not the only one. A feature may be important to the business, but for a first iteration (for example), the level of risk may be too great and thus it may be postponed to the next iteration. An example of this occurred during the planning of this first iteration. One particular feature, known as the management audit, was undergoing review within the business. This meant that there was a large level of risk associated with it. That was, that the management audit process would alter and thus the computer support required by this type of audit would need to change. As we did not have enough time during the first iteration to implement all audit types, this audit was postponed to a later iteration. Thus, the risk here was not technical, but business-related.

Indeed, it was decided to focus on a single, well-defined audit type, for the first iteration. This helped focus on the features to be implemented at this point in time. Essentially, only those features required by the basic "File Review Audit" would be considered. This raised the priority of any such features, while reducing the relative priority of any other feature. To simplify this process, we created two features lists, one for iteration 1, and the other for later iterations. Any feature could have a priority of "high," "medium" or "low," and was placed in one of the two lists. We could thus order the features for iteration 1, and still maintain an ordered list of other features to be looked at during the start of the next iteration.

The final result was that fourteen features were identified for inclusion in iteration 1. These fourteen, and their priorities are presented below (along with a simple description).

As you may note from the above table, not all the features have been categorized as having a high priority. Instead, some features have a medium priority. This provides some flexibility within the iteration. For example, if the high priority features are taking longer to complete than originally anticipated (for whatever reason), then the lower priority features can be moved to a later iteration, thus ensuring that the iteration is completed on time and is delivered to the client in a working form.

Also note that feature F13 relates to the creation of DTD files and sample XML files for use by the rest of the application. Although this might not be an obvious feature of the system, it is identified as a separate feature because the other applications that this application interfaces with also need these DTDs. Thus, this is a very significant element of the system in its own right, rather than just a support task for other features.

10.4.2 Feature to Task Mapping

Features represent schedulable requirements and the activity that will realise those requirements. However, there are two issues, with directly allocating features to designers/developers to work on:

1. Typically, they represent large scale "functionality" that would be difficult to monitor except at the highest of levels.
2. Typically, they cut across multiple layers in the architecture requiring modifications to low-level, back-end frameworks as much as to front-end GUI components. These different areas require different knowledge and skill sets that are rarely possessed by a single individual.

Therefore, from the point of view of project planning and project monitoring, features are not an appropriate project-planning tool. Rather, features are implemented by one or more tasks. Tasks may be relevant to one or more features (as some architectural change may support more than one feature) and in turn, features may be relevant to one or more tasks. Tasks are what the developers actually work on, and are what are monitored, and against which progress is assessed.

Table 10.1 Summarised feature list.

ID	Feature	Description	Priority
F01	Architectural changes	Changes to previous architecture required by new requirements.	H
F02	Closed file report generation and printing	Generation of the report currently produced by hand by auditors.	H
F03	Summary and individual report generation	A (possibly optional) feature of the new system is the ability to produce reports on each file.	M
F04	Changes to main frame	With the introduction of the new audit type various changes will be required to the screens displayed within the application.	H
F05	Audit assembly	It will be necessary for a user to create an audit by selecting appropriate files to review.	H
F06	Loading an audit	The new type of audits must be loaded	H
F07	Writing out audits on completion	As well as loading the new file review audit it will also be necessary to save the file review audits.	H
F08	File review audit type	A major feature of the new system is a new type of Audit – the File Review Audit.	H
F09	File review summary	Part of the new type of file review is the ability to generate an on screen summary review of all the files reviewed as part of the "File Review Audit."	H
F10	Case file checklist	A major part of a file review is the Case File Checklist that provides a series of questions that will guide the auditor.	H
F11	Cost assessment	Another important aspect of the File Review process is the generation of the Cost Assessment information.	H
F12	Checklist summary information	A (potentially optional) feature of the new system is to add summary quality information.	M
F13	DTD and XML files	A new feature of this system will be the definition of additional DTD files to represent file review audits and individual file reviews.	H
F14	Reviews	When an audit is reviewed changes may need to be made to a completed audit.	M

Note that work packages help to group together individual tasks both for allocating work to actual team members and for organising tasks relative to features. However, the tasks that are monitored in detail within the project plan, are just the tasks that individual designers and developers will undertake. These tasks are schedulable and monitorable tasks of typically between 3 and 8 person days duration.

So how are features matched to tasks? This is a process of analysis that involves all the technical team members. During this process, we examine each feature and try to determine what it will take to implement that feature, what steps we will need to perform and what we will need to back up the more obvious tasks of each feature. This is in itself an iterative process that will require refinement, as our understanding of the set of features improves.

The end result is that a set of tasks is identified, that will implement the features listed in Table 10.1 and produce a deliverable system. Note that all tasks are numbered using the following pattern:

<indication of area of system>T:<task number>

Thus, a task dealing with printing is: PT:02

Meaning P for *Printing* and 02 for the second task in the printing related tasks. The other tasks are D for *Design*, A for *Architecture*, B for *Business* objects, M for *Management* of data, G for *GUI* components, I for *Integration* and T for *Text* documentation.

The following table presents each of the features, the tasks that implement the features and a brief description of the tasks. Note that, at this point, no consideration is given to the ordering of the tasks; instead, the tasks are grouped together in a logical manner. Hence, all the data management-oriented tasks are listed together (Table 10.2).

As you will note from the above table, some tasks do not directly relate to any particular feature. These are tasks such as constructing test release systems, providing documentation, etc. These are so because these relate to the overall system and to the production of the final working system rather than an individual feature. For example, providing a user manual allows potential users of the system

Table 10.2 Feature/task relationships.

Feature ID	Task ID	Task description
All	DT01	Familiarisation with existing system and impact of new features
F09	DT02	Impact on Architecture of File Review Summary
F01/F04	DT03	Review of and design for, architectural changes
All	DT04	Test plan and specification for system
F01	AT01	Implementing architectural changes
F14	AT02	Audit review process support
F08/F06/F05/F13	MT01	Review of, and design for, Data Access Manager (DAM) changes
F06	MT02	Implement DAM Changes – reading
F07	MT03	Implementing DAM Changes – writing
F05/F08	BT01	New Audit Type (File Review Audit)
F09	BT02	Design and Implement File Review Summary classes
F10	BT03	Design and Implementation of case checklist classes
F11	BT04	File Review cost assessment classes
F12	BT05	Adding Checklist summary information
F04	GT01	Design and Implement Changes to Main Window
F05	GT02	Designing and Implement Audit Assembly GUI classes and behaviour
F06	GT03	Designing and Implement Loading a scheduled audit GUI classes
F11	GT04	Design and Implementation of Cost Assessment Window classes
F10	GT05	Design and Implementation of "Case file check list window"
F08	GT06	Design and Implementation of Audit Details Window classes
F09	GT07	Design and Implementation of Audit Summary Window classes
F02	PT01	Designing and Implementation of Report generation classes closed file
F03	PT02	Designing and Implementation of Summary and Individual file Report Generation classes
	IT01	Alpha Build and System Testing of system
	IT02	Beta build and System Testing
	IT03	Release Candidate Build, System Testing and User Acceptance Testing
	TT01	User manual document
	TT02	Installation manual

to have a document that explains how this complex piece of software should be used. It also illustrates the need for such documentation, whether the system is being developed in an agile manner or not. Remember, the final end-users don't care as to how it was produced, but just whether it helps them to do their job (and for them, a user manual is very important). However, note that following the agile principles, the creation of the user manual is scheduled postproduction of any software. Thus, we will not need to re-write any part of the user manual during this iteration, due to a change in the software being implemented. Of course, it may need revision during subsequent iterations, but so will other parts of the software!

10.4.3 Ordering Tasks for Iteration 1

Having identified the tasks to be performed, we then need to think about how these tasks will be ordered. In a pure XP project, this might be left to the developers to determine; however, as we are applying an FDD approach, we will provide an initial plan of the ordering of the tasks. This can be done in numerous ways, but the essence of the practice is to consider the dependencies between tasks (an issue often ignored in projects taking an extremely agile approach). This provides a dependency graph illustrating how the tasks relate. This does not need to be done electronically as we are still trying to be agile, and anyway the dependency graph is not our aim per se, rather it is a temporary tool to help in the ordering of the tasks. Therefore, the dependency graph can be created on a sheet of A4 using a pen or pencil, or on a whiteboard, etc. Personally, I tend to prefer whiteboards, as it is easy to rub out the pen-marks and good at being viewed by multiple people.

The dependency graph is not the only influence on ordering, as the priority of the features that the tasks related to was also taken into account. Therefore, an attempt was made to place medium priority feature-oriented tasks to the back of the dependency graph. During this process, one important issue became apparent. Feature 14, which provided the ability to review completed audits, although only a medium priority, needed to be accounted for early on, if it was to be included at all. In discussion with the on-site client and the Business, it was decided that this was an important feature and its priority was raised too high.

Once we had the dependency graph in a state with which we were happy, we then needed to take into account the developers who will be working on the tasks. In this case, pair programming was not used as a standard way of developing; rather each task was initially allocated to the developer with the most relevant experience for that task. This resulted in a dependency graph with resources attached to each task.

Next, the dependency graph was used to order the tasks on a per developer-basis. Any discrepancies relating to the amount of work allocated to one particular developer were then addressed with tasks being moved among the developers. Note that this was done with the agreement of all the developers and was not laid down from on high.

The resulting set of tasks were then entered into (a simple) project diagramming tool. Note that we did not use a heavy-weight project-planning tool, as it was not considered necessary and that it would be an impediment to our agile approach.

In fact, we used the simple Gantt charting features of Visio to create a Gantt chart that could be easily changed, but against which progress could be monitored.

10.4.4 The Gantt Chart for Iteration 1

The following Gantt chart provides a detailed break down of the tasks to be performed for iteration 1 of the project. Note that the "Person Days" column relates to the number of person days spent on the task, whereas the "Elapsed Duration" column relates to the elapsed time spent on the task. Thus, a task of 12 person days, worked on by three people would have an elapsed duration of 4 days. Equally, an ongoing management task has an elapsed time of 65 days, but the number of person days spent on this task is 13 (see Figure 10.2).

In the Gantt chart presented in Fig. 10.2 some buffer has been left within this plan for unscheduled events (such as holidays and illness). We have not tried to have everyone utilizing 100% of the time. We believe that this reflects reality; as well as allowing developers time to expand their experience. However, in the context of an agile development, it also reflects the need to allow for pair programming time. Earlier I stated that "In this case, pair programming was not used as a standard way of developing" at the time you may have thought this was an odd way of

ID	Task Name	Start	End	Elapsed Duration	Person Days	Resource Name
1	DT01: Familirisation	09/09/2002	11/09/2002	3d	12d	All
2	DT02: Impact on existing architecture of new Audit Type	12/09/2002	16/09/2002	3d	3d	Steve
3	DT03: Impact on architecture of Summary information	12/09/2002	17/09/2002	4d	4d	John
4	DT04: System test plan and specification	12/09/2002	17/09/2002	4d	4d	Will
5	MT01: Review of, and design for, DAM changes	12/09/2002	16/09/2002	3d	3d	Ben
6	AT01: Implementing Architectural Changes	18/09/2002	23/09/2002	4d	4d	John
7	AT02: Audit Review Process Support	24/09/2002	03/10/2002	8d	8d	John
8	PT01: Designing Report generation classes for closed file	04/10/2002	14/10/2002	7d	7d	John
9	PT02: Design and Implementation of Summary and Individual file reports	15/10/2002	28/10/2002	10d	10d	John
10	MT02: Implement DAM changes for loading	17/09/2002	24/09/2002	6d	6d	Ben
11	MT03: Implement DAM changes for Writing	25/09/2002	02/10/2002	6d	6d	Ben
12	GT04: Design and Implement of cost assessment window classes	03/10/2002	14/10/2002	8d	8d	Ben
13	GT05: Design and Implement of "Case File Checklist" window classes	15/10/2002	29/10/2002	11d	11d	Ben
14	GT07: Design and Implementation of Audit Summary Window	30/10/2002	11/11/2002	9d	9d	Ben
15	BT01: New Audit type	17/09/2002	27/09/2002	9d	9d	Steve
16	BT02: Design and Implement File Review Summary Classes	30/09/2002	08/10/2002	7d	7d	Steve
17	BT03: Design and Implement case checklist classes	09/10/2002	22/10/2002	10d	10d	Steve
18	BT04: File Review Cost Assessment classes	23/10/2002	04/11/2002	9d	9d	Steve
19	BT05: Adding checklist summary information	05/11/2002	14/11/2002	8d	8d	Steve
20	GT01: Design and Implement Changes to Main Frame	18/09/2002	23/09/2002	4d	4d	Will
21	GT03: Designing and implementing loading a scheduled audit gui classes	24/09/2002	27/09/2002	4d	4d	Will
22	GT02: Designing and Implement Audit Assembly GUI classes	30/09/2002	11/10/2002	10d	10d	Will
23	GT06: Design and Implement Audit Details Window classes	14/10/2002	25/10/2002	10d	10d	Will
24	IT01: Alpha build and System testing	15/11/2002	19/11/2002	3d	9d	Steve/Ben/Will/John
25	IT02: Beta Build and System Testing	20/11/2002	29/11/2002	8d	18d	Steve/Ben/Will/John
26	IT03: Release Candidate Build, System testing and User Testing	02/12/2002	12/12/2002	9d	14d	Steve/Ben/John
27	TT01: User manual document	02/12/2002	06/12/2002	5d	5d	Will
28	TT02: Installation manual	09/12/2002	09/12/2002	1d	1d	John

Fig. 10.2 The Gantt chart for iteration 1.

phrasing the fact that we weren't applying pair programming (hey, we never said we were doing Extreme Programming!). But it was actually intentional. This is because the development team was encouraged to employ pair programming techniques when they thought it would be to their advantage. For example, when they were concerned that they were straying into unknown territory, or needed to work out a difficult algorithm, etc. This approach worked very well (not least due to the particular group of developers and the dynamics within the team) but needs to allow time within the schedule for developers to leave the task they are working on and to pair program with a co-worker. Ironically, it means that the more experienced software engineers were given the largest buffers to allow them to work alongside more junior developers more often (although I can vouch from personal experience, the benefits can be attained the other way around as well).

10.5 Post Delivery

The software developed for the client was delivered on time and with all features implemented. It was then presented to a group of users who would act as champions of the software within each region of the UK. This group of users were trained on the software and were provided with the user manual and then let loose. They used the software in parallel to the existing systems for a time (partly for legal reasons). As others in their regions saw the new software, more users came on board. This approach was taken, as this was an iteration 1 delivery which was complete in itself, but not complete in terms of the whole business press, and thus some tasks needed to be performed manually. While this was happening, the team embarked on iteration 2. As before, the feature list for the iteration was refined, tasks identified and work begun. By the time this iteration was complete, the users of the iteration 1 delivery were able to provide valuable, real-world feedback on the usability of the system. The comments then formed the basis of iteration 3. This allowed the users to see that they were actually being listened to and that their views mattered.

10.6 Summary

This chapter has illustrated how a project using a Feature Driven approach, within an agile framework, can be planned (and presented to a client unfamiliar with agile methodologies). It also illustrates how being agile does not mean hacking, or not planning. Indeed within the framework of FDD, agile modelling and extreme programming become well planned, well controlled and monitored, and clearly organised operations. This is not to say that the same cannot be said for a pure XP project. However, as the size of the project grows, the use of techniques such as FDD can make life much more manageable!

Agile Methods with RUP and PRINCE2

11.1 Introduction

In this chapter, we will consider how some of the agile techniques talked about thus far can fit with more traditional software engineering methods. In particular, we will focus on the Unified Process (also known as the Rational Unified Process or RUP) and PRINCE2.

The Unified Process is a design framework that guides the tasks, people and products of the design process. It is a framework because it provides the inputs and outputs of each activity, but does not restrict how each activity must be performed. Different activities can be used in different situations, some being left out, others being replaced or augmented. It was originally developed by Ivar Jacobson, Grady Booch and James Rumbaugh at Rational. They originally developed the Unified Modelling Language (or the UML) and then went on to create the Unified Process as the process side of their unification efforts (prior to the UML and Unified Process there were a number of competing but similar methods available including OMT, the Booch method and Objectory (Booch, 1994; Rumbaugh et al., 1991; Jacobson et al., 1992). All of these methods (which the authors were each heavily involved in) provided inspiration for UML and the Unified Process. For more details on the Unified Process, see Hunt (2003) and Jacobson et al. (1999).

PRINCE, which stands for *Pr*ojects *in* Controlled *E*nvironments, is a project management method covering the organisation, management and control of projects. PRINCE was first developed by the Central Computer and Telecommunications Agency (CCTA), now part of the UK's Office of Government Commerce (OGC) in 1989 as a UK Government standard for IT project management. The latest version of the method, PRINCE2, is designed to incorporate the requirements of existing users and to enhance the method towards a generic, best practice approach for the management of all types of projects.

In the remainder of this chapter, we will consider the relationship between agile modelling and the Unified process (or RUP). We will introduce the RUP and then consider how modelling is handled within the RUP and how agile modelling can augment the RUP process. We will then consider how feature-driven design fits with RUP before discussing how agile methods relate to the PRINCE2 method.

11.2 Agile Modelling and RUP

The Unified Process or the Rational Unified Process (sometimes known as RUP) (Jacobson et al., 1999; Hunt, 2003) is a framework for handling the whole lifecycle of a software development project. It is referred to as a framework because it allows the overall suite of activities to be customised and modified as required for a particular type of application (this is illustrated in Figure 11.1).

Why then is the Unified Process called a *process* and not the Unified Framework? It is called a process because its primary aim is to define:

- Who is doing what?
- When they do it?
- How to reach a certain goal (i.e. each activity)?
- The inputs and outputs of each activity.

It is thus an engineered process. In fact, it is comprised of a number of different hierarchical elements (see Figure 11.2). In terms of the agile movement, it is towards the heavyweight end of software methods and thus may not initially appear compatible with processes such as those that have come out of the agile movement.

The Unified Process is actually comprised of low-level activities (such as finding classes), which are combined together into disciplines formally known as workflows (which describe how one activity feeds into another). These disciplines are organised into iterations. Each iteration identifies some aspect of the system to be considered. How this is done is considered in more detail later. Iterations themselves are organised into phases. Phases focus on different aspects of the design process, for example, requirements, analysis, design and implementation. In turn, phases can be grouped into cycles. Cycles focus on the generation of successive releases of a system (for example, version 1.0, version 1.1, etc.).

This process is iterative and incremental and is adaptive in that it is responsive to changes in business or user requirements as well as to feedback from users. It is

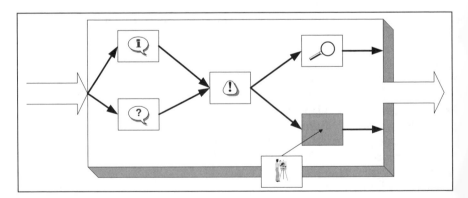

Fig. 11.1 The Unified Process is a framework.

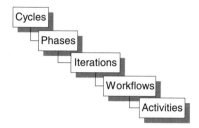

Fig. 11.2 Key building blocks of the Unified Process.

in these respects that aspects of the agile movement can be introduced into RUP as we will see later.

The Unified Process, although a sound basis upon which to base the development process, is a framework which explicitly recommends modification where appropriate (again helpful from the point of view of introducing aspects of the agile movement).

11.2.1 Overview of the Unified Process

There are four key elements to the philosophy behind the Unified Process. These four elements are:

- Iterative and incremental,
- Use-case driven,
- Architecture-centric,
- Acknowledges risk.

Iterative and Incremental

The Unified Process is iterative and incremental, that is, the design process is based on iterations which address either different aspects of the design process or more the design forward in some way (this is the incremental aspect of the model). This does not mean that the Unified Process is a process based on rapid prototyping. Any prototypes that are developed in the Unified Process are used to explore some aspect of the design. This could be to verify some architectural issue, different design options, assess a new technology, etc. Indeed, the use of an iterative and incremental approach in the Unified Process requires more planning (rather than less planning) as compared to approaches such as those based on the waterfall model (as was indicated when we discussed Feature-Driven Development in Chapter 9).

Essentially, the following holds with the iterative approach in the Unified Process:

- You plan a little.
- You specify, design and implement a little.

- You integrate, test and run.
- You obtain feedback before the next iteration.

The end result is that you incrementally produce the system being designed. While you do this you explicitly identify the risks to your design/system Unified Process front and deal with them early on (see later). Note that this does not mean that you are hacking the system together nor are you carrying out some form of rapid prototyping (you are not). However, it does mean that a great deal of planning is required, both upfront and as the design develops.

Use-Case Driven

The Unified Process is also use-case driven. Remember from earlier that use-cases help identify who uses the system and what they need to do with the system (i.e., the top-level functionality). Thus, use-cases help identify the primary require-ments of the system. One problem with many traditional approaches is that once the requirements have been identified there is no traceability of those require-ments through the design to the implementation. Instead designers (and possibly implementers) must refer back implicitly to the requirements specification and make sure they have done what is required of them. This is then verified by test-ing (by which time it is often too late to make any major modifications if the functionality is either wrong or missing).

In the Unified Process, use-cases are used to ensure that the evolving design is always relevant to what the user required. Indeed, the use cases act as the one consistent thread throughout the whole of the development process as illustrated in Figure 11.3. For example, at the beginning of the design phase, one of the two primary inputs to this phase is the use-case model. Then explicitly within the design model are use-case realisations that illustrate how each use-case is supported by the design. Any use-case that does not have a use-case realisation is not currently supported by the design (in turn, any design elements which do

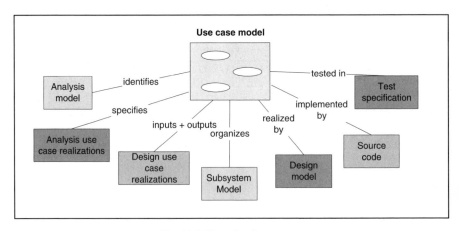

Fig. 11.3 The role of use-cases.

not in some way partake in a use-case realisation do not support the required functionality of the system!).

To summarise the role of use-cases they:

- Identify the users of the system and their requirements.
- Aid in the creation and validation of the system's architecture.
- Help produce the definition of test cases and procedures.
- Direct the planning of iterations.
- Drive the creation of user documentation.
- Direct the deployment of system.
- Synchronise the content of different models.
- Drive traceability throughout models.

11.2.2 Lifecycle Phases

The Unified Process is comprised of four distinct phases. These four phases (presented in Figure 11.4) focus on different aspects of the design process. The four phases are Inception, Elaboration, Construction and Transition.

The four phases and their roles are outlined below.

Inception. This phase defines the scope of the project and develops the business case for the system. It also establishes the feasibility of the system to be built. Various prototypes may be developed during this phase to ensure the feasibility of the proposal. Note we do not focus on the development of the business case in this book; it is assumed that the system to be designed is required and a business case has already been made.

Elaboration. This phase captures the functional requirements of the system. It should also specify any non-functional requirements to ensure that they are taken into account. The other primary task for this phase is the creation of the architecture to be used throughout the remainder of the Unified Process.

Construction. This phase concentrates on completing the analysis of the system, performing the majority of the design and the implementation of the system. That is, it essentially builds the product.

Transition. The transition phase moves the system into the users environment. This involves activities such as deploying the system and maintaining it.

Each phase has a set of major milestones that are used to judge the progress of the overall Unified Process (of course, with each phase there are numerous minor milestones to be achieved). The primary milestones (or products) of the four phases are illustrated in Figure 11.5.

Fig. 11.4 Four phases of the Unified Process.

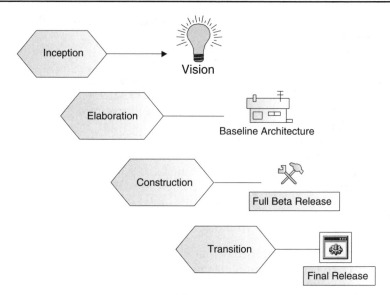

Fig. 11.5 Major deliverables of each phase.

A milestone is the culmination of a phase and is comprised of a set of artefacts (such as specific models) that are the product of the disciplines (and thus activities) in that phase. The primary milestones for each phase are:

Inception. The output of this phase is the vision for the system. This includes a very simplified use-case model (to identify what the primary functionality of the system is), a very tentative architecture and the most important or significant risks are identified and the elaboration phase is planned.

Elaboration. The primary output of this phase is the architecture along with a detailed use-case model and a set of plans for the construction phase.

Construction. The end result of this phase is the implemented product that includes the software as well as the design and associated models. The product may not be without defects as some further work has yet to be completed in the transition phase.

Transition. The transition phase is the last phase of a cycle. The major milestone met by this phase is the final production quality release of the system.

11.2.3 Phases, Iterations and Disciplines

There can be confusion over the relationship between phases and disciplines. Not least because a single discipline can cross (or be involved in) more than one phase (see Figure 11.6). One way to view the relationships is that the disciplines are the steps you actually follow. However, at different times we can identify different major milestones that should be met. The various phases highlight the satisfaction of these milestones. For example, during the Elaboration phase, part of the

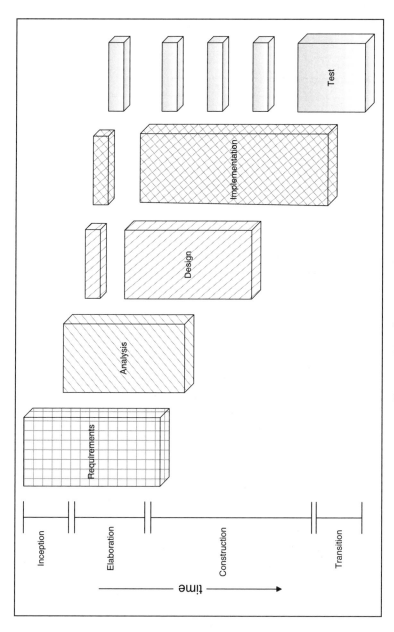

Fig. 11.6 Disciplines versus phases.

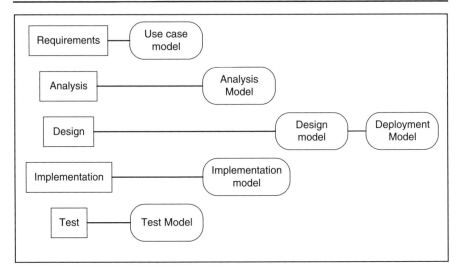

Fig. 11.7 Discipline products.

requirements, analysis, design and even implementation disciplines may act. However, the emphasis at this time, within these disciplines, will be on elaborating what the system should do and how it should be structured, rather than the more detailed analysis, design and implementation which occur during the Construction phase.

The five disciplines in the Unified Process are Requirements, Analysis, Design, Implementation and Test (as indicated in Figure 11.6). Note that the Design, Implementation and Test disciplines are broken down in the Unified Process. This is to indicate that elements of each discipline may take place earlier than the core parts of the discipline. In particular, the design, implementation and testing of the architecture will happen early on (in the Elaboration phase). Thus, part of each of the Design, Implementation and Test disciplines must occur at this time.

The focus of each discipline is described below (their primary products are illustrated in Figure 11.7).

Requirements. This discipline focuses on the activities that allow the functional and non-functional requirements of the system to be identified. The primary product of this discipline is the use-case model.

Analysis. The aim of this discipline is to restructure the requirements identified in the requirements discipline in terms of the software to be built rather than in the users less precise terms. It can be seen as a first cut at a design; however, that is to miss the point of what this discipline aims to achieve.

Design. The design discipline produces the detailed design that will be implemented in the next discipline.

Implementation. This discipline represents the coding of the design in an appropriate programming language (for this book that is Java), the compilation, packaging, deployment and documentation of the software.

Test. The test discipline describes the activities to be carried out to test the software to ensure that it meets the users requirements, that it is reliable, etc.

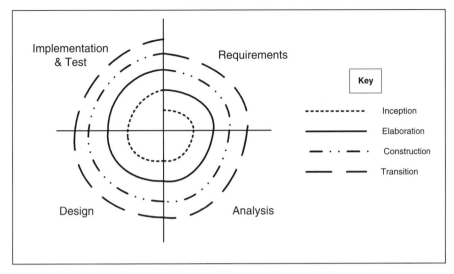

Fig. 11.8 The Unified Process is a spiral.

Note that all the disciplines have a period when they are running concurrently. This does not mean that one person is necessarily working on all the disciplines at the same time. Instead, it acknowledges that in order to clarify some requirement, it may be necessary to design how that requirement might be implemented and even implement it to confirm that it is feasible.

In actual fact, this acknowledges that the Unified Process is a spiral (as indicated by its iterative and incremental nature). This is illustrated in Figure 11.8 (note as a phase moves around the spiral multiple iterations may occur; we have assumed only one iteration in this figure for simplicity sake). As can be seen from this diagram, the five disciplines are involved in each of the four phases. Each phases moves around the various disciplines producing outputs that feed into the next phase. Each phase examines the requirements (to a greater or lesser extent). Each phase involves the analysis discipline, the design discipline and so on. This is in fact one of the Unified Process' greatest strengths, it represents a practical iterative design method, which is held together by an architecture and which acknowledges risk Unified Process front and makes it one of the driving elements of the whole design process. It then ensures that what is being produced will be relevant to users of the system by holding everything together via use-cases. Indeed, it is the use-cases that help a designer identify what should be performed in any particular iterative.

11.2.4 Modelling and the Unified Process

Unfortunately (or may be fortunately), the Unified Process does not describe a modelling methodology as such. Thus, you are free to employ your own approach to modelling.

Let us first review a few important points about the Unified Process. First, it is a framework that encourages you to adapt it to your own needs. In particular,

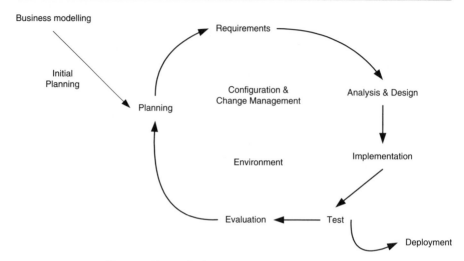

Fig. 11.9 The Unified Process iterative and incremental.

you should not slavishly produce the deliverables from all disciplines unless they are actually useful.

Secondly, the Unified Process actively encourages an iterative and incremental approach to software development (as illustrated in Figure 11.9). Indeed, it is one of the key elements of Unified Process. However, this can be lost in the detail when organizations implement the Unified Process themselves. In particular, it is easy to end up with an approach that promotes each discipline as part of a waterfall-based methodology (partly this is because such an approach is more familiar to those who try to move to the Unified Process and thus an easier fit with what they already know). However, as illustrated in earlier chapters of this book, the incremental and iterative aspects can easily be emphasised instead.

Thirdly, there is nothing in the Unified Process that assumes that *all* the modelling must be done upfront. Indeed, if you adopt an incremental and iterative style, then each iteration will generate its own set of models. Some of these models may replace existing ones, others may augment them and some may be completely new.

This brings us nicely onto the role of Agile Modelling within the Unified Process. There is very little in the Unified Process that actually describes how you should model. In this book, we have examined how to identify the elements of a model, how to refine those elements and what the elements are (for each type of model). However, we have not, until now, discussed how you go about building up a large model for a complex software system. Such a model may encompass years of person time, client and server architectures and technologies, multiple editions of the software, etc.

The Unified Process contains nothing that explicitly or implicitly prohibits the use of Agile Modelling (and remember Agile Modelling is more a philosophy than an actual method). Indeed, there is much in the Unified Process that actively promotes a style of development that naturally encourages an Agile Modelling approach.

However, it is too simplistic to suggest that all you need to do is to plug Agile Modelling into the Unified Process. The following lists some of the adaptations you should consider to the Unified Process to promote the integration of Agile Modelling:

- You may need to lower the emphasis on "use-case driven," although the style is still model-centric and still iterative, it is harder to determine all use-cases upfront and agile model is less use-case focussed.
- Use-cases should be used to help identify the core of the architecture and potentially the elements of the first iteration. The use-cases form the basis of your starting point (but are a subset of all the potential use-cases that could have been identified).
- Subsequent iterations need to identify their own use-cases (or requirements) that will help to focus and drive that iteration.
- Treat the architecture as the key to enabling the integration of the results of Agile Modelling, but be careful not to try to design in all eventualities and "what ifs" – you may never need them and the architecture may have evolved by the time you do, so that they are obsolete.
- The architecture is still the key to the infrastructure, but now Agile Modelling works within the spaces left by the architecture.
- Don't go over the top with the architecture. In particular, select appropriate models and views as necessary for your projects requirements.
- Don't go over the top with design patterns! They can be very useful but you need to know where and when to apply them and they can make software more complicated.
- The architecture is more interested in the contracts between areas than with a fixed skeleton of code (this skeleton itself may be subject to incremental and iterative modelling and implementation).
- The architecture itself can be modelled in an agile manner. That is, the architecture is not fixed, it may well change and evolve, but this change will be controlled and will be effected in an agile manner (only those areas that need to change should change). Other aspects of the "architecture" may not be fleshed out (or even designed) until they are actually needed.
- The iterations and increments are more than likely to be smaller rather than larger. That is, each increment may represent a sub release of a software system (say from 1.4.1 to 1.4.2) rather than a full release of a software system (from say 1.4 to 1.5).

The key philosophy underlying the above is to try and only do what you need to do in terms of modelling for each iteration in the Unified Process and that Agile Modelling can help you to do that. Of course, this is where experience is so important. That is, knowing what must be done upfront and what can be left until later is not a hard and fast science. For example, security in a web application is a very code case. Trying to factor this into an existing system may require major redesign of the whole system. So, although security may not be an important criterion for initial builds, it might be good to design it into the initial architecture. This of course does conflict somewhat with what the agile movement states you should do, but you certainly don't want to engineer in a design that might actually stop security features being added later.

11.2.5 Agile Modelling and Documentation

It is important to realise that adopting an agile modelling approach to your modelling task does not mean that you do not need to produce documentation. Rather documentation encompasses the models you create just as it would have done before. The issue is that you only create just enough models (and by implication documentation actually) to support the tasks required. For example, in general, the documentation you need while creating a software system is different from the documentation you need once that system is built and you need to support it. On a recent project, for example, we were taking a system we had built previously for a client and adding a set of new features and a new class of information to be managed. One of the documents written earlier described how the existing architecture and classes would need to be revised and refactored for the new requirements. This document was of great use during development but was obsolete at the end of the project. What was needed now was a documentation to support future maintenance of the system – not a document describing how to migrate from a previous (and now historical) version of the system.

To conclude this section, agile models and their associated documentation are "lean and mean" and fulfil a specific purpose. They are intended to be good enough for those who should be expected to read them.

11.3 FDD and RUP

Agile Modelling is not the only agile methodology that can be usefully applied to a software project that is employing the Unified Process. Feature-Driven Development (discussed in the last two chapters) is another method with things to offer an RUP project.

One area in which we have found it beneficial to amend the Unified Process is to make it also Feature-Centric (Coadet al., 1999; Carmichael and Swainston-Rainford, 2000; Carmichael and Haywood, 2002). Feature-centric means that each iteration centres on the identification and realization of system features. A feature is a schedulable requirement associated with the activity used to realize it. These requirements may be user-related requirements, application behaviour requirements or internal requirements. The features can then be grouped into workpackages that can act as the basis of the planning required to monitor and manage the software development process.

Another aspect that I have found again and again can be applied to the Unified Process from Feature-Driven Development is the application of fixed timescale iterations. Clients like to know when they will get the next release. This means that they can plan their own acceptance testing, deployment and training schedules.

Associated with the concept of fixed timescale iterations, we have found that clients are very willing to consider the priorities of features and to order them. This means that if we find that an iteration will be unable to implement all the features originally planned for that iteration, we are able to work with them to determine which features will move to the next iteration or be returned to the list of features that will one day be required.

In fact, what we have tended to do is to a wrap up a Feature-Driven Development project within the outer wrappings of a Unified Process project. This means that the Unified Process gives support for early project initiation activities, high-level management support and ongoing software support operations. In turn, the Feature-Driven Development aspects allow us to focus on the primary task of the project, providing software that adds value to the clients within the timescales and budgets available.

For example, earlier it was stated that the iterative approach within the Unified Process essentially has the following steps (which actually look remarkably oriented towards the agile movement anyway):

1. You plan a little.
2. You specify, design and implement a little.
3. You integrate, test and run.
4. You obtain feedback before next iteration.

The Feature-Driven Development process therefore essentially handles these steps. This is illustrated in Figure 11.10 where the design, implementation and test disciplines have been subsumed by the Feature-Driven Development process. Thus, we do not have a big up-front design, followed (possibly in parallel) by the implementation and then the testing. Rather we have iterations comprising planning, design, implementation and testing in an incremental and iterative fashion. Indeed, the typical approach is to have multiple tasks during which a bit of design, implementation and testing occur. To indicate that the iterations managed by the FDD process may be of different sizes, the boxes being subsumed by the FDD process are presented in different sizes.

It is worth refreshing why Feature-Driven Development is very useful for adaptive, incremental software development projects. It helps you to regain control of the software development process. Part of this is the use of feature-centric planning, part of it is the use of timeboxing within each iteration, and the final aspect is being adaptive. These three things make Feature-Driven Development bring real added value to the Unified Process.

11.4 Agile Methods and Prince2

The PRINCE2 method describes how a project is divided into manageable stages enabling efficient control of resources and regular progress monitoring throughout the project. The various roles and responsibilities for managing a project are fully described and are adaptable to suit the size and complexity of the project, and

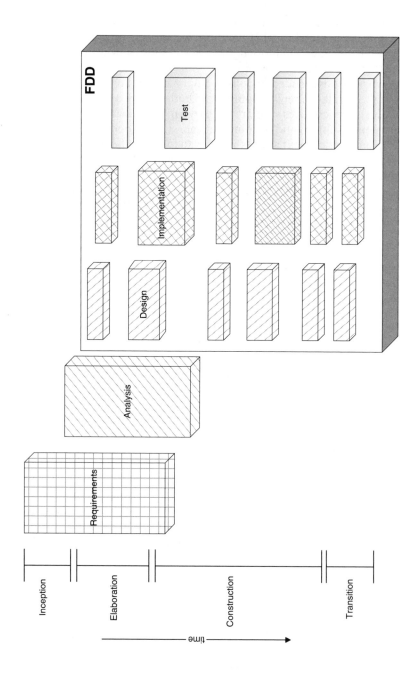

Fig. 11.10 Integrating Feature-Driven Development with the Unified Process.

the skills of the organisation. Project planning using PRINCE2 is product-based, which means the project plans are focused on delivering results and are not simply about planning when the various activities on the project will be done.

Because an iterative or incremental approach may at first sight appear less controlled than an approach such as PRINCE2, some have perceived that this means that PRINCE2 and such approaches are inconsistent. However, this is not the case. Indeed, if you consider the emphasis of the Feature-Driven approach, then similarities with some aspects of PRINCE2 can immediately be seen. For example, product (or feature)-based planning, the involved partnership of users and developers and the strong emphasis on the underlying business need (or case).

Care is needed, however, in using the two methodologies together. Those who have used PRINCE2 to control their Feature-Driven, timeboxed project have found that an unyielding approach – applying the method straight from the manual – can lead to duplication, overlap and conflict.

Table 11.1 makes it clear that the iterative approach includes some project management content while in turn PRINCE2 maintains a view of the whole project (whereas the iterative approach plans out each iteration at the start of that iteration). In addition, the iterative approach fixes the length of an iteration in terms of time and then attempts to achieve a prioritised list of features. Some features may not be implemented in the time available and will "return to the pot" for the next iteration.

The general philosophy to combining a PRINCE2 approach with an iterative one is that where there is no overlap between the methods, you must refer to the appropriate approach. In general, this means that project management related issues will be handled by PRINCE2 and development related issues by the iterative approach.

What does this mean? For example, PRINCE2 does not require management stages to match technical ones. A management stage may consist of a number of timeboxes. Thus, a phase may or may not map to an iteration. If it does, then fine. The first task in an iteration is then to determine the exact set of features to be addressed. However, the general set of features to be addressed during the phase should have been identified (although in the end not all may be implemented).

In terms of roles, the internal project manager might be the Team Manager PRINCE2 role. PRINCE2 assigns project assurance functions to the Project Board members, and each member fulfils this role from his or her own perspective. The

Table 11.1 PRINCE2 and FDD relationships.

	PRINCE2	Iterative/Feature-Driven Design
Organisation	Project board and assurance	Project manager
Project structure	Stages	Timeboxed increments/iterations based on features
Outputs	Management products	Iterative releases
Quality	Quality plan	Test specification, plan and report per iteration
Flexibility/change	Time, cost	Features
Control	Issue management	Timeboxing, feature selection and management

Project Board may delegate project assurance responsibilities to an independent Project Assurance Team (which may have been set up to carry out project assurance for any or all projects). In an iterative approach such as that advocated in this appendix, the Project Assurance Team may be redundant because of the far closer relationship and involvement of the business and the users in selecting the features to be addressed, the visibility of the progress within an iteration and from the deliverables of an iteration. Each iteration is carried out to a fixed timescale with a fixed budget and decisions are always based on the business benefit of the features being addressed.

Products produced as part of the PRINCE2 process are *management* and *quality* products. They relate to the effective and efficient management and control of the project and to project quality, respectively. Most products within the Feature-Driven approach are *specialist* products, that is, they are either descriptions of features, or descriptions of how the system operates with these features (use-case documents), or the techniques to be used. There are, however, some products that are either completely management products or contain project management sections (such as the outline plan for all iterations, and the detailed iteration plan) and some quality products (such as the Test specification, test plan and test report for a particular iteration).

To avoid duplication of effort, the recommended approach is that high-level management and quality products should be the province of PRINCE2 and that detailed iteration planning and quality monitoring should be the province of the iterative approach.

Managing and controlling an iterative project using PRINCE2 is fundamentally the same as for any other PRINCE2 project. The purpose is to enable each level of the project management team to:

- Demonstrate to the next level up that the project is on track to a successful outcome (that the project will deliver products that are fit for business purpose on time and within budget).
- Identify early anything that may prevent this.

To do this, there are mechanisms for controlling and tracking both the PRINCE2 aspects (project management) and the products of an iteration (frequent reporting of the progress of features). In PRINCE2, management and control are done at each project stage and everything depends on how the project is broken up into stages. PRINCE2 defines major control points through the life of the project, as follows:

- Project initiation,
- End stage assessment,
- Regular highlight reports,
- Exception reports,
- Mid-stage assessment,
- Project closure.

The results from each iteration can feedback into the monitoring and reporting stages of PRINCE2.

11.5 Summary

In this chapter, you have seen that just because a method does not declare itself to be part of the agile movement (although many are now trying to jump on that bandwagon) does not mean that agile practices cannot be introduced or that agile concepts cannot be of benefit. Indeed, the RUP can greatly benefit from many of the practices defined for agile modelling. It helps to reduce the big up-front design syndrome that can blight RUP projects. It also helps to control the amount of documentation/models produced and the frequency with which they are revised. In turn, methods such as the RUP provide a welcome structure for (in particular) larger software projects that can be rather too unwieldy to managing in a purely XP manner.

The end result of combining agile methods with processes such as RUP is something that (if handled appropriately) can provide the overall management often required by large long-lived projects with the agility and responsiveness required in the modern development world. From real world experience, I have applied a combination of the Unified Process, with Feature-Driven Development and agile modelling with aspects of XP to software development projects. Admittedly, the end result is not an XP project, nor is it a purely Feature-Driven Development project, but it has worked, produced tangible results on time and within budget and has fitted in with our clients' needs and requirements – what more can be asked!

12

Introducing Agile Methods into Your Organisation

12.1 Introduction

Okay, so if you have got as far as this in the book, it is likely that you are quite keen to implement an agile approach. However, you must now persuade people within your own organisation that they should consider doing this. This may be no mean feat in its own right. To help you, this chapter discusses how you might approach the process of persuading an organisation that they should consider applying agile practices.

12.2 Selling Agile Methods

If you want to introduce agile methods into your organisation, you have to sell the concept of agility to that organisation. It is possible that you may be in the privileged position of being the decision maker regarding the software development approach to take (although in general that will be unlikely). However, even if you are the decision maker you need to get others "on side" in order to make it work. Of course, if you are merely someone who is trying to influence the decision makers, then you have an even bigger need to "sell" the idea of agile methods.

Although programmers think in terms of code and requirements and design, companies (or at least the groupings that represent companies such as senior management, etc.) tend to think in non-programming terms. Thus, if you want to sell agile methods, you need to focus on the results that can be obtained from being agile rather than the methods that are embodied within the agile movement. This may also be true as the methods themselves may make risk-averse managers think more than twice about the approach.

Thus, in selling agile methods to an organisation, you need to avoid discussions regarding techniques (and often in particular about eXtreme Programming as this may conjure up all the wrong connotations for managers – extreme hackers!) and sell the results that can be obtained. From their perspective, the results can include:

1. Software can be developed on time, within budget and be of real use to the end users.
2. This gives the organisation, the customer and the team a competitive advantage.

How many end users have complained that the software they got was late, over their budget and didn't do what they wanted (possibly because they didn't tell the developers what they really wanted but none the less . . .).

Agile methods really do help "get the right software right!" That means, clients will keep coming back, new clients will be won and the business should boom! (at least from the organisation management's point of view).

There are growing case studies that have been reported to back these claims up (see the Agile Universe Conferences and the Agile Movement Website). However, you will still need to convince management that these advantages can be won within your own organisation. In many cases, this means proving it with a project of your own. As management wants to avoid unnecessary risks, it makes sense to propose a small project run in an agile manner as a test case.

Finally, if you are not a primary decision maker within your organisation, then you need to get someone who is on your side. That someone needs to be your Agile Methods Champion – someone who will fight for your cause at the right level of seniority within your organisation. Without that person, in many organisations, you are doomed to failure before you even start.

12.3 Identifying a Suitable First Project

This raises the question – what is a suitable first project? You need to pick an appropriate project. This project needs to be one that will show off the benefits of an agile approach, by that I mean that if the project could be successfully implemented with your current processes, then where is the advantage to be found? However, it must also not be so challenging that the project is likely to fail given the timescales, budgets and resources available, whatever methods were used. If this is the case, the agile approach adopted may well be blamed for the failure when it was actually the project itself that failed. Of course, a counter argument to this might be that agile methods should be able to deliver something – and that is true, but this is the first agile project to be done within the organisation and experience has yet to be gained – so let's be fair for a minute!

The questions, therefore to ask about a project, to consider whether it is a suitable candidate to be a first agile project, include the need to assess the risk, client, nature and size of the project. We will consider each below.

Firstly, the level of risk attached to the project should not be too high. That is, overall the project should not be so risky as to make it almost a failure before you start. However, in addition, it should not be so risk-free as to be mundane and completely predictable (as you are therefore less likely to need to be agile). Another feature of risk is that it should not be too risky for the company (or indeed client). That is, it should not be a business critical project that if it fails will cripple the organisation or the client. Remember, this is your first agile project and it may well go horribly wrong!

Secondly, the client for the project needs to be "on board" with regard to adopting an agile approach. Remember, within any agile method, the involvement of the client is not only essential but also a crucial part of the constitution of the team. Without the on-site client you may very well wander from what they need, be unable to answer important questions and fail to produce what they require. Even if the client is on board they can make an on-site customer representative available to you (even if this is in a virtual manner). If not, then as willing as they may seem that are unwilling to commit fully to your endeavour.

Thirdly, the nature of the project must be suitable. If this is a green field software solution, within which some of the requirements are at best liable to change and at worst still unclear, then you may well be onto a major winner. As agile methods explicitly acknowledge these features, you will be able to show how you can respond to these changing requirements using an agile approach.

Finally, the project need not be too large. Ideally, a team of three or four dedicated and talented software engineers should be able to accomplish the task in hand within 3–6 months. Anything larger and it is likely that it is too big for a first project. Anything smaller and you don't have enough time or people to really get to grips with agile methods. Of course, you need to get the right people in the team, who are not only talented but also willing to adopt an agile approach.

12.4 Promoting an Agile Culture

You will need to promote an agile environment at least within your project if not wider a field within your organisation. You need to ensure that everyone involved with the project is working in an agile manner. It is of little good to you if your immediate team works in an agile manner, but when you try to book some system support time (for example, to help set up an appropriate test environment) you find that you have to book this 8 weeks in advance and they can't do anything for you right now. This is particularly true if you are working on a 2- or 3-week release cycle!

So, what can you do to nurture a culture of agility? Firstly, start small – with a small project, a small team and small(ish) aims. Ensure that everyone is familiar with the aims and objectives of the agile movement. However, you can't be too rigid in your application of your chosen agile method – you need to introduce it gradually. Also don't worry too much about "getting it right;" your understanding of how to apply the principles within a particular approach will evolve. So, let the project become more agile as your understanding and experience grow.

Finally, drive home the fact that it's the software to be developed which is the primary goal of all these and that what the customer wants comes first. This may sound obvious but as has been indicated earlier in this book, this can be hard to achieve. You will also need to fight to ensure that the customer is involved, remains involved and remains interested!

12.5 Building an Agile Team

If you are able to select the software engineers who will comprise your team, then you are very lucky and have a big advantage. You need to try to get the best software engineers you can (don't we all?) but in this case you really need to ensure that it is not their technical ability that causes the project problems (as they will have enough to do learning about being agile!). Note that I have used the term "Software Engineers" here and not programmers. The reason for this is that you need to get people who can see the bigger picture, who can deal with clients directly, can analyse requirements, carry out agile modelling, implement solutions and test them. Developers who only consider themselves as programmers will have too big a learning curve to climb in the short time available for the first project!

However, you need more from your first team. They need to be team players – people who can literally work in a team. They need to be able to communicate (sometimes tricky test for developers) as they will need to understand, share and explore the new agile methods. They will also need to be able to work together in small groups analysing, modelling, designing and implementing the solution.

Which brings us nicely to another point; they need to be practical. That is, they need to be good at identifying a problem and finding a solution – they need to be doers. Remember, you have only a small team and a short time available. So, you can't carry anyone.

Ideally, the software engineers also need to be interested in new techniques and willing, in particular, to try out an agile approach. That is, they need to be open-minded and not enter the process refusing to adopt agile methods. This does not mean that they have to agree to all that a particular agile method proposes without question, but that they will adhere to it for the current project period. Of course, post project, having them question what was done, why and how it may be improved, can be extremely useful.

12.6 Adopting Agile Processes One at a Time

Adopting an agile method takes time. You can jump-in and try everything at once but it makes life a little less stressful if you adopt the practices of your chosen approach one at a time. This helps your team to gain experience in the effects of a particular principle. It also helps with concerns that the organisation may have with regard to agile methods, such as lack of investment in upfront analysis and design, as well as a reduced emphasis on documentation.

By adopting one principle at a time, elements close to the heart of the organisation can be left in place. A good place to start, is in the adoption of the XP approach to unit testing. Personally, I have found that this approach to testing is useful whatever may be the project, whether it is agile or not! By adopting an agile approach to testing (i.e., by introducing testing frameworks such as JUnit and exploiting ideas such as test first implementation, etc.) this helps to develop a different developer mindset and also paves way for refactoring, encourages immediate feedback to changes in the system and helps highlight differences between the development and production environments.

Of course, it takes time to learn how to do effective unit testing and particularly how to design the test first. But, if this is the first practice being adopted, then it makes life less hard. Developers may well get carried away with defining tests that can result in a large number of essentially duplicated tests. These can be identified, as developers may notice similar tests in different parts of the system or as they read tests to understand codes. This is normal and can be "refactored" out of the tests as the project progresses.

Which practice is adopted next tends to depend on which approach you are working with. For example, I tend to look at introducing modelling practices next based on Agile Modelling. With the intention of letting people get familiar with, and learn about modelling in pairs or in small teams for short specific purposes. However, if you are adopting a primarily XP approach, then you might select to introduce the refactoring practice next.

In isolation, a single refactoring operation is often quite simple to do and to test. However, producing larger scale effective refactoring operations can be a lot harder. In addition, within XP, the aim is to refactor whenever a situation warrants it. Getting used to this and actually doing it in the right way (including ensuring you understand what the code needs to do before changing it and testing it thoroughly) takes time to get used to. In general, in software development, we tend to adopt a "if it is not broken, don't mend it policy" which can at first seem to be at odds with refactoring. However, refactoring should be applied when the code is broken with respect to one or more of the requirements or XP practices (such as simplicity). Of course, adopting refactoring implies that you have adopted unit testing fully, as this is the only way in which you can guarantee that the software still provides the same functionality as it previously did.

You can also adopt the concept of "Keeping things as simple as possible" (or at least as simple as is required to serve their purpose). Everyone can agree to this practice (i.e., no one should over-complicate software) but of course the temptation to factor-in implementation details that may be required in the future can be difficult to resist. Thus, the team needs to learn to avoid adding-in code for future requirements (this is where the test first implementation can really help). It is also necessary to be careful of design patterns. Although they are very useful, they can make the software more complex than it needs to be. It is better often to factor-in design patterns as and when needed.

12.7 Managing Existing Processes

One big issue that can be encountered when introducing agile methods is that of existing heavyweight processes and the process owners. In many cases, "it must be done using this method because we have ISO900X and it says we use this method," etc. can be a difficult organisational hurdle. Your only option here (unless you are given dispensation to ignore the process) is to try to work with the process owner. See if they can identify any problem areas they currently have and discuss how an agile method might help. If they are willing to try to see how an agile approach might address their problems, then you can start to introduce agile practices a bit at a time (in order to solve perceived problems).

12.8 Working with Distributed Teams

Physically distributed teams do not exactly fit with agile processes. If your team is distributed (even within a building, let alone between different physical sites), then ideally you want to collocate them. If you cannot do that, then you may be able to use collaborative tools to help you get around the problems. However, you will also need to choose a process into which you place the agile methods which support distributed teams. You might also consider marking some people as mobile. That is, they move between the physical locations of the project team to improve communications, etc.

12.9 Get Some Experience

Finally, there is nothing as good as having someone around who has done it before. Someone who can say "ah, but if you do that. . . ." This can be obtained either by moving someone into the team who has worked on agile software development projects or by hiring someone (on either a permanent or temporary basis) for the duration of the project.

13

Tools to Help with Agile Development

13.1 Introduction

As with many things in life, the right set of tools can make a huge difference to an agile development project. There are a number of tasks that can be made much easier and simpler by employing the correct supporting tools. In this chapter, we will look at some of the tools available and how they can be used. All the tools we will look at are open-source and freely available. This is not to say that only open-source tools can be of help, merely that these tools do not cost anything to obtain and therefore the initial up-front costs involved are minimal. This means that if you wish to experiment with an agile project and want some tools to help you do that you should have little trouble obtaining them. In some of the cases, they are also commercial tools that can be used instead and depending upon your environment you may decide to/need to use those instead. Personally, I have found these open-source tools more than adequate.

13.2 What Tools Do You Need?

So what tools should you use in support of an agile project? To answer this question, let us first consider what tool requirements Agile Software Development imposes on us. Some of these requirements are presented below:

1. We should be able to refactor software simply and easily. For example, in Java if we move a class from one package to another we would want package statement of classes to be updated and all references to that class to be modified, etc.
2. It should be possible to modify existing software securely in the knowledge that we can role back to an earlier version if it all goes horribly wrong.
3. We should be able to track changes in the system.
4. We should be able to run and re-run test suites simply and to review the results easily and immediately.
5. If we are undertaking to perform Agile Modelling, then we should be able to reverse engineer code into models simply and with a minimum of fuss. We should be able to modify code or models and keep both in sync. We should be able to update models without the need to heavy weight tools.

6. Ideally, we also want something that will tell us when we need to create a new build. For example, something that notices that new code has been released into the central repository and initiates the build process automatically.

The tools listed below are those that I have found to be particularly useful in the projects I have worked on. They represent the most common areas that can benefit from tool support within an agile Java development project:

1. An IDE that can be integrated with the other tools proposed, which supports refactoring and iterative development.
2. A lightweight modelling tool to help with Agile Modelling.
3. A build tool to allow simple and rapid rebuilds of the system as and when necessary.
4. A version control system to handle the frequent and rapid changes introduced into the software and to allow the software to roll back when necessary.
5. A test framework to handle the unit tests so important to agile software development.

You do not need any of the above of course. It is quite possible to use *Vi*, *Emacs* or *NotePad* to edit your programs and to manage or maintain builds, versions of software, test suites, etc., without any additional tools – but it does make life easier!

In the remainder of this chapter, we will consider the following tools:

1. The Eclipse IDE (into which all the remaining tools can be plugged),
2. Omondos' modelling plug-in for Eclipse,
3. ANT: the build tool for Java,
4. The CVS version control system,
5. The JUnit Java test framework.

Of course, these are not the only tools available, there are other open-source tools (most notably tools such as NetBeans for Java and CSharp Stuido for C#), low-cost tools (such as JCreator) and fully commercial tools such as JBuilder and VisualStudio. In general, the commercial tools are the most sophisticated and require the least effort to set up/configure and use (although this is not always the case). The point is that you will greatly benefit from using an appropriate set of tools and using free ones to at least get you started can be a great advantage. Personally, these open-source tools meet most, if not all, of my requirements on almost all projects.

13.3 Eclipse: An Agile IDE

Eclipse is an extremely powerful open-source IDE that can be used for developing projects in a variety of languages. It is primarily known as a Java IDE and in this guise it offers facilities on a par with commercial tools within an open-source framework. It can also be used for developing C, C++ and C# applications – thus, offering a common IDE for a variety of development languages.

Eclipse was originally developed by IBM but was moved to an open-source model to widen its appeal and the base of developers working on it. Not only is it an open-source system but it is also an open platform that allows additional tools to be plugged into it to extend its basic functionality. The Omondo UML diagramming tool described later in this chapter is one such plug-in.

An example of using Eclipse to develop Java code is presented in Figure 13.1. Note that Eclipse colour codes Java, and can be configured to insert default templates for Java classes and interfaces. An example of part of a Main class, containing a main method, is displayed.

As an IDE, Eclipse offers the standard suite of features we expect, including:

- Syntax analysis of code as it is entered
- Integrated context-sensitive help system
- Auto-complete
- Pop-up function/procedure prototypes
- View source of supplied components
- Ability to run applications from within the tool
- Integrated debugger
- Variety of wizards for creating different types of Java element
- Integration with version control systems (for example, CVS)

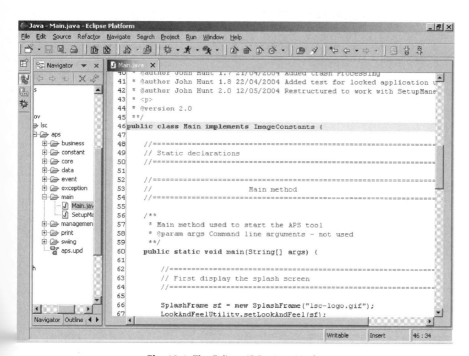

Fig. 13.1 The Eclipse IDE – Java Mode.

- Sophisticated, context-sensitive, search
- Various perspectives (including code, class, inheritance, etc.)
- Integration with Java development tools such as ANT, Junit, etc.

Eclipse is also fast, lightweight and relatively small. It is written in Java and is thus cross platform (allowing developers on a variety of platforms to all use the same IDE).

From the point of view of an agile development approach, one of the best features of Eclipse is its support for various refactoring operations. It is possible to refactor the location of packages, classes and interfaces, to refactor class and interface names, methods, variables and constants. In many cases, Eclipse provides a refactoring wizard that will automatically perform much of the mundane work associated with refactoring. For example, if a developer refactors a method name, Eclipse will search for all references to that method name and will change those references to the new name. It will also search through any Javadoc referencing the method and make changes within the Javadoc comments. It can also search through non-Java files and make changes as required. This is particularly useful for XML files that are used to configure J2EE applications and which may reference Java classes, interfaces and their methods.

An example of the refactoring options available to a developer is illustrated in Figure 13.2. In this example, the user has selected a particular interface and brought up the right mouse menu. On this menu is an option to "Refactor." This

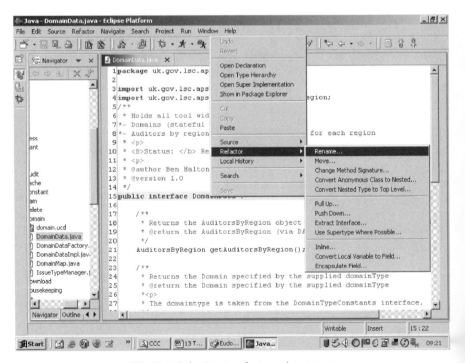

Fig. 13.2 Selecting to refactor a class name.

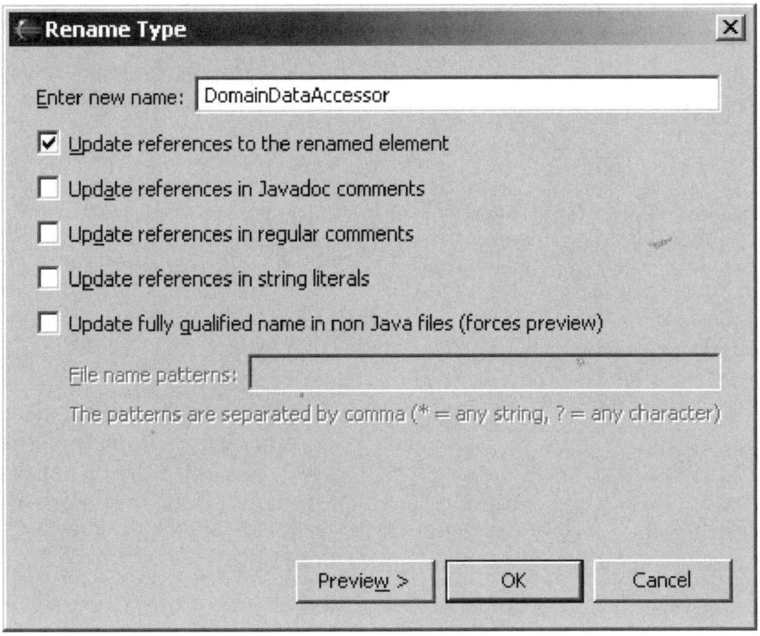

Fig. 13.3 Class/Interface rename dialogue.

results in a more detailed menu being displayed. In this case, the user has selected to rename the interface. The resulting class/interface name change dialogue is displayed in Figure 13.3. Note that this dialogue not only allows the user to enter the new name of the interface but also to select where Eclipse will look to make changes.

13.4 Lightweight Modelling within Eclipse

Within an agile project, we want lightweight tools that aid the development process, rather than impede it. Modelling tools, all too often, feel like that are just such an impediment. They can often feel "clunky" and awkward to use and cause problems if and when code is generated from them or reverse engineered into them.

Within an agile context (and particularly within an Agile Modelling context), what is required is a modelling environment that is natural to use and as lightweight as the code editor within the IDE being used. Both Eclipse and JBuilder include such modelling environments. As we are focussing on Eclipse, this is the environment we will consider.

As it comes "out of the box," Eclipse does not include a modelling environment. However, it is an open platform that encourages the development of plug-ins for various tasks. Thus, modelling tools have been developed that can be plugged into Eclipse to support round trip modelling. One example of such a tool is Omondo.

Omondo have developed EclipseUML. This is a visual modelling tool, which is fully integrated with Eclipse. Two versions are available: a free version which is suitable for single-user developments and allows evaluation of EclipseUML and a commercial version which extends the basic version to support team-based developments and version control systems such as CVS. The team-based version is capable of managing hundreds of simultaneous connections and so is adapted for large software development teams.

EclipseUML has support for live bi-directional (byte-code) model and code synchronisation. Thus, as a change is made to the code, it is made to the model. In turn, any changes made to the models are reflected in the source code underlying the model. Thus, the effort of creating a model is counter balanced by the immediate availability of the source code for that model. An example of a model generated from Java source code is presented in Figure 13.4.

A modelling tool such as EclipseUML is ideal for an agile project as models can be generated as required from source code, models are automatically kept in sync with the source code and changes to models are immediately reflected in the source code (with no additional actions required). Thus, the emphasis is on creating the source code rather than building models for the sake of modelling. It also encourages a move to the source code earlier as the source code is immediately available at all times.

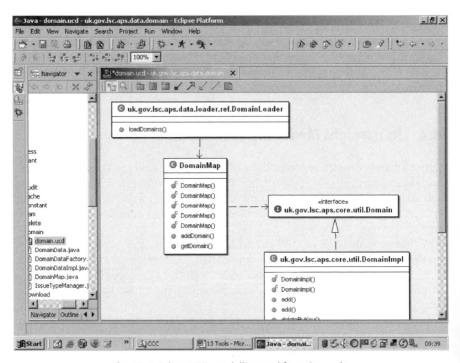

Fig. 13.4 EclipseUML modelling tool from Omondo.

13.5 Building Applications with ANT

ANT is the Java build tool; it is *make* (plus much more) for Java. It allows a developer to specify what components need to be built, when and into what format.

Every quality IDE, from the open-source projects (*Emacs, NetBeans, Eclipse, Jedit*) to the commercial offerings such as *IntelliJ IDEA* and *JBuilder* now have high-quality ANT integration either built-in or available as a download. Indeed, it is getting to the point within the Java world where many Java developers expect to be able to use ANT as a basic part of their development environment. Indeed, in many cases, if you download an open-source project, you will find an ANT script has been provided to allow you to build that project.

However, there are still many organisations and situations in which Java developers are unaware of ANT and what it can do. In this section, we will outline what it can do and highlight its integration with the Eclipse tool.

Using ANT, it is possible to:

- Extract all the current source from a version control system such as CVS.
- Compile all the Java code in a system.
- Automatically generate a build number, provide a build date stamp, add a version number to a property file, etc.
- Jar that code up into a single file.
- Copy that jar to a deployment location.
- Generate the Javadoc for the compile system.
- Copy the Javadoc to an appropriate location.
- Create Web Archives (WARs).
- Create Enterprise Archives (EARs).
- Deploy WARs and WARs to servers (such as Tomcat or JBoss).
- Start up servers such as Tomcat and JBoss.

ANT is written in Java and uses XML configuration files to control its build process. These build files, called "build.xml" by default, control what ANT does and how it does it. Each build file contains one project and at least one (default) target. A target describes an ANT activity such as the compilation of some Java code, or the creation of a Jar file (or both). An example of a ANT build file for a simple project is presented in Figure 13.5. This illustrates the basic ideas. The root element of the build file is the "project" element. This element specifies the name of the project and the default target (that is what should happen if the user merely types "ANT" on the command line). It also indicates the base or default-working directory for the ANT execution process.

The ANT build file example in Figure 13.5 also illustrates the definition of three different targets. For example, it defines the target "compile." This is the default target run by the ANT process. This compile target updates a property file using the property file element (this allows the current release status, version and date to be added to the core.properties file). It then initiates the javac program using the javac element specifying the source, destination and *classpath* attributes. Note

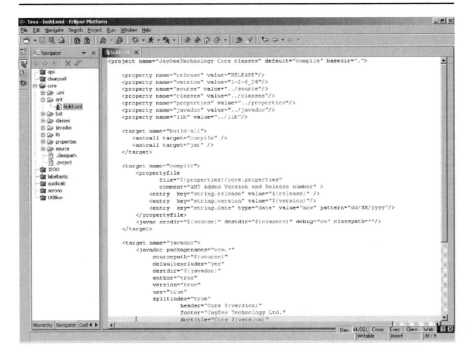

Fig. 13.5 An ANT build.xml file in Eclipse.

that the source and classes attributes are defined by ANT properties. These are similar to variables in a program and are set at the top of the build file.

It is also worth looking at the "build-all" target above the "compile" target. This target allows the compile target and the jar target to be called one after another. This illustrates ANT's ability to have hierarchical targets. To run the "build-all" target (or any of the non-default targets), ANT must be invoked with the name of that target, for example:

ANT build-all

Eclipses' ANT support allows ANT processes to be executed from within the Eclipse tool. This allows you to create and run ANT build files from the Eclipse Workbench. These ANT build files can operate on resources in the file system as well as resources in the workspace.

You can interactively configure the ANT process, add ANT tasks, set ANT properties, etc., from within Eclipse as illustrated in Figure 13.6.

Once a build file has been configured, it can be run from within Eclipse. To do this, the build file is selected in the Navigator view and the right mouse button used to initiate the "Run ANT" option. This displays the ANT dialogue presented in Figure 13.7. This dialogue lists the targets available for the build file and allows other data such as properties and the class path to be set.

Output from an ANT build file is displayed in the console view in the same hierarchical format seen when running ANT from the command line. ANT tasks

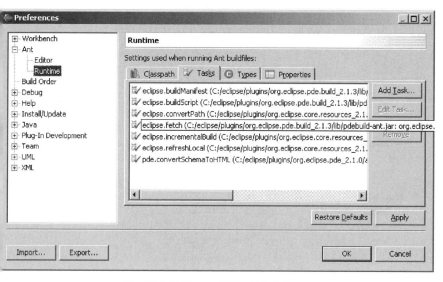

Fig. 13.6 Setting up ANT within Eclipse.

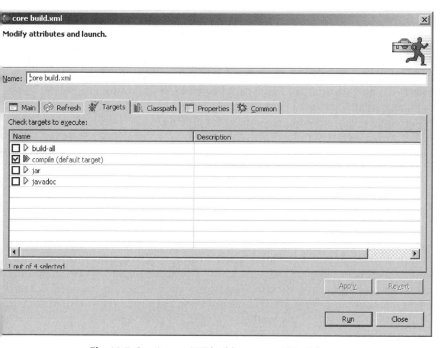

Fig. 13.7 Starting an ANT build process within Eclipse.

(for example, "[mkdir]") are hyperlinked to the associated ANT build file, and javac error reports are hyperlinked to the associated Java source file and line number.

13.6 Version Control with CVS

CVS is the Concurrent Versions System, the dominant open-source network-transparent version control system. CVS is useful for everyone from individual developers to large, distributed teams:

- Its client–server access method let developers access the latest code from anywhere if there is an Internet connection.
- Its unreserved check-out model to version control avoids artificial conflicts common with the exclusive check-out model.
- Its client tools are available on most platforms.

CVS is used by popular open-source projects like <u>Mozilla</u>, the <u>GIMP</u>, <u>XEmacs</u>, <u>KDE</u> and <u>GNOME</u>.

13.6.1 So What Is It All About?

That is all well and good, you might be saying, but what does it do for *me*? First the basics: A version control system keeps a history of the changes made to a set of files. For a developer, that means being able to keep track of all the changes you've made to a program during the entire time you've been developing it. Have you ever lost a day's work due to an errant keystroke at the command line? A version control system gives you a safety net.

Version control systems are valuable for anyone, really. (After all, who couldn't use a safety net?) But they're usually used by software development teams. Developers working on a team need to be able to coordinate their individual changes; a central version control system allows that.

13.6.2 Code Central Station

Individual developers who want the safety net of a version control system can run one on their local machines. Development teams, however, need a central server so that all members can access to serve as the repository for their code. In an office that's no problem – just stick the repository on a server on the local network. For open-source projects, it's still no problem, thanks to the Internet. CVS has built-in client–server access methods so that any developer who can connect to the Internet can access files on a CVS server.

CVS maintains a history of a source tree, in terms of a series of changes. It stamps each change with the time it was made and the user name of the person who made it. Usually, the person provides a bit of text describing why they made the change as well. Given that information, CVS can help developers answer questions like:

- Who made a given change?
- When did they make it?
- Why did they make it?
- What other changes did they make at the same time?

CVS available on a variety of platforms include Windows, Linux, Unix, VMS, Mac OS, etc.

13.7 Testing with JUnit

Testing is a key aspect of an agile development approach. It is of course quite possible to generate an appropriate set of unit tests without the use of any form of support. However, the application of a standard testing framework has a number of benefits. These include:

1. *Standardised test format.* This means that all developers use the same test format, follow the same rules for creating tests, manage those tests in the same way, etc. This allows tests to be easily understood by other developers as well to allow for code and knowledge sharing.
2. *Repeatable tests.* Automated tests supported by a testing framework are more repeatable than manual tests because they execute in exactly the same way every time – no matter who the developer is. Typically, they are also easier to initiate – there is no "so how do I run your tests again?" Finally, testing frameworks can provide simple but effective reporting tools to allow the results of tests to be easily and simply verified.
3. *Tried and tested frameworks.* The last thing we want is to have bugs in our testing framework such that bugs in the tests hide potential problems in our code. Using an established and well-tested framework can help to overcome this.
4. *Potential tool support.* It would not be beyond the bounds of feasibility to create my own testing framework and to use that on any software project I undertook. However, this would not be a widely used framework and thus would be unlikely to have direct support within any particular IDE. Using a well-established testing framework, however, may allow such support to be exploited within your chosen IDE.

JUnit is an example of a standardised, well-established testing framework. It was written by Erich Gamma and Kent Beck and is modelled on the xUnit testing framework (essentially, the J in JUnit indicates that it is a version of the xUnit pattern for use with the Java language – other examples are the CUnit and CppUnit versions for C and C++, respectively).

JUnit provides a simple way to explicitly define repeatable unit tests and test suites. It is written in Java and so can be easily integrated into any Java development environment. It is also possible to integrate JUnit into ANT to automate regression test suites.

JUnit comes with three different ways of running tests (referred to as TestRunners) depending upon whether you wish to run a Swing, AWT or non-graphical test runner:

- a textual TestRunner – it is the fastest to launch and can be used when you don't need graphical feedback on test results.
- graphical TestRunners – these provide graphical feedback on the results of running the test and can be either Swing or AWT based.

One of the IDEs which provides direct support for JUnit is Eclipse. It provides a set of wizards which greatly simplify writing JUnit tests and test suites. We will look at this feature of Eclipse in subsequent subsections below.

13.7.1 JUnit within Eclipse

JUnit is now such an important feature of the Java development world that a number of the IDEs available have included JUnit support. For example, Eclipse includes direct support for JUnit. Of course, you do not need to use Eclipse to use JUnit, but having direct support (including a number of JUnit wizards does make life a whole lot easier). The key to Eclipses support for JUnit is the plug-in facility

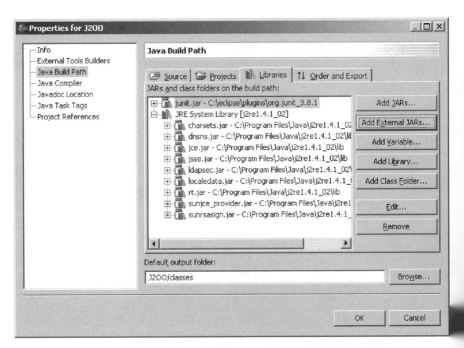

Fig. 13.8 Adding the JUnit.jar file to an Eclipse project's build path.

within Eclipse. This allows additional tools and wizards to be created for Eclipse and "plugged in" to the IDE in a simple and standard way.

Support for JUnit can be found within the Eclipse plug-in architecture.

13.7.2 Adding JUnit to an Eclipse Project

Within Eclipse you need to add the JUnit jar to the project build path. This will then allow the code generated by Eclipse for the JUnit tests to be compiled. It will also add the junit.jar file to the runtime classpath for the project so that any run configurations you create will automatically be able to access the JUnit framework.

The junit.jar file is added to the Java build path in Eclipse 2.1 by opening up the project properties and selecting to edit the Java build path. You can then select to add an External Jar file to the build path. In Eclipse 2.1, you will find the junit.jar file under the eclipse\plugins\org.junit* directory. By selecting the junit.jar file and adding it to the Java build path you should end up with the dialogue presented in Figure 13.8.

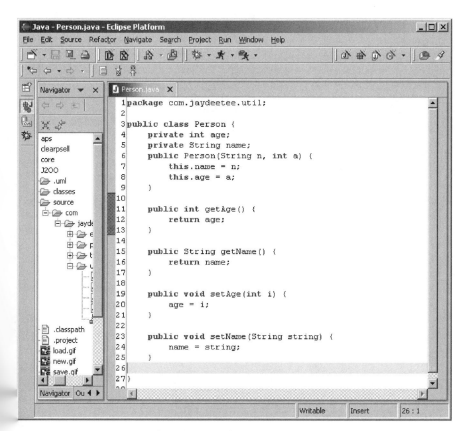

Fig. 13.9 A simple Java class to test.

If you have successfully added the junit.jar file to your project build path, then you are ready to start to use the JUnit plug-in wizard.

13.7.3   Using the Eclipse JUnit Wizard

To create a TestCase class using the JUnit framework, you can use the JUnit wizard provided as part of the JUnit plug-in. Selecting to create a new class for a package can do this. In the following example, I have created a simple class *Person* in a package *com.jaydeetee.util*. This class is illustrated in Figure 13.9.

The Person class has two instance variables for name and age that are accessed via setter and getter methods. It also provides a constructor which allows these values to be initialised. Obviously, this is not a particularly complex class; however, it is sufficient to illustrate the ideas being presented here.

We are now in a position to create a JUnit test case for the class Person. To keep things simple, we will place the test class within the same package as the class being tested (in reality you might well wish to place the test class within its own test package hierarchy).

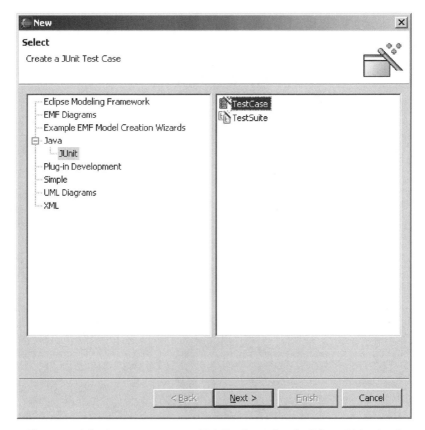

Fig. 13.10 Selecting to create a new JUnit TestCase using the Eclipse JUnit wizard.

To create the test class, we use select the "New" menu option from the pop-up menu available off the package *com.jaydeetee.util.* This menu option allows new classes, interfaces, etc., to be created. In this case, we select the new Java JUnit option. This presents the dialogue presented in Figure 13.10, which allows the user to select to create either an individual test case or a whole test suite. For the moment, we will select to create a single test case.

The result of selecting to create a new JUnit TestCase is the dialogue presented in Figure 13.11. Amongst other things, this dialogue allows us to define the name of the test case (by convention we will call this test case after the name of the class being tested followed by "TestCase," thus this test case is called PersonTestCase). It also allows the class being tested to be specified, i.e., Person. Additionally, it allows the user to select how they wish to view the results of running the test case (we have selected to use the Swing-based GUI to view the results). We have also selected to generate setup() and teardown() methods. These can be used to set up any test environment and remove the test environment (for example, these might be used to set up some data in a database which will be used by the tests and then to remove that data from the database).

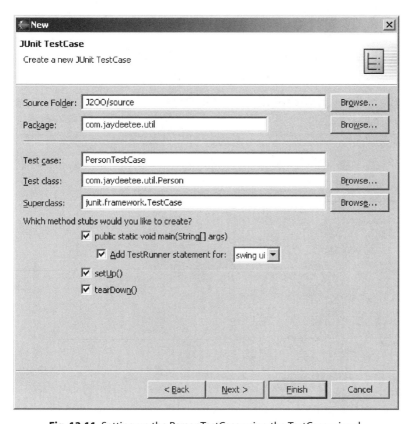

Fig. 13.11 Setting up the PersonTestCase using the TestCase wizard.

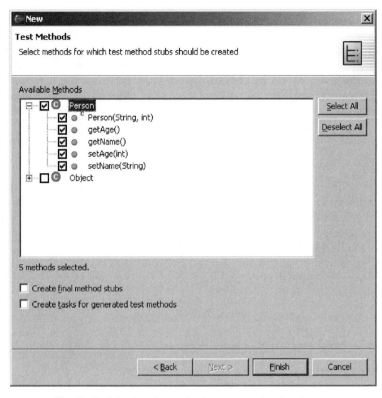

Fig. 13.12 Selecting the methods to test on the class Person.

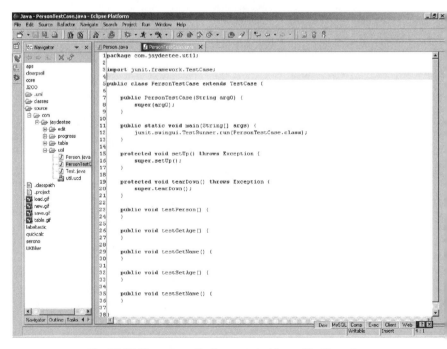

Fig. 13.13 The automatically generated PersonTestCase class.

```
public void testGetAge() {
    Person p = new Person("John", 40);
    assertEquals(40, p.getAge());
}
```

Fig. 13.14 A simple test method.

Having entered the data to define the basics of the test unit, the user can then select the "Next >" button to specify which methods on the class Person should have tests written for them. This is done in the "Test Methods" dialogue presented in Figure 13.12. In this example, we have selected to test all the setters and getters and the construction of a new instance.

The effect of clicking on "Finish" in the Test Methods dialogue is that the Eclipse JUnit plug-in generates the Java code necessary to implement a JUnit test case. The resulting code is illustrated in Figure 13.13.

Note that it has created a subclass of the JUnit class *TestCase*. This super class provides all the functionality required for this *PersonTestCase* to work within the JUnit framework. Also note the main method. This main method has been defined to start up the JUnit swing test runner application with the *PersonTestCase* class as the provider of the test methods.

It then provides setup() and teardown() methods that can be extended for the Person class. Finally, it provides null implementations for the various methods to test within the Person class. Note the convention that a test always starts with the name "Test"<Something>. This allows JUnit to automatically find methods

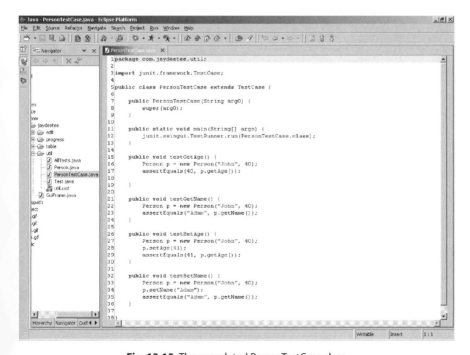

Fig. 13.15 The completed PersonTestCase class.

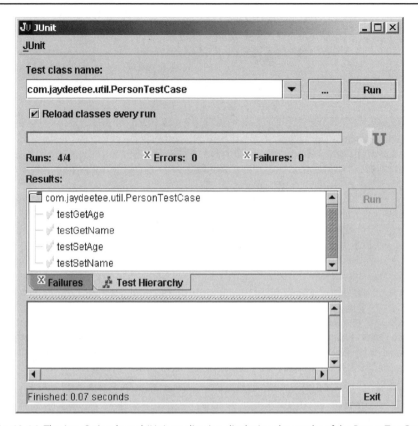

Fig. 13.16 The Java Swing-based JUnit application displaying the results of the PersonTestCase.

to run in a test. This convention can be ignored but adding methods that don't follow this convention to a test is more work.

We are now in a position to implement the various tests. We can do this by setting up a particular situation and then testing the result of some activity, etc. For example, in Figure 13.14 we are testing whether a new instance of Person has been initialised with the correct value (or indeed that getAge() can return the appropriate value). This is done by creating an instance of the class Person and then calling the assertEquals method. This method takes two parameters, the value I expect to be returned by getAge() and the actual value returned. If they are equal, the test is passed; if they are not, then this test fails and the failure will be reported by the JUnit framework. Note it is possible to have more than one test within a method to check various different values, etc.

There are a whole range of assert methods including assertEquals, assertTrue, assertNotNull, assertNull and assertNotSame. Unfortunately, there is no assert-NotEquals!

The finished test case for the Person class is presented in Figure 13.15. We have removed the setup() and teardown() methods as they are not needed in this situation.

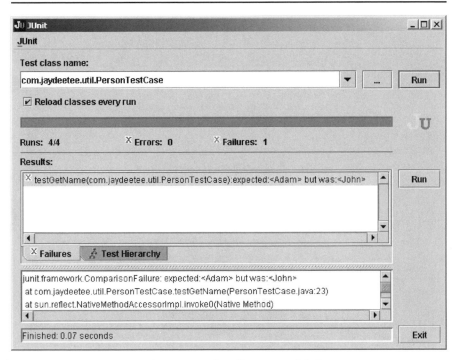

Fig. 13.17 The JUnit interface illustrating a failed test case.

We are now in a position where we can run this test case. This is done by running the PersonTestCase main method. The result of doing this is illustrated in Figure 13.16. This is the JUnit swing interface. It lists the tests performed and the result of the test. In this case, all tests have been passed.

If we now change one of the tests so that they fail and re-run the test case, we can see what happens when a test fails. As you can see from Figure 13.17, it is clear that at least one test has failed from the red bar. In addition, we can see which test failed, where and what the values were. That is, it was line 23 of *PersonTestCase* and the value expected was "Adam" but the value returned was "John," etc.

Of course, most systems will be too complex to test in a single test case. To support larger test suites, JUnit provides the TestSuite class. Once again, Eclipse provides a wizard to simply create a TestSuite. Using the New menu option, we can select to create a TestSuite rather than a single TestCase as illustrated in Figure 13.18.

Once again this dialogue allows us to specify the name of our test suite (AllTests in this example) as well as the Test cases that will comprise the test suite (in our case just PersonTestCase). It also allows a main method to be created that will manage the test suite class (such as adding a test to the test suite class). It also allows us to specify the way in which we wish to see the results of running the test suite. Once again we will select the swing GUI from the JUnit framework. Clicking on "Finish" results in the Eclipse framework generating the code presented in Figure 13.19.

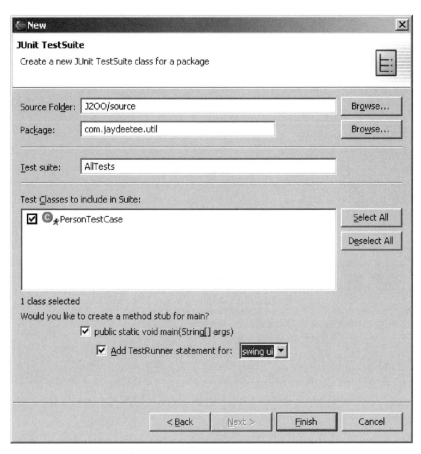

Fig. 13.18 Using the JUnit TestSuite wizard within Eclipse.

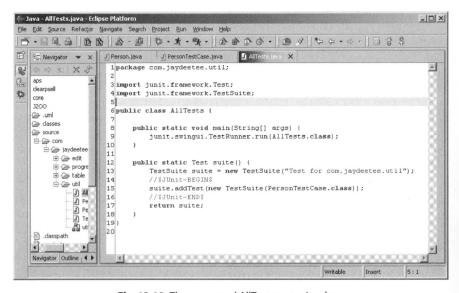

Fig. 13.19 The generated AllTests test suite class.

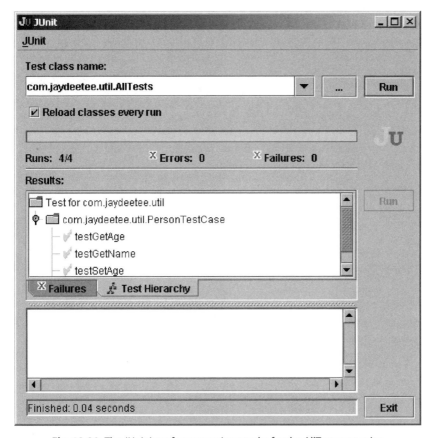

Fig. 13.20 The JUnit interface reporting results for the AllTests test suite.

This is the fully functional test suite and does not require any additional code to be added. Running this main method results in the JUnit TestSuite interface being displayed (as illustrated in Figure 13.20).

Note that in this interface the *PersonTestCase* is presented as an element of the larger test suite in the Results tree.

13.8 Online References

Eclipse – http://www.eclipse.org/
Omondo – http://www.omondo.com/
ANT – http://ANT.apache.org for more details.
JUnit – http://junit.sourceforge.net/
CUnit – http://cunit.sourceforge.net/
CppUnit – http://cppunit.sourceforge.net
CVS – http://www.cvshome.org

14

Obstacles to Agile Software Development

14.1 Introduction

In this chapter, we will consider some of the obstacles that can be encountered when trying to introduce an agile approach into an organisation. We will also try to suggest some approaches to overcome these obstacles (although the suggestions made in Chapter 12 regarding introducing an agile project are still important).

In the remainder of this chapter, we consider the issues associated with management intransigence regarding new development processes. We also address the issue of the "failed agile project" syndrome, that is, what do you do if somewhere else in your organisation an agile project has been tried and failed. Developer resistance is also a major drag factor as well as customer opposition (this later possibility, the biggest stumbling block of all, as you really do need customer involvement in any agile project). Next, we consider contractual difficulties arising from the traditional use of requirements as the basis for any development contracts. Finally, we discuss the lack of familiarity with agile development methods.

14.2 Management Intransigence

The drive towards agile software development often comes from the developers themselves or from developer teams. In such situations, management can represent a significant obstacle to adoption of an agile approach. This can be for a host of reasons that include:

1. Lack of familiarity with Agile Software Development methods.
2. Mis-comprehension of what eXtreme Programming and Agile Modelling offers (such as believing them to be legalised hacking).
3. A feeling of losing control (as agile methods are more dynamic in terms of planning activities than traditional approaches).

4. Remoteness from the actual coalface and thus remoteness from development issues.
5. The need to feel that they have the whole project planned out in advance.
6. Lack of suitability for their own review-and-assessment process. That is, if they are assessed on a more traditional waterfall model, then they may have the production of a detailed project plan as one of their aims and objectives to be completed.
7. Belief that adopting eXtreme Programming (and thus doubling developers up) will actually halve productivity. Although current research indicates that the opposite is actually true.
8. The parapet syndrome. That is, a manager may not want to risk a different approach to that normally adopted (i.e., putting their head above the parapet), as no one may be censured for doing things the standard way, but they may well be for doing things in a different way and failing!
9. The fear of the unknown!

There are no easy solutions to these questions – it all boils down to education. Getting in a consultant who can help deal with their concerns and lack of knowledge can be useful – but that assumes that they are willing to consider an agile approach in the first place. Getting to that point may well be your job. Thus, using books such as this one, the web and case studies may be your only option.

Often, the best solution is to try to adopt an agile approach on a low profile project in which management has little interest. This can then be used as an example of how it worked (assuming it did), to help accept and adopt the approach on other projects. Even better is when another part of your organisation has adopted an agile approach and been successful.

Finally, if you convince senior management of the potential benefits of an agile software development process, then this can "influence" lower level management to adopt it – again it is a case of education (although possibly suitable subtle education).

14.3 The Failed Project Syndrome

In the previous section, I have said that having a successful agile project in another part of your organisation can really help you to convince management of the benefits of the new approach. However, the failed agile project can of course have the reverse effect – i.e. merely proving their belief in the futility of this agile thing!

I have been in this situation when providing consultancy to a client. We talked about the possibility of adopting an agile approach based on feature-driven development method, Agile Modelling, etc. However, one manager suddenly butted in to say that they had already tried this "so called agile approach" and that it had been a waste of time and effort and that the result had been thrown away and re-implemented in a proper manner. The manager in question was most forceful in his condemnation of agile methods. In a bid to retain my credibility with the client in general, I tried to drill down and find out what the issues had been with the project. It turned out that:

1. No one involved in the project had ever done an agile development before.
2. Half the developers were actually industrial engineering students taking time out between their second and third years, and had limited commercial software development experience anyway.
3. The belief appeared to be that you should never comment code (it was self-documenting).
4. They never wrote any documentation (believing it not to be the agile way).
5. They never did any design (as they considered design to be the antithesis of agility).
6. Refactoring appeared to have been an area they considered a waste of time!

Given this, it is not surprising that the project was not a success. Interestingly, in contrast, the remaining project members and some very experienced software engineers successfully redeveloped it. Thus, they had more experience and knowledge of the domain when they redeveloped the project (or refactored it as it turned out).

Of course, my take on this was that they had not really done an agile project (they had achieved something that had some elements of various agile methods, but hadn't carried it through) and may well have failed anyway due to their reliance on inexperienced and untried developers. By explaining why the approach they took had failed, we at least opened the door to future agile software developments (although as it transpired in this case, not on the project being discussed!). And yes, the manager who expressed his concerns regarding agile development methods was the manager of the failed project (but not the successful project!).

So, if you find yourself in this position, there are no guarantees of success, but by dealing with each issue raised by the failed project and addressing them head on, you may convince people of the value in trying again. This is particularly true, if you can point to external projects that have succeeded (for these, look at the agile websites referenced at the end of the book).

14.4 Developer Resistance

Many software developers are at best "comfortable with their current development approach" and at worst "stuck in their ways." In addition, many software developers would consider working in pairs or designing/modelling in teams as not only an aberration, but actually extremely uncomfortable. This is for a number of reasons.

Many (most) software developers have come through the university system during which they have studied a computer science subject. During their degrees, they would have undertaken numerous projects and submitted many pieces of code for assessment. The majority of these will have had stringent rules against collaboration or teamwork. In many cases, it will have been banned completely. In others, it will have been frowned upon potentially with marks divided between those submitting the course work. Only a few items of work will have encouraged teamwork (and I speak here as an ex-University lecturer!). Thus, software developers are trained to work alone and guard against collaboration, etc.

In addition, the software development industry does have a tendency to attract individuals who would prefer to spend long hours in front of a monitor rather than converse with other members of the human race. For such people, programming in isolation to solve tricky technical problems is the height of what they do – make them work in a pair to do this can be the worst torture they could imagine. I do have some sympathy for this attitude, as I can sometimes experience it myself – deluded, as I can be, that I know the answer and just want to get on and program the solution – as that's the fun bit. However, my experience is that usually someone else can contribute something that I have either missed or discounted when I should have included it (and it also keeps me honest!). However, there are some who will never come round to this idea – in which case they need to work on non-agile projects (and certainly not XP projects!).

14.5 Customer Opposition

If you are reading this book, then there is a very good chance that you are involved in software development in some aspect – be it as a designer, developer, project manager, etc. However, it is probably true that you are unlikely to be a customer or a buyer of a software system (not that these people shouldn't read this book!). This is because the users of the software systems we build are not, in general, software developers – they are lawyers, accountants, architects, book editors, opticians, doctors, vets, etc. To be fair, I do not keep up with developments within their areas of expertise; so why should they keep up with ours – and they won't. Thus, presenting a customer with an agile development approach can be daunting.

It is likely that when you present a client with an agile approach, they may be less than ecstatic. This may be for a variety of reasons including:

1. Concern that they don't know exactly what the software will do at the end of the day.
2. Related to this, the lack of a detailed plan that they can review.
3. The level of involvement and commitment required of them.

One really useful thing to have is a "Customer Champion" – someone to push your cause within the customer organisation. This champion may well require education as to what an agile approach is and what benefits it has for the customer. However, if you win an insider, this can be 50% of the battle won. The rest is down to education of the customer regarding the potential benefits of an agile approach to them – remember, the main motivation behind the agile movement is to delivery working/useful software to the customer (rather than large and detailed design documents/planning documents/UML models, etc.).

Remember, you really do need the customer on board when you get to the development stage. The on-site customer (even if a virtual on-site customer) for me is one of the key indicators for success. If you have one, then you are more likely to succeed. Not having one does not necessarily guarantee failure (but it certainly makes it far, far more likely).

14.6 Contractual Difficulties

A very significant issue relating to agile software development methods is that of contractual difficulties. By that, I mean that contracts traditionally have been based around a waterfall software development approach. Thus, the buyer of the software may state exactly what is required, and if all the specified functions are not provided, then the contract is not met. This situation is often exacerbated by the presence of fixed price projects. That is, a supplier must state exactly how much they will charge to provide the required functionality. All of this of course takes place in advance of the software development and may not even involve the actual developers.

How does this fit with an agile approach in which we try to provide fixed length iterations with variable functionality (which is determined based on current requirements, etc.)? The answer to this is not that simple. For example, on a recent project (which actually lasted over 2 years) we had to initially provide a fixed cost quote for the first cut of the software. Once we had done that and were able to prove that we could produce the goods, on time and within the budget, then we could work with the client to adopt a more agile approach in which we fixed the amount of time spent on an iteration and adjusted the requirements per iteration as required by their (changing) business needs. We could do this because the client trusted us.

Therein lies the issue – you need to develop a level of trust between yourselves and the clients in order to adopt an agile approach. This is a two-way street in that you need to trust the clients to work with you (which in some cases can be a novel idea). This is as true for an internal project as it is for an external software development project. However, how do you do this before you have won the contract – indeed how do you win the contract when you might be involved in a competitive bid?

We have found that we needed to make the case for our approach a part of any bid process we are making. This often requires a level of pre-bid education to try to ensure that an agile method will be accepted in an appropriate manner. At times, this has meant allowing an initial iteration to be carried out in a more traditional approach (as described above).

Note that we consider educating our potential clients, with regard to agile development methods, an important aspect of our client relationship. In many cases, software buyers (particularly buyers of bespoke software systems) do not have a particularly high regard for our chosen profession and can often cite previous bad experiences. They may therefore be surprisingly amenable to the potential benefits of an agile approach.

Another potential contractual difficulty can be in acceptance testing. In many cases, a software buyer may wish to specify the set of acceptance tests that must be passed at the start of the project. This may be done to ensure that when the software is delivered, there can be no argument about what constitutes acceptance. In some cases, this may be enforced by the development company itself (again to ensure no arguments of acceptance). However, doing this upfront goes against the agile philosophy – that is, we are not trying to specify exactly what will constitute the final system at the start, as the exact set of features implemented may change as the requirements, their priority and content change. Our solution to this is that each feature for each iteration indicates the set of tests that represent acceptance. This may be formally via an acceptance test plan document or informally based on the understanding of the features. In either case, it assumes a level of involvement from the clients during each iteration to ensure a successful delivery and acceptance of the software. Whilst this can be time-consuming, it can be of great help, as the client is directly involved in each iteration that helps to feed information into the project. In addition, it can help to make sure that the software does what it should, as the interaction between developers and the on-site customer can help in defining unit tests as well as acceptance tests (rather than developers inventing unit tests without reference to the users' needs).

In general, we have found that working with clients so that they understand some of the benefits from their side is essential to the adoption of an agile development method. In particular, we have found emphasising the following to be useful:

1. *The level of control/influence they can exert.* That is, the extent to which the clients can influence what is done when, can sometimes be a major surprise. Software buyers often used to hand over the requirements, and then feel that they lose control of the project, and that they are left out of any project decision made internally. In an agile approach, the client and his representatives should be on board all the time (indeed XP and Agile Modelling require their direct inclusion in the team).

2. *The feedback they will receive.* Returning to the issue of the involvement of the client in the project, in many cases, clients have received very little feedback on the progress of the project. Often what feedback they have received may later prove to at best have been optimistic and at worst a down right lie. As the clients find themselves in the midst of the project, they will naturally receive regular feedback. They will also be able to judge the accuracy of the information they receive as and when releases are made (at frequent intervals).

3. *The adaptability of the project to changing requirements.* One regular issue for bespoke software buyers is the problem of changing requirements. If the requirements document is the basis of the contractual agreement between supplier and customer and subsequently if a requirement changes, then the contract changes. In some cases, this can be a very large hurdle to cross and will require lawyers and protracted negotiations. However, as requirements may be drawn up well in advance of the software development, they may well have changed/may well change in the future. By adopting an agile approach, as requirements change, these changes can be naturally and simply passed through to the project team.

4. *The ability to prioritise features.* A (possibly) surprising advantage of the agile approach to customers is that a low priority feature in a software system can be included but only implemented if time allows or its priority rises. This can be important whether for political reasons (some senior manager thinks it is important but no one else does, so it has to be in the requirements) or in green field software where the importance of some features may be unclear at

the start. As feature's priority is continually revised, then its inclusion (or not in a particular iteration) can be reviewed.

14.7 Familiarity with Agility

One major obstacle to adopting an agile software development is the lack of knowledge of how to start and run such a project. Chapter 12 discussed ways to introduce this approach into an organisation. However, until you have been involved in one or more agile software developments, a great many questions may stop you in your tracks. For example, "how do we estimate the cost of the software to the clients at the start of a project?" "how do we decide how many iterations will be there?" "how do we know what will be in each iteration?" and "how do we decide how long an iteration should be?" There are no right or wrong answers to these questions – although there are answers that may be more right or more wrong than others. We will take up each point in turn and try to discuss why each should not stop you from starting an agile software development project.

How do you estimate the cost of the software to the clients? The issue here may appear to be a question of how can we determine how much this software will cost for us to develop, given that we don't yet know exactly what we will do, when and how long (particularly later) functionality will take to implement. The real issue here is that the focus of the question is wrong. Customers need a budget to work within and so do you. Thus, if the client has a budget of £60,000 and requires the final release in 6 months time, then you already know how much effort you can afford to take on the project. That may or may not be enough to implement all the current requirements (which may be subject to change anyway). However, in general, the majority of software systems do not require all the possible functions that could be put into them, but they do need to remain within their budgets. Thus, what you need to be aware of is what budget you need to work within; and then provide an indication of how much of their specified functionality you currently believe you can achieve within that budget. Obviously, this has issues within competitive bids – but this takes me back to the issue of education – make them understand the issues involved and why you are being open and honest regarding your charges. One way we have handled this is by specifying a daily person rate and indicating how many person days they can buy for their budget, and relating that to the anticipated feature list.

How do we decide how many iterations there will be? This may appear as an obstacle because the question being implied here is "how many iterations will it take to implement *all* the requirements?" Whereas in fact, the issue should be "How many iterations should there be, to enable the clients to receive an appropriate number of releases, and for them to provide feedback to the development team, and to consider the current open questions?" This question implicitly acknowledges that some features may remain un-implemented as time may not allow for them. It also acknowledges that some as yet unknown user-feedback will impact upon that set of features. Thus, the size of each iteration relates more to the overall length of the project, the size and complexity of the system being implemented and the business processes of the client that will allow interim releases to be made.

For example, on one relatively small Java web-application project we had a 2-week iteration cycle; however, on a large two and a half year project, iterations last 3 or 4 months. Thus, the number of iterations was determined as a factor of the length of the project against the length of an iteration (i.e., over two and a half years, we had seven or eight iterations).

How do we know what will be in each iteration? Again this question arises from the more traditional waterfall mind set – it is really saying, "I want to know exactly what will be done in all iterations of the project." Whereas, agile methods essentially say that we will *roughly* decide what features, functions, use cases or user stories (depending on your preferred terminology or approach) will be planned for each iteration, but that only the current iteration will be planned in detail. Then, at the end of the current iteration, we will review the overall plan for the iterations and features, and that the next iteration will then be planned in detail. Thus, we only plan for the next few weeks or months (depending upon the size of an iteration) in detail. This does result in more planning than with a big upfront plan approach, but is actually more effective (both of which can be of real surprises to first-time agile developers). It is also more realistic, as the number of project plans that end up being works of fiction with little relationship to reality is probably too scary to contemplate.

How do we decide how long an iteration should be? This goes back to an earlier question, but is worth considering here again. Each iteration should be large enough to contribute something of value to the end-user, but small enough to allow for rapid and useful feedback from those users. Larger, more complex systems will thus naturally require larger iterations, whereas smaller, less complex systems will be able to achieve "something of value to the end-user" in smaller steps. Although, it is also worth noting that as a project matures, later iterations may be able to achieve more in shorter time periods, as there are larger "chunks" that can be exploited.

References

Alexander, C. *The Timeless Way of Building*, Oxford University Press, New York, 1979.

Alexander, C., Ishikawa, S., Silverstein, M., Jacobson, M., Fiksdahl-King, I. and Angel, S. *A Pattern Language*, Oxford University Press, New York, 1977.

Ambler, S. W. *Agile Modeling: Effective Practices for Extreme Programming and the Unified Process*, Wiley and Son, Inc, New York, ISBN: 0471202827, 2002.

Auer, K. and Miller, R. *Extreme Programming Applied: Playing to Win (The XP Series)*, Addison-Wesley, New York, 2002.

Bass, L., Clements, P. and Kazman, R. *Software Architecture in Practice*, Addison-Wesley, Reading, MA, 1998.

Beck, K. *Extreme Programming Explained: Embrace Change*, Addison-Wesley, Reading, MA, 1999.

Birrer, A. and Eggenschwiler, T. *Frameworks in the Financial Engineering Domain: An Experience Report: ECOOP'93*, pp. 21–35.

Boehm, B. *Get ready for agile methods, with care*, IEEE *Computer*, Jm 2002, 64–69. http://fc-md.umd.edu/projects/Agile/Boehm.pdf

Booch, G. *Object-Oriented Analysis and Design with Applications*, 2nd Edition, Benjamin Cummings, Redwood City, California, 1994.

Booch, G., Martin, R. and Newkirk, J. *Object Oriented Analysis and Design with Applications*, Addison-Wesley, Reading, MA, ISBN: 020189551X, 2003.

Bowers, J., May, J., Melander, E., Baarman, M. and Ayoob, A. Tailoring XP for large system mission critical software development, in D. Wells and L. Williams (Eds.): *XP/Agile Universe* 2002, LNCS 2418, Springer, Chicago, IL, 2002, pp. 100–111.

Budinsky, F. J., Finnie, M. A., Vlissides, J. M. and Yu, P. S. Automatic code generation from design patterns, *IBM Systems Journal*, 35(2), 1996.

Buschmann, F., Meunier, R., Rohnert, H., Sommerlad, P. and Stal, M. *Pattern-Oriented Software Architecture—A System of Patterns*, Wiley and Sons Ltd., New York, ISBN: 0471958697, 1996.

Carmichael, A. and Haywood, D. *Better Software Faster*, Prentice-Hall, NJ, ISBN: 0130087521, 2002.

Carmichael, A. R. and Swainston-Rainford, M. J. Feature Game—A Game for up to 24 players Based on Feature Driven Development, *OT2000 Conference*, BCS-OOPS, Oxford, UK.

Coad, P., Lefebvre, E. and De Luca, J. *Java Modeling in Color*, Prentice-Hall, Englewood Cliffs, NJ, 1999.

Cockburn, A. *Agile Software Development*, Addison-Wesley, Reading, MA, ISBN: 020699699, 2002.

Craddock, A. DSDM and Extreme Programming: Agility with Structure. http://www.dsdm.org/en/publications/newsletter3/dsdm_xp.asp

Fowler, M. *Analysis Patterns: Reusable Object Models*, Addison-Wesley, Reading, MA, ISBN: 0201895420, 1997.

Fowler, M. *Refactoring: Improving the Design of Existing Code*, Addison-Wesley, Reading, MA, 1999.

Gamma, E., Helm, R., Johnson, R. and Vlissades, J. *Design Patterns: Elements of Reusable Object-Oriented Software*, Addison-Wesley, Reading, MA, 1995.

T. Glib. The Evolutionary Project Managers Handbook, Evo Manuscript Distribution Edition 0.1, 1997, http://home.c2i.net/result-planning/Pages/2ndLevel/glibdownload.html

T. Glib. *Competitive Engineering: A New Systems Engineering Approach for Controlling Complexity, Communication Clearly and Challenging Creativity*, Addison-Wesley, Reading, MA, ISBN: 020167498X, 2002.

Grand, M. *Patterns in Java: Volume 2*, John Wiley & Sons, New York, ISBN: 0471227293, 1999.

Grand, M. *Patterns in Java: A Catalog of Enterprise Design Patterns Illustrated with UML Volume 3*, John Wiley & Sons Inc, New York, ISBN: 0471333158, 2001.

Grand, M. *Patterns in Java: A Catalog of Reusable Design Patterns Illustrated with UML*, 2nd Edition, Volume 1, John Wiley & Sons, New York, ISBN: 0471227293, 2002.

Hofmeister, C., Nord, R. and Soni, D. *Applied Software Architecture*, Addison-Wesley, Reading, MA, 1999.

Hunt, J. *Guide to the Unified Process*, Springer-Verlag, Berlin, ISBN: 1852337214, 2003.

Jacobson, I., Booch, G. and Rumbaugh, J. *The Unified Software Development Process*, Addison-Wesley, Reading, MA, 1999.

Jacobson, I., M. Christensen. *Object-Oriented Software Engineering: A Use Case Approach*. Addison-Wesley, Reading, MA, ISBN: 0201544350, 1992.

Jeffries, R., Anderson, A. and Hendrikson, C. *Extreme Programming Installed*, Addison-Wesley, Reading, MA, ISBN: 0201708426, 2000.

Johnson, R. E. Documenting Frameworks with Patterns, *Proc. OOPSLA'92, SIG-PLAN Notices* 27(10), 1992, 63–76.

Kruchten, P. The 4+1 View Model of Architecture, *IEEE Software*, 12(6), November 1995, IEEE. http://www.rational.com/support/techpapers/ieee/

Larman, C. *Applying UML and Patterns*, 2nd Edition, Prentice Hall, PTR, Englewood Cliffs, NJ, ISBN: 0130925691, 2001.

Metsker, S. J. *The Design Patterns Java Workbook*, Addison-Wesley, Reading, MA, ISBN: 0201743973, 2002.

Palmer, S. and Felsing, M. *A Practical Guide to Feature Driven Development*, Prentice Hall, Engelwood Cliffs, NJ, 2002.

Rechtin, E. and Maier, M. *The Art of System Architecting*, CRC Press, Boca Raton, FL, 1997.

Rumbaugh, J. et al. *Object-Oriented Modeling and Design*, Prentice Hall, Engelwood Cliffs, NJ, 1991.

Stapleton, J. DSDM, Dynamic Systems Development Method, 1997.

Wake, W. C. *Extreme Programming Explored*, Addison-Wesley, New York, 2002.

Williams, L. and Erdogmus, H. On the Economic Feasibility of Pair Programming, International Workshop on Economics-Driven Software Engineering in Conjunction with the International Conference on Software Engineering, May 2002 (http://collaboration.csc.ncsu.edu/laurie/Papers/EDSER02Williams Erdogmus.pdf).

Williams, L. and Kessler, R. *Pair Programming Illuminated*, Addison-Wesley Professional, Reading, MA, ISBN: 0201745763, 2003.

Williams, L., Kessler, R. R., Cunningham, W. and Jeffries, R. Strengthening the Case for Pair-Programming, IEEE Software July/Aug 2000 (http://collaboration.csc.ncsu.edu/laurie/Papers/ieeeSoftware.PDF).

Williams, L. A. The Collaborative Software Process, Ph.D. Dissertation, 2000, University of Utah, Salt Lake City (http://www.cs.utah.edu/~lwilliam/Papers/dissertation.pdf).

Online References

Agile Software Development Alliance www.agilealliance.org

Agile Modelling mailing list www.agilemodeling.com

Extreme Programming http://extremeprogramming.org/

XP Universe Web site http://www.xpuniverse.com

Pair Programming Web Site http://www.pairprogramming.com/

Rational Corp Web Site http://www.rational.com/

PRINCE 2 http://www.ogc.gov.uk/

DSDM http://www.dsdm.org/

Patterns web page is: http://st-www.cs.uiuc.edu/users/patterns/patterns

The World-Wide Institute of Software Architects. http://www.wwisa.org

Index